BRANCHES
in the VINE

The Life Story of
Fred and Dorothy Waldock

MARY AMESBURY

Wasteland Press

www.wastelandpress.net
Shelbyville, KY USA

Branches in the Vine:
The Life Story of Fred and Dorothy Waldock
by Mary Amesbury

First Printing – October 2012
ISBN: 978-1-60047-793-5
Cover photo by Rachel Swope, socrates_rms@yahoo.com

Printed in the U.S.A.

0   1   2   3   4

Dedicated to all those on my path who told me to write.

TABLE OF CONTENTS

FOREWORD

John 15:1-13

"I am the true vine, and my Father is the husbandman. Every branch in me that beareth not fruit He taketh away: and every branch that beareth fruit, He purgeth it, that it may bring forth more fruit.

Now ye are clean through the word, which I have spoken unto you.

Abide in me, and I in you. As the branch cannot bear fruit of itself, except it abide in the vine; no more can ye, except ye abide in me. I am the vine, ye are the branches: he that abideth in me, and I in him, the same bringeth forth much fruit: for without me ye can do nothing. If a man abide not in me, he is cast forth as a branch, and is withered; and men gather them, and cast them into the fire, and they are burned. If ye abide in me, and my words abide in you, ye shall ask what ye will, and it shall be done unto you.

Herein is my Father glorified, that ye bear much fruit; so shall ye be my disciples. As the Father hath loved me, so have I loved you: continue ye in my love. If ye keep my commandments, ye shall abide in my love; even as I have kept my Father's commandments, and abide in his love. These things have I spoken unto you, that my joy might remain in you, and that your joy might be full. This is my commandment, that ye love one another, as I have loved you. Greater love hath no man than this, that a man lay down his life for his friends."

The title, "Branches in the Vine," describes how Fred and Dorothy lived life – they were branches connected to the True Vine, Jesus Christ. In every circumstance and in every challenge that they faced they looked to their Savior for sustaining grace. It was His life flowing through theirs that transformed the lives of hundreds of lepers, students, soldiers, hospital workers, businessmen, pastors and missionaries – the poor, the rich, Indian and

American. It was their connection to Christ that made their lives so significant on earth and so influential for eternity.

Theirs were lives of utter dependence on the Lord Jesus Christ. They never dared to go at it alone or to chart their own course. Their duty was to follow the Master. Fred was fond of saying, "Where He leads me I will follow, what He feeds me I will swallow." A humorous statement but based on an attitude of surrender and a determination to obey even when it wasn't comfortable.

As branches they trusted the Vine completely. Dorothy once challenged a group of women with these words: "God's power is developed in His infinite program. Refuse to calculate, speculate or work it out yourself. Leave it in God's hands."

CHAPTER ONE
A Sure Foundation

"Christianity is not just a mere assent of doctrines and creeds, but it is a life given to God for the service of others." – Fred Waldock, March 1982

William Arthur Waldock had served his country as an officer for the British forces during the First World War. He had been a greengrocer in England before the war, but the German air raids had destroyed much of the country and unsettled conditions made life there difficult. So William and his young wife, Gladys Rose, decided to start over in Canada. They immigrated to Canada sometime between 1919 and 1920. They eventually settled in Crossfield, Alberta, a small town of about 800 people north of Calgary.

When William arrived in Crossfield, he worked as the manager of the dry goods section of a combination grocery and dry goods store. He was a methodical businessman.

The couple's first child - Frederick William Waldock - was born in Crossfield January 23, 1922. Seventeen months later Hedley was added to the family. Next, a girl, Grace, was born but she died as a child. The last was another son, Raymond, who was born five years after Hedley.

The family lived in town and William and Gladys attended a nominal Christian church. Sometime in the 1920's an evangelist by the name of Morrie Hall came to Crossfield to hold special meetings. This was a new experience for William and Gladys. Perhaps they were converted at this time or simply rededicated their lives to Christ. They pulled out of the nominal United

Church of Canada (a merger of Methodists, Congregationalists and most Presbyterians) and became part of a group of believers who started a new Baptist church in their community.

Fred was wheeled to church in a baby buggy from a very early age. The matter of church attendance was not even in question – the family went to Sunday school and church every Sunday. William became the Sunday school superintendent and Gladys was a teacher. Theirs was a strict Christian home and it was easy for Fred to think that he was a Christian. He couldn't recall a day when they didn't have family devotions.

The Great Depression ravaged the Canadian economy as it did in the United States. By the early 1930s a third of Canadian workers were unemployed. Factories went out of business or operated far below capacity. People who were still working faced uncertain prospects and deep wage cuts. The depression in Alberta led to cutbacks in the store where William worked.

In 1932 he applied for a job as a manager of a grocery store chain in Three Hills – a town about 50 miles from Crossfield. By the providence of God, William got the job and moved his family to Three Hills. There the family immediately got involved with Prairie Tabernacle and Prairie Bible Institute.

On a Sunday evening in June 1932 at the age of ten Fred realized that he was a lost sinner and needed to personally accept Christ as his Savior. When Fred was in the eleventh grade, Prairie Bible Institute started a Christian high school. Fred knew his parents wanted him to go. But Fred loved sports of all kinds and played on several high school sports teams. He knew there wouldn't be enough students at this new school for even a ball team.

The family prayed about the matter and then Fred was left to make his choice. Fred later related that incident in a sermon. "My parents said, 'You know how we feel about it but you make your own decision.' That was hard. I tried every way to get their sanction – but no, I had to make my own decision. And that was the best thing for me. To have to make decisions is character building."

"I really knew that I should go. Finally, I made the decision and went to the vice-principal and told him of my decision. It wasn't easy, but I felt the Lord's victory in my life. The next three years were spent in the best of Christian environments and I was riding on the joy of Christian fellowship."

Fred and Hedley were charter members at Prairie High School. In the summers the boys helped build at the Institute. The building skills they acquired during those summers were to be used many times on the mission field in later years. The boys also worked with their father in the grocery store. It was here that they learned how to be methodical and thorough in their work. Fred and Hedley were frequently challenged by missionaries from all parts of the world during their youth and Bible school days.

After graduating from high school in 1940 Fred attended Prairie Bible Institute. World War II had begun in Europe in 1938. Canada reluctantly entered the war in September of 1939 when Britain and France declared war on Germany. After one year at Prairie, Fred joined the Canadian army in 1942. Fred was selected for Officer's Training School and was commissioned as a Lieutenant in December 1943. Fred served in the Army for 22 months but did not see combat overseas. In general, relatively few Canadians were shipped overseas during the war.

Fred testifies, "It was during my early days in the Army that I really saw the world in all of its sin. I just couldn't believe that people could be so low. The devil worked hard and I'm sorry to say he won out in my life for a time, but the Lord in His mercy brought me back to Himself. I enjoyed the Army and received fast promotion and for that reason I fought against a medical discharge for an eye condition. The Lord knew best and I was discharged as a Lieutenant (in May 1944) after serving 22 months. Another period of serious backsliding took place, but (after 16 months) I again entered Bible college (in the fall of 1945) and finished my training."

During the war, William and Gladys Waldock joined the staff at Prairie Bible Institute. Both were teachers. William also served as treasurer and Gladys was dean of women.

Sometime during these years Fred read a little book called "Honey-Two of Lisu Land" by Mrs. A. B. Cooke of the China Inland Mission, which had been published for the first time in 1932. This book told the story of the Lisu tribe and specifically of the conversion and subsequent service to God of Honey-Two, a man of this tribe. The Lisu lived in the area now called Myanmar (formerly Burma). Honey-Two was from the Wa States located on the border of southwest China and Burma. This book and the China Inland Mission had a profound effect on Fred's thinking. He felt the Lord's call to China and began to earnestly prepare for that ministry.

Fred and Hedley were not only brothers, they were best friends. They did everything together. During the summer of 1946 Fred and Hedley went to work as counselors at Lake Sammamish Bible Camp near Seattle, Washington. Fred had been encouraged to go by a fellow student at Prairie Bible Institute – Marion Foss. In the providence of God, he met Marion's friend, Dorothy Richter, at the camp that summer.

CHAPTER TWO
A Girl Who Wants God's Best

"May we all be just as faithful as He who called us." – Fred Waldock,
February 1948

Dorothy Louise Richter was born in Wing, North Dakota – the seventh child of Charles Alvin and Ida Marie Richter. The date was February 23, 1924.

Dorothy's parents were married July 16, 1912 in Minneapolis, Minnesota. Charles was 24. Ida was 28. Within 15 months their first child, David, was born in Virginia, Minnesota. Edna was born a year later in Ishpeming, Michigan. Two years later a second son, Frederick, was born in Bismark, North Dakota. Nineteen months later in Sentinel Butte, North Dakota the fourth child, Charles, entered the world. Then came Albert in 1920 and Thomas in 1922. After Dorothy, Florence, the eighth and final child, was born in 1926 when Ida was 41. In fourteen years of marriage, 8 children were born. The family moved at least six times as both Charles and Ida served in the Salvation Army. Charles had attended the Salvation Army College and had risen to the rank of Captain. He was also a minister in the Episcopal Church.

In the summer of 1927 the family moved over 1200 miles to Tacoma, Washington. Dorothy was only three. In 1934 the family began to attend Temple Baptist Church – a new church that stood against modernism and held unswervingly to the Bible as the word of God. They had heard Dr. Powell preach on the radio. The Richter family was distressed by worldly practices in the church that they were attending and were attracted to this new church with its fundamental stand.

They started attending Temple Baptist Church when Dorothy was nine. The church was vibrant – people were being saved every week. In early 1935 when Dorothy was 10 she accepted the Lord as her Savior after a morning service at Temple. She was baptized on Sunday, March 11, 1935 with five other members of her family – her parents, brothers Albert and Tom and her sister Florence. Her brother Charles was saved on April 25th and baptized on June 23rd. Thus all of the Richter family with the exception of the three oldest siblings were baptized in 1935 and became members of Temple Baptist Church.

Temple Baptist had a zeal for missions and this must have impacted Dorothy. Until the mid-1970s the church took an annual missionary offering at Christmas time each year. The church's newsletter in November 1934 contained this challenge: "Instead of giving a lot of worthless, cheap candy to our boys and girls, we ought to teach them to make Christmas an occasion of sacrifice for Christ. The whole idea of Christmas should be unselfish, and if we simply give things to those from whom we expect to receive things in return we have defeated the only real value of Christmas."

The year 1935 was a time of great spiritual growth for the family but it was also the year that tragedy struck. Dorothy's father suffered a stroke during the evening of December 23, 1935. He entered the hospital on Christmas Eve and died shortly after midnight on December 26th. Charles was only 47 when he went home to heaven leaving his wife with eight children – the eldest being 22 and the youngest not quite 10. The Great Depression was still going on during those years. In fact, nearly all of Dorothy's childhood was during the depression era and the thriftiness she learned during these years stayed with her all her life.

In May of 1937 death struck again when Dorothy's oldest brother David died from a blood clot and heart problems. He was just a few months shy of 24 years old.

In high school, Dorothy felt that the Lord was calling her to serve Him. She often talked with her brother Albert about attending the Bible Institute of Los Angeles together. Albert had promised to save money so that they could both go to BIOLA. Albert joined the United States navy in the spring of 1939. Charles, Jr. was drafted into the army in January 1941. Later Al was assigned to a naval base in Hawaii. Then on December 7, 1941 calamity struck the Richter family a third time. Twenty-one year old Albert was on board the U.S. Arizona when the Japanese sank it during the raid on Pearl Harbor. On Saturday, December 20th Ida Richter received a telegram from the department of the navy informing her that Al was missing in action, following the performance of his duty in the service of his government.

Although heartbroken at the probable death of son and brother, the Richters maintained their faith in the Lord. Their Christian testimony was a blessing to both saved and unsaved people alike.

Dorothy graduated from Stadium High School in Tacoma in June 1942. She was very involved in the young people's group at Temple Baptist. Her leadership qualities and take charge attitude were evident even in high school. After graduation she worked to save money for Bible school.

In 1942 Dorothy met Marion Foss, a committed Christian who came to Tacoma to do Christian work among children. The two became good friends and the friendship lasted for the rest of their lives. Dorothy felt that the Lord wanted her to go to BIOLA but Temple Baptist wanted her to go to a Baptist college. Marion and Dorothy spent much time on their knees seeking the Lord's will for Dorothy. As the Lord would have it, Albert in his death provided for his sister's Bible school. His insurance policy was eventually paid and this money enabled Dorothy to go to BIOLA in September 1943. The people at Temple Baptist declared, "Dorothy has been one of our most faithful and consecrated young people. We will surely miss her."

During the summer of 1944 Temple Baptist Church hired Dorothy to do Bible clubs for children in various parts of Tacoma. Her schedule was one morning club, one afternoon club Monday through Friday. In September Dorothy and Florence returned to BIOLA. During the summer of 1945 Dorothy worked at Lake Sammamish Bible Camp as Marion Foss's junior counselor.

In Dorothy's senior year at BIOLA, two missionaries on furlough from India were very influential in giving Dorothy a burden for missionary service in India – a needy and difficult field. Dorothy told the Lord she would go to India if He so led. Dorothy enrolled in the School of Missionary Medicine at BIOLA and sent to Baptist Mid-Missions for application forms. Then she went home for summer vacation, still not completely convinced of her call.

That summer of 1946 she returned to Lake Sammamish Bible Camp.

CHAPTER THREE
Two Lives Blended Into One

"It's no little wonder why the Lord can't use us if we won't resign everything over to Him." –Fred Waldock, March 1947

Dorothy smiled with satisfaction as she looked around Lake Sammamish Bible Camp. She dearly loved this camp and the godly influence it was in so many counselors' and campers' lives. Aunt Ruby Jepson and her husband Annis were pouring their lives into the camp and that was what made it special. It was good to be back for a second summer. Dorothy felt sure that in this atmosphere God would continue to reveal His will for her life.

The staff at Lake Sammamish Bible camp came from various Bible schools in the United States and Canada. In the summer of 1946 there were several students from Prairie Bible Institute located in Alberta, Canada. Among them was a young Canadian named Fred Waldock who had a heart for God and an eye towards the mission field.

During the course of the summer the two future missionaries became acquainted. Soon they became interested in each other and looked for opportunities to spend time together. They volunteered to cook breakfast for the camp each morning - just the two of them. That summer there was quite a bit of lumpy oatmeal and burnt toast as the cooks' thoughts were on other matters. When free from camp responsibilities they took long walks together in the woods.

"Dodo, you know I believe God is calling me to China to work with the tribes in the southwest where John and Isobel Kuhn are working under China Inland Mission," said Fred earnestly.

"Yes," Dorothy replied as she gazed into the eyes of the strong, kind-hearted man she was falling in love with. "And I feel called to India."

Fred's heart was burdened. He was falling in love with Dorothy Richter but it seemed as though the Lord was calling them to different lands. Finally he went to Aunt Ruby Jepson with the problem.

"Aunt Ruby, can I talk with you?"

"Sure, Fred. What's up?" asked Aunt Ruby.

"Well, you see, I'm feeling mighty attracted to Dorothy. But she feels the Lord is calling her to be a missionary in India. And I feel led to China," said Fred looking downcast. "Under the circumstances, I don't know if I should continue to let the relationship grow."

"If the Lord is in it, Fred, He'll make the way clear," counseled Aunt Ruby. "You just have to keep praying for the Lord's will to be done. I'll be praying for both of you too."

"Thanks, Aunt Ruby," said Fred.

When camp was over, Fred stayed in the United States to have more time with Dorothy. He went to her home in Tacoma and met her mother and then accompanied Dorothy back to Los Angeles and the School of Missionary Medicine.

"Fred, we have to be determined to know the Lord's will for our lives," said Dorothy bravely.

"Yes, we can't permit ourselves to get involved out of the Lord's will," replied Fred with a sigh. "But I'm sure praying that it's the Lord's will that we'll be together forever, darling. I sure do love my Dodo," said Fred as held Dorothy's hand.

"You'll write, won't you?" asked Dorothy.

"You bet, every Wednesday and Sunday at the very least," replied Fred eagerly. "And I'll be thinking about you all the time."

The couple prayed together and then Fred began the long trip back to Prairie Bible Institute for his senior year. He felt sure that the Lord would work all this out for good.

Both Dorothy and Fred threw themselves into their studies, determined to prepare themselves well for the work God had for them. They were convinced of their love for each other and prayed that the Lord would work out the difficulties.

In early February 1947 Dorothy was still not sure of the Lord's will. She prayed that the Lord would show her whether she was to go to India or China or neither. At that time Hubert Mitchell had come to BIOLA for a missionary conference. As Dorothy sat in the auditorium she silently prayed, "Lord, if You want me to go to India have the speaker use 2 Corinthians 5:14 -15 – the verse You used to challenge me to surrender my life for India."

Hubert Mitchell stood and strode to the pulpit. Then he began to speak. "For the love of Christ constraineth us; because we thus judge, that if One died for all, then were all dead: and that He died for all, that they which live should not henceforth live unto themselves, but unto Him which died for them, and rose again. 2 Corinthians 5:14 -15."

"Oh, Lord, I do want Your will," Dorothy prayed. And yet, she also wanted Fred. Dorothy rose early the next morning and began her personal devotions. "Lord, I want to be so sure that you are calling me to India. Show me just once more," she prayed. Dorothy began to read her Bible where she had left off the day before. The Lord brought her attention to 2 Timothy 3:14, "But continue thou in the things which thou hast learned and hast been assured of, knowing of whom thou hast learned them." The matter was settled. Dorothy testified, "Then I knew for sure that the Lord really wanted me in India, and I have never doubted that call." With resolve, Dorothy sat down to write a letter to her beloved Fred telling him of how God had assuredly called her to India regardless of whether he was to go or not.

At the same time that God was working in one heart in Los Angeles, He was directing another in Three Hills, Alberta. The candidate secretary for China Inland Mission came to Prairie Bible Institute. He insisted that all candidates have further training. This raised a question in Fred's mind and in the minds of several other students. Fred did not feel the go-ahead to continue pursuing ministry under C.I.M.

At the same time, he heard more about Baptist Mid-Missions – a relatively new mission to him. Fred investigated Baptist Mid-Missions and their work in India and more and more the Lord seemed to be leading along that line. He sat down to write Dorothy about the complications in his going to China and told her he was considering Baptist Mid-Missions and India.

Their letters – revealing the will of the Lord – crossed in the mail. Fred and Dorothy rejoiced in the wonderful way that the Lord was leading them together. Soon after that, Fred learned that Baptist Mid-Missions' work in India was among the tribes in the northeast that were ethnically related to the tribes in southwest China that he had felt called to. The tribes in northeast India were also Mongolian peoples but lived on the other side of the Himalayan Mountains.

Soon Dorothy and Fred were unofficially engaged. As a student at Prairie Bible Institute, Fred was not allowed to become engaged until after graduation. But in their minds it was already settled. By Valentine's Day he had ordered an engagement ring.

Fred sat at his desk to study but could not keep his mind on his books. His thoughts were on the miracle that the Lord was doing to bring Dorothy permanently into his life. Pushing the books aside, he pulled a lightweight sheet of airmail paper from the desk drawer and began to write to his sweetheart.

"February 16, 1947
My Darling Dorothy,
We had a lot of fun playing hockey yesterday morning. The ice was more like slush. Boy I sure saw stars one time. I happened to get a break away and was tearing down toward the goal as fast as possible. Just as I shot the puck I saw I was going to run into the goal post. So I dodged it and as I did someone hit me from behind and I twisted right around in the air and cracked the back of my head right smack against the post. It was only a 2 x 6 I think. It just about knocked me out but I only suffered a lovely headache for the rest of the day. It's all in the game dear.
I was thrilled to read of how the Lord so marvelously and definitely revealed to you His will re India and for confirming your call so assuredly. I praise Him too, dear, that I know I have a girl who wants God's best no matter what the cost. I imagine that was a real testing time to you when you didn't know what I was going to do. I too want to

thank you for your prayers. I believe they played a great part in what has taken place.

When I wrote to the Mission I wasn't sure, in fact I thought you had been interested in central India. But I told them I was definitely interested in the tribes, and then in the next letter from you, you mentioned about the tribes in Assam. To tell you the truth dear, I don't know much about India, as I've never really considered it my place of service. It has always mostly been China. Yet in these last two weeks things about the C.I.M. are quite perplexing. The possibilities of getting out there very soon are rather grim. So I'm all the more assured that it is India. I'm very anxious to hear from Mid-Missions, but again I know the Lord will work it all out.

The Lord has been so good to us and has led us so marvelously that I'm sure everything will work out all right. We must not fret or worry though, dear, but to trust Him and to continue in prayer.

My love for you grows greater every day and I mean it. I don't see how, but it is so. I'll be thinking of you much throughout the day. I sure does love my 'Dodo.'

Always yours for always,
Fred"

In a letter to Fred, Dorothy included a tract called "On Wings of Song" written by Baptist Mid-Missions missionary Leona Barnum. The little pamphlet told the amazing story of how God allowed His message to infiltrate Hindu Manipur State. Leona Barnum was learning the Manipur language in hopes of someday being able to enter this area and teach the people about Jesus. She loved to sing gospel songs in the Manipur language even though her teacher said that her pronunciation left much to be desired. While in Calcutta on a shopping trip, the Holy Spirit impressed her with the thought: "Make a Victrola recording of a gospel song in the Manipur language." Obedient to the Spirit, Leona made a recording of the hymn "Only Trust Him." When her language teacher learned she had made a record he was horrified. When the record arrived in the mail, Leona gave it to her language teacher for evaluation. He played it several times and declared that it was very good and pronunciation mistakes were almost non-existent. The teacher began to play the record for his countrymen. It was the first recording of any kind in the Manipur language. The teacher, who was still a Hindu, asked to take the record with him when he visited Manipur State. The son of the Maharajah ordered a copy of the record, as did many other wealthy Manipuri. The gospel song was played at weddings, funerals and on holy days.

This pamphlet only intensified the burden that Dorothy and now Fred had for the tribal people of northeast India. The couple began to pray the Lord would provide the money for Dorothy to travel to Canada in April for the spring conference at Prairie Bible Institute and Fred's graduation. The night of the graduation Fred intended to give Dorothy an engagement ring. Fred and Dorothy had also sent letters to Baptist Mid-Missions in Cleveland, Ohio asking for an application and recommendations for further training.

Although both of them had very heavy course loads, their love for each other made correspondence a priority. On March 16, 1947 Fred wrote, *"We had a wonderful message this morning on: 'What hinders us from having the authority of God in our lives?' The basic reason is that we refuse to be under His authority. It's no little wonder why the Lord can't use us if we won't resign everything over to Him. I trust dear that we will have that as our motto as we seek to serve the Lord. Our lives will be useless in India unless we are under the authority of Christ, then we will have the authority of Him in our lives.*

I received a letter from Mid-Missions last night. I guess they never even got my other letter so I'm going to write them again about what I told them before. They sent me their last paper, also a history of the work and two other pamphlets so I have plenty to read. I don't see any reason, darling, why I shouldn't go under them, if that is what the Lord wants. I guess I'll have to join a Baptist church. I don't think that should be anything to worry about because our doctrine up here is close to Baptist anyway. Mother and Dad both belonged to a Baptist church. I don't suppose there would be any trouble in me joining a church down in the States seeing as how I'm a Canadian would there? I'll be anxious to hear from Mid-Missions again, when I tell them about you. I told them before but I don't think they received that letter.

We had a good service last night. Two missionaries from Lisu-Land in China spoke. These people of whom they talked are much the same as those to whom we'll be going. My, what a challenge.

My love always,
Fred"

On March 19 Fred wrote, *"My Darling Dodo, it's exactly six months today since I left you in Los Angeles so I think it's about time we met again, huh dear? It's wonderful to know the Lord is leading. I forgot to praise the Lord with you for the way the money (for Dorothy's trip to Canada) has come in; $70 seemed an awful lot to me at first, but again the Lord proved Himself faithful."*

After many weeks of heightened anticipation, April finally came and with it Fred's graduation from Prairie Bible Institute. Dorothy stayed with Fred's mother. As Fred put the engagement ring on Dorothy's finger he wondered if he would ever be as happy as he was at that moment. The two rejoiced in God's sovereign plan for their lives.

After graduation, Fred and his brother Hedley moved to Vancouver and worked in a lumberyard for 87 cents an hour. Both were to be married in early summer so they lived frugally and tried to save as much of their paychecks as possible. Dorothy returned to Los Angeles to finish the School of Missionary Medicine.

In May, Dorothy received a letter from her future mother-in-law. In part it read, *"It means so much to me to see Fred so happy. God bless you both abundantly, and use your united lives for His glory. I am only too glad to see you both going ahead with your plans. So few go to the mission field, and so many have not heard of a Savior for them. As much as I would love to have you home for awhile, I fully realize the Lord's will and work must come first. He will undertake in His own way when you should come this way again. My prayer for both you and Fred, Thelma and Hedley is that the Lord will take you to the field as soon as He sees fit. It is a joy to me that that is the purpose of you all. How wonderfully He has and is working all things out for you. His will is being done. Praise His Name."*

Dorothy graduated from the School of Missionary Medicine on June 5, 1947 and she and her sister Florence returned to Tacoma the following week. Fred remained in Vancouver to work until just before the wedding.

Fred and Dorothy were married on Sunday, July 6, 1947 at 9 p.m. at Temple Baptist Church. Their call to the mission field was apparent even at the wedding. A large banner made by Marion Foss proclaimed "Chosen For Service - John 13:18". The wedding included a prayer of consecration for missionary service.

CHAPTER FOUR
Missionary Appointees

"Each one who has received Jesus Christ as his own personal Savior has the responsibility of seeing that the gospel is given out to others who have never had the privilege of hearing." – Fred Waldock, January 1949

The Sunday after the wedding Fred was baptized and joined Temple Baptist Church. On August 24, 1947 Temple Baptist Church licensed him as a minister for missionary work.

In September Fred and Dorothy moved to Los Angeles so that Fred could take the School of Missionary Medicine course. Temple Baptist Church sent the couple off with a generous love gift. In appreciation for that gift, Fred wrote: *"Dear Friends in Christ,*

Dorothy and I wish to take this opportunity to thank you for your generous love gift to us as we left for Los Angeles to resume studies again in preparation for our missionary work in India.

We are looking to the Lord to make this the most blessed year of our lives, one in which we will grow in the grace of our Lord Jesus and will be better fitted to serve our Lord in the needy field of India to which He has called us.

It is with great anticipation that we look forward to our life work. We can assure you that your gift will be used wisely towards our training. Let me say also that it is indeed a personal joy to belong to a church that desires to see God's purpose and plan fulfilled in the lives of their young people. Most of all we thank you for your prayers, which we feel and know are most essential in the life of any Christian. May God bless you as a church as you minister to Him, and as individuals as you seek to do His will..."

Soon it became apparent that the couple was to be a family. The baby was due in April of 1948.

In February Temple Baptist Church joyfully voted to authorize Fred and Dorothy Waldock as their missionaries. The church paid for the young couple to travel to Cleveland, Ohio to attend the quarterly missionary conference and be interviewed by the General Council of Cooperating Baptist Missions of North America, Inc. known as Mid-Missions.

The church members, as well as Dorothy and Fred, were much in prayer for this interview. If accepted, they would be missionaries, if not – well they didn't want to think about that. God had so marvelously led them together and called them to India that they were convinced that He would also carry them through the doctrinal interview.

Fred and Dorothy arrived early at Hough Avenue Baptist Church in Cleveland. Dorothy, eight months pregnant, was nervous, as was Fred. They did not have to wait long – they were the first candidates to be examined by the General Council. Just before the first general meeting they were told the good news – they had passed and were officially accepted as missionary appointees to India!

After the meeting that night they sat down to write the good news to Temple Baptist Church.

Thursday, Feb. 19, 1948

"Dear Christian friends,

We were looking to India by faith, but now it is fast becoming a reality...Praise the Lord for His continued faithfulness. Our hearts are full of gratitude, first of all for His saving grace, and then for the work He has set before us. There is no greater place of blessing than in His perfect will and especially so if that is in full-time service for Him. The rewards and blessings far outnumber the trials and we realize that there will be many of the latter on the foreign field.

We are also so very thankful for our church and every one of you who have been so faithful in helping us and praying for us. You have a real part in our service for Him. So you who have been praying with and for us join now in a song of praise and thanksgiving and then continue to pray for further guidance as we endeavor to get passports, equipment, etc. Where prayer focuses, power falls.

We are indeed glad to be your representatives in this field of service. You have just as definite a responsibility as we have. May we all be just as faithful as He who called us. Yours for needy India, Fred and Dorothy."

By the end of the conference six individuals were appointed for service in India – the Waldocks, Gertrude Berg, Neva Jones, Glenola Marchel and Isabelle Swanson. Rev. and Mrs. John Wilkens were reconfirmed for service in India at that time.

Such a large influx of new workers was good news for the India field. The Baptist Mid-Missions work in Assam had been started thirteen years earlier in 1935 by Dr. and Mrs. Galen Crozier who by that time were nearly seventy years old. The Croziers had worked in India since 1899 but their former mission board had forced them to retire. But Dr. Crozier's burden for the Manipuri people would not retire. By God's providence the Croziers eventually joined Mid-Missions and began a new work in Assam.

Perhaps Fred and Dorothy learned of some of the earlier work in India from Leola at that conference. Dr. Crozier and his wife Mabel began the work in Assam in 1935. They met Manipuris in the marketplace and conversed with them in their native tongue. The interest in the gospel was strong among the Manipuri who were denied the gospel in their native state located next to Assam. The people purchased more than 600 copies of the gospel of John within just a few weeks of the Croziers' arrival. Land was purchased at Alipur – a rural area thickly populated with Bengali, Manipuri and tribal peoples of Hindu, Islamic and animistic beliefs.

A dispensary was opened and the sick and blind came to get healing for their physical and spiritual needs. There were setbacks in those early years. One night the dispensary and other buildings were destroyed by fire. But victories came too. Manipuris began to accept the gospel and God provided the Croziers with missionary colleagues – Leona Barnum in 1938 and Jim and Joyce Garlow and Julia Rose in 1939. Jewell Earnhart and Rachel Funk arrived in May 1940. Dr. and Mrs. Lilburn Burrows and the Delos Priors came too. As the available personnel increased so did the outreach. A leper colony was established and outreach began in various villages.

A church was organized and grew as outreach was conducted in the surrounding villages. Scripture translation continued.

Before World War II, Mid-Missions' missionary force in India had grown to a dozen workers.

The future of the India work looked very promising until World War II invaded Northeast India. In May 1942 the British ordered all missionaries to evacuate Assam. The missionaries scattered to various parts of India and back to the homeland. At the urging of Dr. Crozier, Dr. Burrows volunteered his services to the British military.

But the missionaries would not be deterred from their God-given responsibilities. By November, Rachel, Leola and the Croziers were back at Alipur. In 1944 Miss Barnum went on furlough. The Burrows and Garlows left for much needed rest in 1945. As Dr. Crozier visited the sick in the villages, Mrs. Crozier worked on translating the New Testament into Thadou Kuki with the help of a language consultant. After that, she and another helper did major revising of the Manipuri New Testament which had been translated earlier. From 1945 to 1947 Rachel helped with the checking and revising.

India was given her independence from Britain in 1947. The new government was slow in granting permits for missionaries to return. Those that had gone home during the war were not able to get visas to return. Then the Croziers and Rachel received word that Dr. Burrows was on his deathbed. In February 1947, Lilburn went home to be with the Lord during an operation in the veterans' hospital in Columbia, South Carolina. Mrs. Burrows resolutely determined to continue her missionary service and made plans to return to India with her daughter, leaving the two older boys in the United States for schooling.

The revision of the Manipuri New Testament manuscript was finished in May 1947 and the next day Rachel had word of her booking for the USA for furlough. Again the Croziers were left alone in Assam. The needs of Assam were still as great as ever but at 81 years of age Dr. Crozier was slowing down, albeit unwillingly. Thirteen years had been invested in Assam under Mid-Missions and many souls had been won to the Savior. Two churches had been started – one in Manipuri and one in Bengali. Dr. Crozier was determined by God's grace to see the work continue. A hospital needed to be built and other outreaches accomplished for the Lord's glory.

Hope for additional coworkers was rekindled when James and Joyce Garlow received permits to return to Assam in the fall of 1947– the first received in seven years. After many months of consecrated prayer, word was received at the Mid-Missions Home Office on December 22, 1947 that visas had also been granted to Leola Barnum, Beulah Burrows and a new missionary, Doris Bruce. How they all rejoiced and thanked the Lord of the Harvest for answered prayer.

Soon after the conference in Cleveland, these women sailed for India. The Croziers plans were to leave India in April 1948 to come to the United States with the intent of passing their burden for the tribes of Assam on to a younger doctor.

After the exciting Mid-Missions conference Fred and Dorothy joyfully returned to Los Angeles. They could hardly believe it! Now they were missionaries! And in just a few short weeks they would be parents. On April 26, 1948 David Arthur Waldock entered the world.

Fred graduated from the School of Missionary Medicine in June 1948. The family made a quick trip to Tacoma, Washington and Temple Baptist Church before going to Canada for Wycliffe's linguistics school. By the first of October they were back in Tacoma. On October 17th Temple Baptist Church voted to begin support of the Waldocks as the church anticipated by the Providence of God that the family would soon depart for India.

Fred and Dorothy prayed that God would provide for them to sail not later than January 1949 so that they would be in India before the extreme hot season began. A great need was a passport and visa for Dorothy. The Canadian government had already provided Fred's but Dorothy's was delayed.

As they sought the Lord in prayer about a sailing date they were also asking Him to provide a rather significant amount for outfit and passage. Less than two years before they had thought that $70 to get Dorothy to Fred's graduation was a step of faith. Now they were praying that the Lord would provide almost $1,200 for passage to India. Temple Baptist Church was in the middle of an ambitious building project. Would they be able to help with outfit and passage money at the same time?

Fred and Dorothy dearly loved their church family and were very interested in seeing the building go up. They had little to give financially to the project but Fred lent his time and his muscle. He worked tirelessly on the building when they were in Tacoma. In November the little family traveled much, speaking in Baptist churches about the need in India.

Each year Temple Baptist Church took a missionary offering at Christmas time. It was determined that this year the church would especially seek to honor God by providing for the Waldock's needs. People also purchased items of equipment for the missionaries.

An article in the church newspaper, The Temple Tidings, encouraged the congregation to give sacrificially toward the missionary offering. *"It would be difficult for any of us to make a choice and settle the question as to what is the most important thing for us to do right now for we have so many exceedingly important matters before us. Yet it would be likely that all of us would agree that the missionary offering is of such importance that it should take the lead in our hearts and minds this week. It isn't necessary for us to remind you of the work and workers involved. Fred and Dorothy Waldock must be prepared and sent away to the mission field at the very first part of the year. They are getting everything together now and expect to sail about the latter part of January or the first part of February. This offering is the basis of their supply, humanly speaking, and if we do not bring our hearts into a large place in this time of giving, other sacred causes may have to suffer. We realize that this offering will have to be made in sacrifice, at least many of our fine people will have to do without something they need to make this offering what it ought to be. It is a matter of our deepest concern that we shall not fail our Lord nor any of His great work in this effort. How much do we love **Him**?"*

In faith at the end of December Fred booked passage for the family for the month of February. The total cost of the ticket for the three of them was $1,134 – which is the usual price of one ticket by ordinary travel. But Fred was able to secure passage on a freighter with a passenger deck through Washington Travel Bureau.

The offering at the end of December was less than what was needed and a second offering day was scheduled. "Complete the Sacrifice Day" was set for January 9, 1949. On January 3rd one couple, after much prayer, determined that they simply had to do more to help Fred and Dorothy get to the field. The husband approached the pastor on Monday and said, "We can't go – but we want to help send Fred and Dorothy." With that declaration he opened his wallet and emptied it of its contents. He gave $45."

In response to the gifts of equipment from individuals in the church, Fred wrote the following thank you note.

"*Dear Friends,*

'For unto whomsoever much is given, of him shall be much required.' (Luke 12:48) Each one who has received Jesus Christ as his own personal Savior has the responsibility of seeing that the gospel is given out to others who have never had the privilege of hearing. God has called us to go; it is your privilege and responsibility to enable us to go by giving and praying. The task is equally as much yours as ours according to God's Word.

We thank you from the bottom of our hearts for all that each one of you has done for us already. We would like to thank each one of you personally but that is impossible at this busy time of packing and preparing to go. As we use each item we will be thinking of you who gave them and we trust that your giving will create in you a real prayer interest for us. We dare not go without God's people standing behind us in prayer.

May we always be found faithful in using all that the Lord has given us both spiritually and materially.

Labors together in Him, Fred, Dorothy and David Waldock."

The special offering on January 9th amounted to $632.80. However, the Waldocks could not take advantage of the sailing on January 28 because Dorothy's visa had still not arrived. Believing that all things work together for good to them that love God, they set their sights on a sailing on March 2nd out of Seattle.

Dorothy's visa arrived on January 27. A special day of prayer was held at Temple at the end of January. Another was held on Friday, February 18th. The Lord's presence was felt by many that attended the Lord's Supper service held at the conclusion of the day of prayer. On Sunday, February 20th during a fellowship hour honoring the Waldocks, God did an amazing thing. Twenty-two of Temple's young people came forward indicating their surrender of life to full-time Christian service!

Finally the day for departure arrived. A group of friends from Temple Baptist Church joined with Dorothy's family to see Fred, Dorothy and David off at the Greyhound Bus station. The

Waldocks took the bus to Portland, Oregon where they met the S. S. Canada - the freighter that would take them to India. The ship set sail on March 3, 1949 with twelve passengers. As the ship pulled out of the harbor, Fred and Dorothy remembered the verse that God had given them when He united their lives and called them to serve Him in India. John 15:16 had became their life verse. "Ye have not chosen Me, but I have chosen you, and ordained you that ye should go and bring forth fruit, and that your fruit should remain: that whatsoever ye shall ask of the Father in my name, He may give it you."

CHAPTER FIVE
On the Way

"I don't believe that any young person who says he hasn't been called would ever say that again, if he once saw the faces of these people, with their hunger for the something that only the Gospel can give them." –
Fred Waldock, March 1949

The ship's course was to cross the Pacific from Longview, WA to Manila, Philippines. But this trip across the Pacific turned out to be anything but tranquil. Once on the high seas, hurricane winds and terrific storms buffeted the ship for days on end. As the ship rolled and tossed, Fred and Dorothy succumbed to seasickness. Nearly one-year-old David maintained his sea legs better than his parents did, making it difficult for them to keep watch over him. It was almost more than Dorothy could manage to keep her son in clean diapers. As the nausea took hold, both Fred and Dorothy lost weight. For twelve days the S. S. Canada struggled until finally the storm blew itself out. Blown off course and running late, they docked in Japan. It had been a rough beginning - an experience they would never forget.

In Japan, Fred and Dorothy's eyes were opened to the need of missions in a most vivid way. The destitute look on the faces of the people impacted them deeply. They were appalled by the poverty around them. The clothes that the Japanese people wore were so old and worn that the missionaries could not tell the original pattern because there were so many patches.

Fred and Dorothy saw a wonderful opportunity for the gospel in Japan. Fred commented, "You know, Dorothy, I don't believe that any young person who says he hasn't been called would ever say that again, if he just once saw the faces of these people with their hunger for the something that only the Gospel can give them."

"If it were not for the fact that the Lord has shown us that our duty is in India, I would say we should stay here and do missionary work," said Dorothy, as the two walked around the city.

"It certainly is a needy place," agreed Fred.

Fred and Dorothy took the opportunity of being in port to send word back to the home church. Fred wrote:

"But they that wait upon the Lord shall renew their strength: they shall mount up with wings as eagles; they shall run, and not be weary; they shall walk and not faint." Isaiah 40:31

"We can thank the Lord for this verse afresh as we make this trip. It seems it is taking a much longer time than we had expected but we are confident that the Lord is in it. We have an opportunity to wait upon Him and renew our strength. And then there is a great opportunity to get all the rest that we need in a physical way. Although I must say that we are getting tired of just sitting around waiting for the boat to take us on our way.

When we left home we didn't think that we were going to Japan and here we are still in Japan. We will arrive in our last port today. Actually by this time we were supposed to have been leaving Manila, but instead we won't even get there until Sunday, and we will be there for three or four days. As it looks now we will not arrive in India before the 20th of April but the Lord knows, and we know that He will continue to lead us as He has done already.

We have had a few opportunities to speak to the passengers and crew members. They are a very good bunch but the things of the Lord are of no interest to them. We are asking an interest in your prayers on behalf of our testimony to them. We have been conscious of your prayers a great deal thus far. We praise the Lord over and over for your backing in prayer."

In another letter they wrote, *"We are asking the Lord to teach us much from Himself these days of traveling and to prepare us both physically and most of all spiritually before we get to Assam. As we near the field, our responsibility seems even greater and ourselves much weaker. He must work in us and through us if we are to bear fruit.*

Don't forget to pray for our arrival in Calcutta that we may get through customs without having to pay a great deal of duty."

One night after supper while Fred and Dorothy were in their cabin, David slipped quietly out of the room. The adventurous toddler headed toward the steps. His cries alerted the young parents that he had escaped. In terror they followed the sound and discovered David at the bottom of a flight of steel steps. Fred flew down the steps and picked up his son. The Lord had certainly protected David because he wasn't even scratched and he stopped crying in just a few minutes. Back in their room the family knelt to thank the Lord for sparing David from harm.

The trip from Japan to Manila, Philippines and on to Calcutta was largely uneventful and the family was able to rest much in anticipation of the strenuous adjustment to life in India before them. They arrived safely in Calcutta on April 21, 1949 – almost seven weeks after leaving Portland, Oregon.

As they stepped off the boat in Calcutta their senses were overwhelmed by the masses of people. Everyone seemed to be pushing and shoving. Although it was only April, this was nothing like springtime in Tacoma. The air was hot and humid. Fred and Dorothy tried not to be shocked at the poverty, filth and dirt on the streets, and by the people who lived on those streets. The noise of thousands of people speaking foreign tongues was exotic at first but then quickly added to their confusion. Fred removed his hat and wiped the sweat out of his eyes. So this is India. Heat. Insects. People. People everywhere. Satan and his demons have ruled here for centuries. Fred could almost feel the spiritual oppression as he leaned against the rail of the ship. Fred clutched David a little tighter in his arm, returned his hat to his head and squeezed Dorothy's hand to give her assurance.

They had arrived in India. The land of their call. And they would move forward dependent on the One who had called. "Faithful is He who calleth you, Who also will do it."

The immediate challenge would be to find the missionary that would be meeting the ship and then to get through customs. It would be a long process, no doubt. Out of the corner of his eye, Fred spotted a white man waving his arm. It was veteran missionary Jim Garlow. Fred acknowledged Jim with a wave. Welcome to India.

After what seemed like days rather than hours, the Waldocks were finally cleared through customs. "India is the land of delay," explained Garlow. "You'd better get used to it."

Jim Garlow took the young family to the train station. They would go directly to Darjeeling in the northeast of India for language school. Once they were settled in a compartment, Garlow cautioned them, "Don't open this door for anyone until you get to Darjeeling." Darjeeling, located in northeastern India near the border of Nepal and Sikkim, was more than 400 miles from hot and steamy Calcutta. On the way, some people tried to break into their compartment. But the young missionaries put their trust in their faithful Rock and Fortress. Perhaps the words of Psalm 31 gave them comfort, "In thee, O Lord, do I put my trust; let me never be ashamed: deliver me in Thy righteousness. Bow down Thine ear to me; deliver me speedily: be Thou my strong rock, for a house of defense to save me. For Thou art my rock and my fortress; therefore for Thy name's sake lead me, and guide me."

David celebrated his first birthday five days after they landed in India. For the first six months they were assigned to language school where they studied Bengali. Darjeeling is located in the lower Himalayas at about the 6,000-foot level. From a distance it looked like a fairyland with castle-like structures appearing to hover in the clouds and the Himalayas in the distance.

In June Fred and Dorothy wrote, *"We never cease to thank the Lord for His goodness to us and for the way He meets us daily."* Their language school was not without problems. Good tutors were scarce and progress was slow at first. Some of their luggage was held up as well. The rainy season, June through October, had also begun.

In September 27-year-old Fred and three other fellows went hiking in the Himalayan Mountains. They trekked to the 12,000-foot level where they hoped to have a spectacular view of Mt. Everest located on the border between Nepal and Tibet. Fred related the story to Dorothy who by this time was six months pregnant with their second child; *"It was a very hard trek as we traveled from 4,000 feet to 10,000 feet in seven miles the first day. The second day we had fourteen miles to go, six miles were downgrade and eight miles were up. And I do mean up. We were four tired lads when we reached the summit. The air gets very thin after 10,000 feet and the going is slow. We were disappointed when we got to the top because we had a cloudy day and couldn't see anything of Everest from that vantage point."*

In October the India field council met to discuss how best to expand the work in India. When the five veteran missionaries (Rachel Funk, Leona Barnum, Jim and Joyce Garlow and Beulah Burrows) met with the nine new recruits (Fred and Dorothy, Doris Bruce, Neva Jones, Isabelle Swanson, Glenola Marchel, John and Cora Wilkens and Connie Olds) in Banskandi they looked to the Lord for the future direction of the India field. The Lord had provided new laborers for Assam and the time was ripe for expansion.

Discussion at that field council meeting concerned buying 1,000 acres of an abandoned tea plantation for the establishment of a leprosy and agricultural colony. Dr. and Mrs. Crozier had established a leper colony at Alipur. Houses had been built to accommodate them and there was also a small clinic and a TB ward. Dr. Crozier had dreamed of building a full-scale hospital at Alipur but a lack of missionary workers, and especially a doctor, had slowed down the expansion. But now the missionary force had grown again and Dr. Crozier had recruited a young doctor and his wife for India. Dr. and Mrs. Quentin Kenoyer from Indianapolis would be coming out to India in about a year. So now there was a need to move the leprosy patients to make room for building a general hospital and a nurses' training school at Alipur.

Fred wrote, *"If we feel as a Mission that we can take over this new place, we (Fred and Dorothy) will more than likely be sent there...From what we have heard of the place, it will be ideal in every way for the work among the new tribes. It was originally to be the site for a tea garden but evidently it didn't go through. There is a fine building on the land and much of the land is broken and ready for cultivation. According to Jim Garlow it is almost self-propagating. It will cost considerable but they will accept small payments. The opportunities are great for work in this tribe and as yet they have never been evangelized. This is a great responsibility if the Lord should lead us to take over this site, and we will certainly need wisdom from Him."*

Since Fred and Dorothy had completed the course in missionary medicine, they felt led to help with the start of the work at Makunda Leprosy Colony. After the field council meeting, Fred and Dorothy moved to Jorhat located in one of the districts north of Cachar District. Fred taught in the Christian school there and took opportunities to witness to the police patrol and others. While in Jorhat they continued to pray about the matter of taking on the work of the leprosy colony.

The young missionaries in a strange land had much to adjust to. Dorothy wrote home to her mother. She wrote:

October 29, 1949
"Dearest Mommie,

We received your letter sent October 20th in just 7 days – not too bad, huh? Mail evidently comes faster here than to Banskandi. We are moved into our new place but it is kind of bare in spots because we have so little furniture. Mr. Cook loaned us a dining room set, wicker settee and wicker chairs, beds, etc. so we do have that much. We are using our kerosene stove and it works fine.

David likes it here and has a great time running from one end of the house to the other. His ayah (nanny) is very good at watching him while he is out of doors so I don't have to worry. It isn't like home – you just can't let the children outdoors a minute alone because of snakes, bugs, et cetera. We haven't seen any snakes here because they keep the grass cut short but you can never tell.

It's still very hot here especially during the days but David doesn't seem to mind. I can take a nap in the afternoon and wake up wringing wet but David takes his every day and doesn't seem to be so hot when he wakes up.

Our new cook is the brother of our ayah but he's a lemon. She is willing to do anything and he tries to get out of everything...People at home may think we are lucky to have servants but it would be far less strain to live without them. You always have to watch them for stealing and cheating you when they do the shopping. We've had reports that this cook is light fingered so we especially have to keep tabs on him. If he doesn't work out better we're going to get someone else. If I could just get a boy to help me I could do the cooking part fast enough using the kerosene stove and then I'd still have time for language study.

We are thankful for the ayah though, as it is a big relief to know that David is safe when he is out playing.

Fred has already started his schedule. He teaches Bible Doctrine three mornings a week in the Bible school and has had to speak twice up here so far. Next week Mr. Cook will be going to a two-week conference so Fred will substitute for a couple more classes for him.

Tuesday morning we start lessons with our new Bengali teacher from 8:00 to 10:00 a.m. six mornings a week. We hope to make some good progress before leaving here. Most of the people talk Assamese around here so except for a few phrases we are learning, we can't talk to most of the people. I know how to tell the ayah to give David a bath, wash his clothes, or hands or face and tell her she may go home and when to come back but other than that I have to point and show her. The cook can understand Bengali and also some English which is his only good point!!

Must close and get some other letters off before noon…

All our love and kisses,

Fred, Dorothy and David"

In another letter dated Saturday, November 26, 1949 from Jorhat she tells more of her new life in India.

"Dearest Mommie,

Just finished having my Bengali lesson so thought I'd write to you while Fred is shopping and David is outside playing. You could never realize the difference here in weather now. Just last week it was terrifically hot around noon. Now this week it has been cold and cloudy all day. This morning I left David's warm P.J. top on him and put a sweater over that to keep him warm. There's no way of heating this big place except a small fireplace in the front room. They say that after this rainy spell we're having this week it will warm up by noon each day but the evenings and mornings are really quite cold. They always told me that India is a land of extreme climates and I'm beginning to find out!

We are still waiting to hear from Jim (Garlow) if he got the tea estate. The girls from our station who were supposed to come up here for a medical conference changed their minds so didn't come. Thursday was Thanksgiving and we talked about inviting someone to dinner but everyone had their houses full of guests for the conference so I just decided to skip it as long as Fred is Canadian anyway. But that afternoon he had the cook bake a pumpkin pie and then he bought a chicken that we roasted in parchment paper and we had a small Thanksgiving dinner anyway.

Yes, we still have that cook. He did a pretty good job for about a week so we thought we'd keep him but he's been lousy for the last three days again – meals never on time, if he doesn't want to cook something he just doesn't and helps himself to anything he wants, apparently. Last night we wanted to start a fire in the fireplace but he had taken all the sticks we had saved for it and then blamed it on the ayah. I have to keep everything locked up in the pantry and then put out just enough for each meal. They deliver bread every other day here – nice white bread – but we used to run out at least one meal before it came. This time I locked up the bread because I saw him take some and now we are a whole loaf ahead...

I don't want you to worry about us. We really don't have it hard. Servants are the most trying but they are a little bit of help sometimes!! We are going to have string beans out of our own garden for dinner tomorrow. Will probably write you from the hospital next time.

Lots of love and kisses,
Fred, Dorothy and David"

Shortly after that letter their second son, Kenneth, was born December 1, 1949 in the mission hospital at Jorhat. In December the Waldocks learned that the purchase of the tea plantation had gone through and that they would be moving to Makunda to begin work there in the leprosy colony. Christmas that year was spent at the army barracks in Jorhat ministering to the soldiers.

On January 2, 1950 the family moved south again to Banskandi as an intermediate step in moving to Makunda. The trip started out all right. Fred had purchased second class special tickets, which were almost as nice as first class tickets only cheaper. They were supposed to have the same class the whole trip but when they transferred at 9 p.m. that night they discovered the next train didn't have special second class. So the family had to travel second class. As Dorothy entered the coach she was dismayed to see that it was full. Indian men had stretched all their bedrolls out on the seats and there was no room for anyone else.

As Fred struggled to get all their luggage aboard, Dorothy stood there with both Kenny and David crying. Her anger beginning to rise, she shoved a Muslim man's feet over and sat down with Kenny. The man did not budge. He just stretched out full length and covered his head with a blanket. Dorothy shoved him aside a little more and continued to sit. A couple of the other men were a little more kind and tried to make room for them.

When the luggage was on the train, Fred put Kenny's basket on some suitcases and got him settled and put the bedroll on some other things in the aisle and David slept there. Then Fred put paper on the floor and rested his head on the end of David's bed and there he slept. Dorothy crawled into her little corner on the end of the bench and put her feet over on David's bed and then everyone was settled for the night. Three windows were out of the coach and one of them right by Dorothy's head but they were all wrapped up in blankets so they did not suffer. They tried to transfer trains the next morning at 8 a.m. but that train was full to overflowing so they had to wait four or five hours for another. Even the next train couldn't take the bigger freight so it came on another train. The missionary men had to make another trip into Silchar for it the next day. There was some danger in traveling at this time as well because of the growing dissension between Hindus and Muslims. Recently riots had broken out in various places in their vicinity. Such was travel in India in 1950.

"January 5, 1950
Banskandi P.O. Cachar District, Assam

"Dearest Mommie,
Sorry this is late but I suppose you realized we were at last moving. We left Jorhat Monday and arrived here at Banskandi on Tuesday. We didn't tell the doctor we were going because he said not to go before the 15th but when the Lord answered so definitely in my health so that I could go, I didn't see how we could wait that long. That sure wouldn't be much faith, would it? I had perfect peace in coming and I don't think I am any worse off for the trip. David had a bad cold before we left and still has it but I think he would still have it if we had stayed there too. It is so much warmer here it seems and not any of that heavy dew in the mornings and evenings. It's really a nice climate in winter – warm enough in the middle of the day to wear a cotton dress without a sweater.
I don't think all missionaries give the worst side of the field although I suppose a lot do. There are a few nice things about India but

if I was here just for secular work I'm afraid I would choose to go home. But when the Lord takes care of you and provides for you, it isn't so bad.

I'm sure getting tired of moving but we aren't through yet...Jim has already moved 15 lepers down to Makunda to start work. He will be back on Saturday and as far as I know all the Waldocks will move down next Tuesday instead of my staying here.

Then in April we have to move back to Darjeeling for language school. What a life, huh? It keeps us moving and broke! It's a blessing we have such good kids, though. Both Kenny and David slept on the last trip and were so good. Kenny is almost completely over his jaundice now and gaining about 10 ounces a week.

It's seven minutes to six and I hear the first cheep out of Kenny so guess he is waking up for his supper. Wish you would pray we could get a good ayah. The one we had in Jorhat was only fair but she wouldn't come with us. They say they are almost impossible to get at Makunda but maybe we can get someone to train. I don't know. It's impossible to study or get anything else done without one. Will write more when we get settled at Makunda.

All our love and kisses,
Dorothy, Fred, David and Kenny"

CHAPTER SIX
Beginning at Makunda

"Even in trying circumstances and hard places His grace has proved sufficient and His blessings have far exceeded and surpassed hardships."
– Fred Waldock, May 1951

The Waldocks moved to Makunda in mid-January and began to get a look at their new home. It seemed to them an ideal spot in many ways. Their bungalow, which was built for the tea planters, was never completed by the planters but was quite nice. It was of concrete construction with a thatch roof, which made for coolness in the hot season. The missionaries planned to make it into living quarters for two families and perhaps one or two of the single women until other houses could be built.

The house sat right on the top of a hill overlooking the rice fields, lush green jungle and small villages on every side. The view was beautiful, the sunsets glorious. The Makunda property was about a section and a half and consisted of rice land, jungle, three rivers and many small villages.

In less than a ten-minute walk in any direction were villages of Manipuris, Bishnapuris and Bengalis. When Fred, Dorothy and the children went for walks, the people ran out to see them. They were friendly and anxious for the missionaries to come visit them in their villages. Of course, the children were a big attraction and the people were delighted when two-year old David smiled at them and gave them their own greeting.

As a result of those walks and of the giving out of tracts both in the villages and in the bazaar, quite a few people came to the bungalow to talk and to read the Scriptures.

Fred wrote to Temple Baptist Church:

"Dear Dr. Powell and Friends at Temple:

Greetings from Makunda. Yes, we are now occupying the bungalow on this estate about which we have been praying and writing for so long. The Lord has marvelously answered prayer and in spite of obstacles and setbacks we can now say that Makunda is ours – that is, as a mission. The final papers are almost ready for the previous owner's signature after which he will pack his grip and catch the first means of conveyance out. As he puts it 'I'm fed up with the place.' But we know without a doubt that God had this place all planned for our work out here, for which we praise Him.

I'm sure you will be interested in a few things concerning Makunda. Our other station at Alipur was all but crowded out so it was time to expand and not only that but we wanted to reach more of the people of this vast land who have never yet heard the Gospel.

There is over a section of land, some is rice land under cultivation, which will supply all of the rice for the leper colony and mission compound both here and at the other station. There is much jungle land but from it we are able to get all of our wood for building purposes and all the necessary thatch for the roofs. And not only that, there is plenty of wild game of which we have made use of already. I have shot two deer and quite a few wild chickens so this helps a lot with our food problem as well as saves on expenses. Of course, it is fun too.

There are three rivers running through the estate and in the course of time, we are planning on stocking them with fish, as it is one of the main foods for the natives. In short, it will be entirely self-supporting.

The entire estate cost only 60,000 rupees (approximately $15,000). Of course that sounds like a lot, but we have visited some of the surrounding tea gardens and their bungalows alone cost from 75,000 to 100,000 rupees, so you can see that the Lord certainly did work on our behalf. I might say that we missionaries out here are undertaking to pay for this ourselves through the funds that the Lord sends out to us. I mention this because some have written and asked how it will be financed.

The greatest challenge is the vast number of villages just at our doorstep who sit in the darkness of sin and false religion. Our constant cry is, 'Oh, if we could only speak the language better.' Already the people are coming to us both for medical aid and to hear us read to them what little we know of the Bible stories in their language. Do pray for us that we will soon be able to give them the Word of Life. We just long to be out in their villages telling them of the Lord Jesus.

We are quite remote out here with just a very few white people around at all and they are tea planters. I rode 28 miles on my bike the other day to get a few things for the table. The distance wasn't too bad, but oh the roads, or should I say, trails. After the rains start we will have to walk three miles to our bungalow as the river washes out the bridge, so we will stay put for those months, as far as possible.

In April we will again go to Darjeeling to continue in language school. Dorothy will stay until the end of September as it is too hot to bring the children down to the plains in this terrific heat, but I will come down as soon as school is over in July in order to be on the station...

Thank you one and all for the cards and greetings during the Christmas season and also for the cards for Kenny. God has been good to us in giving us another son and we do thank Him. We are well and happy in the Lord. We often pray for you all, in fact daily, and we are keenly interested in the progress of the church building. God bless you. We would love to have a letter from a number of you. We are quite isolated here so letters will be greatly appreciated, but above all continue to pray for us.

Lovingly, your missionaries,
Fred and Dorothy Waldock"

Fred and Dorothy continued to doggedly work at learning Bengali. They met with their language tutor at a table outside the bungalow.

There was also a lot of hard physical labor involved in working with the nationals to cut roads through the jungle, to plant more rice fields, vegetables and fruits and to make bricks and build buildings. At the same time they were stretching their language abilities to witness and to hold morning Gospel services before giving out work assignments to the laborers. They strenuously prepared to teach Sunday school classes and hold regular worship services each week.

The leprosy patients from Alipur were transferred to Makunda. They helped build the bamboo and thatch-roofed houses for themselves and for the other patients.

Fred wrote an article for the Mid-Missions newsletter, "*At the present time, we are continuing with language study and occupying the station. Mr. Garlow, our senior missionary, comes down for a few days at a time to keep the workers busy clearing land, cutting timber, cutting thatch, building houses for lepers, etc. We have enough bamboo, thatch, lumber and rice land to take care of both of our stations but it takes a lot of work and money to get it all started. Eventually we expect to have two or three hundred lepers settled on one end of the land. We believe God has wonderfully undertaken for us in providing such a mission site and we are trusting Him to supply the needs.*

The greatest challenge that faces us is the host of villages practically on our doorstep and as yet without a gospel witness. The fear, the bondage, superstition and unrest can only be solved by the message and power of the Lord Jesus. Pray that we might be used of God to win some, yes many, to the Lord."

Fred and Dorothy enjoyed watching the sunsets but it was to them a spiritual picture as well. As they watched the sun setting and the darkness falling they couldn't help but feel the greater darkness that these dear people were in. They felt that they were scarcely able to do more than look, but how they longed to soon be out among them telling them of Jesus, the only One who can dispel the complete darkness that has blinded them for so long.

In the jungle there was a constant struggle against the environment. Makunda is located on a low plain near sea level. Mosquitoes filled with malaria sought bodies in which to deposit their poison so they had to sleep under mosquito nets that stifled any air that might have been moving. Ants – big and little, white and red – chewed through bamboo furniture and precious books. Mold was a constant problem. Life was very primitive with no running water and few conveniences. They used a wood-burning stove for cooking and the refrigerator ran on kerosene. All their water had to be boiled first. Dorothy frugally tried to make their food supplies last as long as possible. The climate was not pleasant. Sometimes temperatures were 100 degrees with 100 percent humidity. And yet, for all the challenges, Fred and Dorothy were glad to be there - doing the work the Lord had called them to.

There never seemed to be enough hours in the day. In April they headed back to Darjeeling for more language training. In mid-June disaster hit the city. In one 24-hour period, 17.3 inches of rain fell, and the ground simply could not contain it all. The torrential rain continued for six days. Consequently the hillsides began to give way in great earth and rock slides, some of them 1,000 feet long. There were over 100 slides in 25 miles of road. The road heading out of the city was irreparable. Darjeeling was cut off from the outside world for months. Electricity and communication systems were destroyed.

As soon as they were able, Fred and Dorothy sent a cable back to Temple Baptist Church with this message: *"ALL SAFE. SERIOUS LANDSLIDES. DARJEELING CUT OFF FROM SUPPLIES FOR WEEKS. LOVE."*

Despite being cut off from the outside world, there were no food shortages except sugar, which was already a rationed item in India. Outside of a few inconveniences, like the lack of water and no electricity, they were not in need. Electricity was restored within a month.

Fred returned to Makunda on July 1st but Dorothy and the boys remained in Darjeeling where the heat of the summer was not so oppressive.

On the evening of August 15th the Garlows (who were in Darjeeling on holiday) and Dorothy were sitting and talking when they heard the window rattle. At first, they thought that it was someone knocking until the lights and then the whole house began to sway. They pulled their children out of bed, wrapped them in blankets and stood in the doorway, not knowing what else to do. It was dark outside and pouring rain. Hills and large trees were above and below them. It had been just two months since the landslides and they could not help but wonder what was going to happen this time. After several moments of rocking, it stopped and some time later they put the children back to bed. Two more long shakes were felt that night but no damage was done.

It was several days before they learned that the center of the earthquake was in Assam. Railroad lines were broken and no communications were coming through to tell them how their station had been affected. Eventually they heard from Fred who had been alone at Makunda. He reported that the house had been shaken quite hard and that the beams had begun to creak, but that there was no damage. A series of blasts had been heard and the village people reported that Silchar, the largest city in their district, had been bombed. In reality, the earthquake caused similar blasts all over Assam.

How thankful they were that the Lord had spared the Mid-Missions stations. Thirty thousand square miles of Assam were badly shaken or flooded and over 2,000 houses were destroyed and thousands of others damaged. One section of the National Highway of Assam was badly damaged and sunken for a distance of 12 miles. Many of the tribal villages in the hills were completely destroyed by serious floods. Rivers changed their courses. Bridges and roads were washed out, cutting off communications and food supplies.

Through these times their hearts were encouraged anew by God's presence and by His Word. Psalm 46:1-2: "God is our refuge and our strength...Therefore we will not fear, though the earth be removed, and though the mountains be carried into the midst of the sea."

In October the entire family returned to their home at Makunda and continued with the work of turning the jungle into a productive colony. Just mere living at Makunda took much time. In Fred's eyes that became far too great a problem at times, but it was a reality that had to be reckoned with. It was with joy that they began to see spiritual fruit.

Abaram, a leprosy patient with severely crippled hands and feet, was one of the first ones to accept Christ at Makunda. He and another patient in the leper colony confessed Christ in one of the Sunday services. Others were becoming interested in the gospel. The patients learned a number of hymns and choruses and enjoyed singing, "What a Friend We Have in Jesus," "Just as I Am" and "Take the Name of Jesus with You."

Towards the end of 1950, Fred and Dorothy were required to travel to Calcutta to take their first-year Bengali exams. David and Kenny and their ayah stayed with Beulah Burrows at Alipur. At Makunda, the Garlows and Doris Bruce remodeled the bungalow to better meet the needs of both families.

Fred wrote of his impressions of Calcutta in a Christmas letter to supporters: *"In this great city we see every type of human being and every type of culture and religion. Men, women, boys and girls who are beggars, laborers, rich business men, poor peddlers,...blind, lame, distorted, filthy outcasts – all throng the streets of the city. Some of the buildings on the main streets are beautiful, huge, and spotless; and right next door to them may be a hovel. Yes, India is the land of extremes, fears, and bewilderment. Yet those who are the captives of sin are the very ones that Jesus came to free, to make them children of the true God and fellow heirs with Himself. What a wonderful Savior!"*

The multiple moves and language school expenses took a toll on the Waldocks' finances. As the months went on, their account at Baptist Mid-Missions went deeper into the red. After much prayer and concern about the matter, Fred felt that it was the Lord's will that they ask Temple Baptist Church, their only supporting church, for a loan of $500. The church gladly provided the sum. Fred promised to do his utmost to pay back the loan as soon as possible. They were trusting that the Lord would send in extra gifts from month to month.

In April 1951, Fred returned alone to Darjeeling for three more months of language training. This time, Dorothy and the boys stayed at Makunda. It was not easy for the family to be separated at this time, because Dorothy was expecting another child that would be born in late June.

Fred wrote from Darjeeling in May 1951:

"Dear Dr. Powell and Temple Loved Ones:
'The blessing of the Lord maketh rich and He addeth no sorrow.'
How thankful we have been in the Lord during these past two years in India for His abundant mercy and grace toward us. Even in trying circumstances and hard places His grace has proved sufficient and His blessings have far exceeded and surpassed hardships. How true it is that each time we go through trials the closer we are drawn to the Lord, and He becomes sweeter and dearer to us. It is our prayer that all such trying circumstances which befall us will work out to a deeper and closer walk with the Lord.

A verse of a poem has been running through my mind lately. It goes something like this:
'Must I be carried to the skies on flowery beds of ease,
While others fought to win the prize, and sailed thro' bloody seas?
NO – I must fight, if I would reign; increase my courage Lord;
I'll bear the toil; endure the pain, supported by Thy Word.'

And I trust that it shall be the prayer of our lives, as well as the song of our lips, as then the Lord will be able to use us to bear fruit for His holy Name. For the immediate time, please pray for Dorothy and the boys in Makunda and for me in my language school here in Darjeeling. Our language opportunities have not been good but we are continuing to work and trust the Lord. Again we praise God for our church and pastor, and for what they are doing for us.

Yours for souls in India,
Fred and Dorothy"

Fred hoped to be able to concentrate more on his language studies while he was alone. They had not been able to find good teachers and the Bengali spoken around Makunda was not the polished Bengali he was learning in his classes. The tyranny of daily tasks at Makunda had also stolen time from language study. All in all, Fred was disappointed about his progress in the language.

Dorothy and the boys went up to Shillong when the hottest part of the year approached. Gordon Dean Waldock was born in Shillong, India on June 23. Fred was away from the family preparing for his language exams in Calcutta which he took a few days later.

One day after all the Waldocks had returned to Makunda, Fred and an Indian guide were deep in the jungle when they heard something big crashing through the trees behind them. It was a rogue elephant – and it was coming straight for them!

The Indian man ran up a hill but Fred in his heavy boots could not run as fast and was tiring quickly. He had gotten out of shape during the three months of language school. He ran until he thought he would collapse. The Indian man motioned to Fred that he should run in a zigzag fashion through the bamboo. The elephant would have to slow down to try to catch the scent and Fred would have a chance to get away.

So Fred ran, zigzagging through the bamboo until he was exhausted. He finally evaded the pursuing elephant.

Years later when he was on furlough, he related the story to his mother in Alberta, Canada. His mother became excited and inquired, "Fred, what day was it exactly? Do you remember?"

"Why is the date important, Mother?" asked Fred after he told her the approximate date and time.

"One night I was unable to sleep. I was so very burdened for you. I could not rest until I prayed for you and received assurance from the Lord that He had heard my prayer," she answered, with awe in her voice. "The time difference between Alberta and India is 12-1/2 hours. I do believe the Lord burdened me to pray for you at just the time you were fleeing that elephant."

The work continued at the leprosy colony. A treatment shed was built and more houses were added. Fred often woke up as early as 4:30 in the morning to do correspondence and the like before breakfast so as to escape the heat of the day. The strain of financial challenges continued to wear on their hearts.

There was much physical labor involved in the colony. Some of the lepers were able to work – others were confined to bed. Leprosy was a dreaded disease in India. Many advanced cases of leprosy were horribly disfigured. The earliest symptom of the disease is a loss of sensation in a patch of skin. The lack of feeling in the affected part often leads to unnoticed injuries. Damage to the nerves causes muscles to become paralyzed. Infection sets in. This infection results in scar tissue and absorption of the bone.

Some of the patients were responding to the gospel, but others were not. In the last three months of 1951, there were reasons for rejoicing. The Manipuris had been very slow to accept the Gospel even after hearing it for a number of years. However, now several young men had been coming and asking for teaching and some took their stand for the Lord despite opposition from their families. Fred began teaching a class for two Christian patients and other interested ones to instruct them further in the riches of God's word.

Some of the boys in Dorothy's Sunday school class for leper children were also saved. One of those boys was 12-year-old Sanat. Sanat was born in a small village to very poor peasant parents. They made their living by begging. If they were fortunate enough to get a little money or food given to them, they ate. Then Sanat's father died and his mother was left alone with several small children. But God, in His mercy, provided another daddy for Sanat. This time it was a tea garden coolie who at least had a certain amount of money and food to meet the family's needs.

But Sanat's family was on the tea garden only a short time. One day the garden doctor said that Sanat and his older sister must get off the tea garden immediately. They had leprosy. Trouble upon trouble – what should they do? The parents took them to Dr. Crozier's leper colony at Alipur just a few miles from their home. The separation was hard; but for Sanat and his sister Bishaka, it meant food, clothing, medicine and best of all the opportunity to hear for the first time, the good news of salvation. Bishaka accepted Christ as her Savior first. Then Sanat was transferred to the new colony site at Makunda. When they asked him if he was a Christian, he said "yes" but he could not give "a reason for the hope within." But in a Sunday school class he learned the way of salvation for himself.

His work in the colony was to take the colony cows out to the fields each day to graze. Often he sat out near the cows with a slate or a simple Bible story book. In this way, he practiced his reading and writing and reviewed his Bible verses. Sanat's lowly birth and dreaded sickness was God's mercy and plan for him.

The Sunday before Christmas 1951 they had a service for the patients and showed them colored slides of the Christmas story. That was followed by a similar service on their front veranda for about 30 compound workers. That was the first time many of them had heard the Christmas story and the plan of salvation; so it was a real thrill for Dorothy and Fred to present it to them. As a result of that service more of the compound children came to Dorothy's Sunday school class.

After breakfast and stuffing geese for Christmas dinner, they went down to the colony for a Christmas service. All the patients had on their newest clothing. Donated items such as a girl's lavender or yellow sweater or a bathrobe that was now worn as a coat were treasured by the patients. Anything that was colorful and kept them warm – no matter how old it was, how it fit, or how ridiculous it might look to the missionaries – was a delight to the patients' hearts. The cold season isn't long in Assam but the patients suffered because of their physical condition if they did not have warm clothes.

After the service the missionaries distributed fish, sugar, brown flour and candied balls made with popped rice mixed with molasses to each patient for his Christmas dinner. It was the first meat for many of them since the year before when Fred and Jim Garlow had been able to kill a deer. Recent attempts at deer hunting had been unsuccessful.

Dorothy wrote in a prayer letter dated January 8, 1951, "*One day as I was giving medicine to some villagers, one of the Christian boys and a non-Christian boy were listening to the villagers' long story of all their troubles – much sickness in the family, etc and both of them told these villagers to believe in Jesus, God's Son, and He would help them! Pray for this non-Christian, whose name is Sanathan, that he may publicly confess Christ as his personal Savior. He lives with the other Christian boy and shows an interest. We feel that the Lord has sent us these patients – not only to be given help for their bodies – but that they may come to know the Great Physician as their Savior.*"

In March 1952, the Waldocks asked for special prayer from the home church that they would have strength and protection during troublesome times in their area. One day while Fred was away from the colony some of the tenants beat Jim Garlow. The tenants were attempting to force the missionaries out so that they could claim the land for themselves.

Fred and Dorothy wrote a long letter to Temple Baptist Church:

"*Dear Dr. Powell and Temple Friends,*
'That ye might be filled with the knowledge of His will in all wisdom and spiritual understanding; that ye might walk worthy of the Lord unto all pleasing, being fruitful in every good work, and increasing in the knowledge of God; strengthened with all might according to His glorious power, unto all patience and long suffering with joyfulness.' Colossians 1:9b-11.

These verses came with a letter some time ago and what a blessing they have been. This truly is our hearts' desire and prayer. I wonder at times how worthy our walk is. Whether or not it is always 'unto all pleasing.' Self is a terrible master and tries in so many ways (and I think they are multiplied on the mission field) to try and get us to please ourselves. In a day that is filled with problems of every nature and adverse circumstances unless the Lord fills us with the knowledge of His will in all wisdom and spiritual understanding we are sure to fail and become utterly discouraged. Then – patience – how many times a day I get checked about this! But again the wonderful provision that we have in Christ, "strengthened with all might, according to His glorious power, unto all patience and longsuffering with joyfulness."

Patience with joyfulness. I find it at times rather easy to exercise patience on certain lines or shall I call it "endure patience" because joyfulness is absent. Patience and longsuffering with joyfulness. "I am come that ye might have life and that you might have it more abundantly." Truly victory is ours in Christ! If it weren't for such blessed promises as these, one would easily become discouraged and defeated.

I think I can safely say that we think and pray for you daily with very few exceptions. The friends at Temple are very dear to us and close to our hearts. We know that you are praying for us. How many times your prayers have been answered only eternity will reveal. We wish to thank the church again for the added support that you have been sending us for the past few months. As the boys are growing up and the cost of living in general increasing, we certainly thank you for this practical help.

We wish we could invite some of you folks to come and visit us out here. I'm sure you would be surprised at many things, shocked at others and thrilled at others. I'll try to describe to you a typical Sunday here with us in our jungle home.

As this is the hot rainy season, sleep sometimes is very unrestful because of this awful sticky heat. However, we manage to get up around 6 a.m. Sometimes we actually feel as though we hadn't slept at all, but after a good wash pep begins to arise. Three little hungry live-wires are dressed and washed for breakfast. On Sunday morning just before we eat our breakfast we always pray for services at Temple.

After breakfast, final preparations are made for Sunday school and for the leprosy services for the patients at the little temporary hospital. Dorothy, Doris Bruce and Joyce Garlow have Sunday school with our own children and the neighboring tea garden children when they are home.

Jim Garlow and I, at this same time, hold a service for patients in the hospital. They are hospitalized because of their ulcers and general rundown conditions. So far we just meet in a little corner of the dispensary because of yet we have no church. Try to imagine these hot days, with sweat running off your elbows and your clothes actually soaked with perspiration sitting in this little room, about 9 x 9 feet with about 20-25 leprosy patients. *The stench is so strong at times that you can hardly bear it. These leprous sores have a terrible odor.*

But then – forgetting that – think of the joy and thrill of singing together with them and telling them the old, old story of Jesus and His love. If ever a man needs to be loved it is a leper in India.

We have seen the Gospel message work in these men's lives. You can see the change on their faces. I think of one especially. What a hopeless case he was less than a year ago, both physically and spiritually. But now the radiance on his face and the difference in his body is miraculous. Our hearts say 'thank you Lord for bringing us here, if just for this one man!' I heard him pray for the first time the other day and it touched my heart.

If such as that won't bring tears of joy to your eyes, I don't know what will. These men know what salvation means. They really love the Lord and thank Him from the very depths of their hearts. This particular man is still very crippled and walks with a cane but walks about a mile and a half each way to these services twice every Sunday.

After the meeting we visit with the very sick ones and try to encourage them in the Lord. No, they aren't all Christians by any means but the interest is growing and gradually the way of salvation is becoming clear.

The children are ready for a nap by midday and after they are quiet we try to read a while or write letters but often it is so hot that we, too, succumb to 40 winks. It is a custom in this land to have tea around four o'clock in the afternoon. It is usually welcome and sort of gives a reviver after the hot part of the day.

Again we get ready for the afternoon service for the patients. We practice some of their tunes, and what a job, but they love to sing them. About 5 p.m. we gather for an hour and a half and tell them again of Jesus and His love and power to save them from their sins and fear of death.

At this time Dorothy has a service in the house for some of the women around the compound. How blinded some of these people are by fear, superstition and religious rites. But the Holy Spirit is breaking through and the ones and twos are becoming interested. I'm sure you will never fully understand the joy there is of seeing one of these poor, unwanted people accept the Lord Jesus – you just have to see it for yourselves. A few have been saved in the past six months and others are showing keen interest. Recently we baptized three and there are many more awaiting baptism after more teaching. So praise God with us for these results.

After the service we come home for supper, have devotions with the boys and settle down to letter writing and sometimes reading.

There are many things upon our hearts for prayer as well as praise. We daily need the wisdom and strength of the Lord.

The Lord has provided a good language teacher – the first in three years – so for the next three months it is all out on language study to try and pass our second year exam. The work increases daily but we must get six hours a day in concentrated study while we have a teacher. Since Garlows have been away on holiday it has been impossible to keep up to this standard but the Lord can quicken our minds for the remaining days ahead. So pray for added strength for this task.

Then too, the Mission is facing great financial problems as the work grows and reaches out. We need at least four houses immediately to house our missionaries, besides many other heavy running expenses. Let's pray that the givers at home can keep up to the Lord's progress in our work out here.

Yours in His joyous service,
Fred and Dorothy Waldock"

One of those saved at about this time was Prasanna Malakar, a former Hindu priest who had suffered with leprosy for about 20 years. When he came to Makunda his body was full of ugly, draining sores and his long hair and beard did not add to the attractiveness of his appearance. Medical treatment greatly improved his body and the Great Physician wrought a wonderful transformation of his soul. Prasanna observed the lives of the missionaries closely so that he might learn to walk carefully with the Lord. He gave up smoking and cut his hair and beard. He grew spiritually and developed a gracious and tactful manner of witnessing to his fellow patients.

As he sat on a stool and told his life story to missionary Doris Bruce, he had a sad expression until he came to the account of his conversion. At that point he rose from his stool and his face fully glowed with the glory of the Lord. The prayer of each of those at Makunda was that this transformation of body and soul would be repeated in many hundreds of lives.

Fred and Dorothy requested special prayer for the Field Conference held at Alipur in October 1952. The trip going there was a memorable one but the Lord protected them. It was during some of the worst flooding in Assam in 18 years. The group from Makunda could not get through by jeep so they transferred to the train. Then in Silchar, just 12 miles from the Alipur station, they were forced to seek refuge for the night at the Welsh Mission bungalow because the ferry would not cross the river after dark. Sleeping on the floor or on mats, the heat and mosquitoes were so intense that they got little rest.

The next morning they engaged 15 bicycle rickshaws with their drivers to take all of them and their luggage out to the river between Silchar and Alipur. Much of the way they drove through water up to the floorboards of the rickshaws and in places the current was so fast that they could see and feel themselves being swept sideways. At these times, the drivers quickly jumped off and pushed the cycles. In some of these places the area was so widely flooded the drivers just had to guess where the road might be.

Then to climax it all, they came to a wide breach in the road where the current had swept away a whole section and the waters were rushing through. Jim Garlow went back to town for boards to lay across the road. With fear and trembling, each one walked across the three thin planks. Then they got back into the rickshaws and went through yet more water to reach the river. They had to bargain for almost an hour before they obtained a large-sized rowboat to take them across. The mission jeep was waiting for them on the other side. It took two loads to get everyone to the station. Again they went through water, in one place so high that the fan belt had to be removed. They were all thankful for the Lord's provision and protection along the way.

The conference was a time of real blessing and spiritual refreshing in answer to the prayers of many. Each of the messages made the missionaries search their hearts and confess sin and failures. The messages also gave them a renewed desire for closer fellowship with Christ their precious Lord and Master.

By autumn 1952 there were 25 missionaries on the Assam Field, in comparison with the five that had been on the field just three years before when Fred and Dorothy had arrived. That year at the conference, Fred was elected Field Council President and Dorothy was selected to oversee the language committee. Plans were approved for building the first unit of the leprosy hospital at Makunda. The missionaries also decided to build a church for the leprosy colony with a "clean" section for those not infected with leprosy.

Reflecting back on their first three and a half years in Assam, Fred and Dorothy were encouraged. A fully functioning leprosy colony was now a reality. By God's grace the foundation had been successfully laid and now they looked forward to building on that foundation to the glory of God.

CHAPTER SEVEN
Perseverance

"If ever a man needs to be loved it is a leper in India." – Fred Waldock,
September 1952

Fred was determined that in all the work of building and
maintaining the station that the one essential thing – the
missionaries' personal fellowship with the Lord - would not be
neglected. He wrote, *"The devil would love to see us weaken on this
point and then he would be in like a flood to trip us up and thwart our
purpose of preaching the Gospel and reaching the lost for the Lord Jesus.
To this end we are looking forward to our Spiritual Life Conference
which is to be held at Alipur on March 26-30. We would ask that you
folks at home would join us in prayer that the Lord will visit us in real
power and that our hearts and lives will be revived. Unless the Lord
Himself meets with us, it will be in vain. It's my earnest prayer that the
Lord will do something new in our midst at this time; we need it."*

The Conference began with prayer meeting at 6 a.m. The
Lord's Spirit was with them in giving them a deep longing for His
working in their hearts. The meetings lasted four days and there
was much confession of sin and heart searching from the first
meeting to the last, no matter what the message. It was clearly a
visit from the Lord. How they were led to rejoice in the fresh
realization of the power of Christ's blood in cleansing and giving
them daily victory.

There was always much going on at the leper colony. The
patients worked according to their capabilities. Some worked in
the fields, some removed seeds from cotton, others wove baskets

and others learned to knit. A chapel period with much Scripture memory work was also a daily part of that schedule.

The new leprosy hospital unit was dedicated to the Lord in June 1953. By that time the leper population at Makunda had risen to nearly 160 patients. Many were finding help for their physical bodies and some were also finding spiritual life.

Fred and Dorothy were often called on to help with the medical work because of the training and experience they received at the School of Missionary Medicine at BIOLA. They were even drafted to assist with surgeries and to work in the dispensary.

The 1953 Field Council meeting was again held at the Alipur station. Dorothy described the trip in a letter to Temple Baptist Church, *"We piled into the jeep September 10th and if you could have seen us you would know why I said 'piled.' The bottom layer was lunch, umbrellas, thermoses, topis (sun hats) and small hand luggage. The next layer was adults and on top were children of various sizes. It's amazing what a jeep can hold! Of course, there are no sides to hinder our bulging out and the jeep can't go fast enough for anyone to fall out easily. We stopped for lunch and shopping along the way and made the trip of 70 miles in six hours."*

This was Fred's first experience leading the annual field conference and the Lord undertook for him in a wonderful way. Fred was re-elected as chairman of the field council and Dorothy was re-elected chairman of the language committee.

At the conference, it was confirmed that the Waldock's furlough was to be delayed until the fall of 1955 – nearly six and a half years from their arrival in the country. Before coming to India, they had been under the impression from correspondence with Mr. Fetzer at the Baptist Mid-Missions Home Office that their first term of service was to be three years.

"We had promised to stay here at Makunda until the Garlows got back (from furlough) but when we promised they had said they would go home this fall, but they decided later not to go until spring. Now it is settled that Garlows will go next April (1954) and we will remain until the fall of 1955. This does present some problems not counted on when we left home. For one thing David (five years old) is not as well as he should be and must continually take vitamins, iron preparation and cold vaccines. He has an enlargement of the heart with a murmur possibly

due to his frequent bronchial attacks that he has had since coming out here. It may even be advisable to keep him in the hills for three or four months the next two summers.

Then there is the added expense of the boys' (David and Kenny) schoolwork. We are teaching them with the Calvert Correspondence Course.

We thank the Lord for the way the Sunday school classes at Temple have helped out with clothing and other things because we certainly didn't bring enough with us for such a long stay."

In a week or ten days Fred will be going to Calcutta to meet three new missionary women. Several extra gifts were sent this month making it possible for me to go with him and get some very necessary dental work done. Then when we return I have to go to Alipur for surgery. I have a large tumor-like growth on my leg just below my groin.

We have lots of hopes and plans for the fall and winter months. It is the beginning of our cool season now and with it comes new energy and ambitions. Fred and I want to make regular visits to the villages around here this winter. He has been teaching some interested Muslims for some time and I have been teaching some Hindu women both in their village and here at the house on Sunday afternoons. Fred also has several classes and meetings in the Colony weekly. This year I am afraid he will have a good amount of traveling to do in connection with the Mission work.

We hate to think of not seeing you Temple friends as well as our loved ones for another two years, but we pray the Lord will keep you well and in His love until we come home. Fred's mother, although she is able to be up a little at home, cannot do anything without her heart acting up. Her condition is such that she may go at any time although we pray the Lord will keep her for us if it be His will. We would like to see her once more and have her see the children.

May the Lord continue to bless you in the work there. We follow with great interest the life of the church and its members. We thank the Lord continually for you and your prayers and your making it possible for us to stay here.

With much love in Christ,
Fred, Dorothy and boys"

New Year's Eve brought real joy to their hearts when their ayah and another girl from Dorothy's Sunday school class were baptized in the pond below their house. The following Sunday four leprosy patients were baptized.

Fred wrote an article for "The Harvest," the publication of Baptist Mid-Missions, describing the work in India.

"How our hearts are encouraged and filled with praise when a Hindu, Moslem, or animist tells us he is now a believer. The angels in Heaven rejoice and so do we. To hear a former holy Hindu, ridden in body by the dreaded disease stand up with a beaming face and testify of the saving grace of the Lord Jesus certainly thrills our hearts. We are thrilled again when we witness the baptism of these believing lepers. How their faces illuminate as we assure them of the love of the Lord Jesus for them.

At the dispensary at Makunda the Word is given out daily and many receive the gospel message both by the written word and the spoken word. Had it not been for the medical ministry many men, women, boys and girls would still be on the road to a Christ-less grave.

Our hearts are heavy for those who see the light and witness it in others but whom, mainly for fear, withstand and refuse to acknowledge their sin and need of a Savior."

Fred wrote of the absolute necessity of prayer in maintaining and advancing the work of evangelizing Assam.

"God's work can never progress unless the Holy Spirit has full sway in the lives of each worker. He cannot flow through blocked channels. The problems that often confront the work are beyond human wisdom, but God is omnipotent. The future is dim. But has He not called? Has He not chosen? Has He not sent? And has He not promised? Then let us work together in this great responsibility of evangelizing the lost in Assam."

The article contained the first picture of the leprosy colony hospital at Makunda. The first unit had been built and was already overflowing by the time of the writing of the article. Building in India was not easy. They had no lumberyards so they had to go to the jungle and get the trees cut, have an elephant move them to a suitable place for sawing, and then take them to the building site. Rocks in Cachar are conspicuous by their absence, so it was necessary to burn bricks to substitute for rocks in the building of the foundations.

In the past two years the work as Field Council chairman had become increasingly heavy. The problems of administration at Makunda were overwhelming in addition to the bookkeeping and correspondence, which took hours of time. When the Garlows returned to the United States for furlough in June, Fred felt the burden even greater.

Fred wrote, *"These, all added to the former duties, thrust one upon the Lord. 'But God is able to make all grace abound toward you; that ye, always having all sufficiency in all things, may abound to every good work.' 2 Corinthians 9:8.*

God's plan is for all the saints to share in the spreading of His Word, so we don't hesitate to ask, yes even beg, for your concerted prayer on our behalf. This will be our sixth summer in India and the long, hot and sultry seasons are telling on our bodies. Pray for your missionaries in Assam this summer as never before. Pray that God will guide us and give us wisdom and understanding as we fulfill His commission for our lives."

Yours for souls in Assam,
Fred and Dorothy Waldock"

Fred wrote of an increasing resistance to the gospel in a letter dated June 15, 1954: *"For the past few months we have been going through a time of stiff opposition to the Gospel. The Sunday schools have been going down in number and it is like pulling teeth to get patients out to the Sunday afternoon services. I know that some are definitely under conviction. There are those in the colony who are Hindu leaders and they have an influence which is very detrimental. It is for these men that we are asking special prayer. If the Lord can get some of them and if they really become soundly converted, then I think there will be a day of reaping. It has been a time of heart searching for us, too, because we realize that as long as there is sin in the camp the Holy Spirit cannot use us. The devil uses so many little things to upset us missionaries and how easily we fall. The Lord has been blessing us in our special Bible study and prayer meetings together. We also meet for concentrated prayer before the services on Sunday afternoon."*

More and more lepers came to Makunda to seek help, sometimes two or three in one day. Fred and Dorothy's hearts were heavy. The colony could not support any more. Fred wrote an impassioned plea to the people at Temple Baptist Church urging them to adopt a leper for $6 a month.

"I wish you could see them. Such distorted and unlovable bodies, helpless and much worse – hopeless. See their forlorn and anxious expressions on their faces as they cry for mercy. I wish you could see

them as they feel even the missionary won't help them. It is all that I can do to face them and tell them, 'No, I'm sorry.'

Sick, homeless, friendless, dirty, smelly, unwanted LOST lepers. Oh friends, Jesus died for them. He loves them. Do you? For just $6.00 a month we don't have to say 'no' to them. We can say, 'Yes, we have room for you. Come with me.' What a joy to receive these patients and tell them of the love of the Lord Jesus, to tell them that Jesus died to save them from fear and hell, that He wants to be their Savior, their friend."

This adopt-a-leper program worked very well. So many responded to their call for individual patient supporters that the missionaries at Makunda were able to take in quite a few new patients for treatment and to hear the Gospel.

As summer moved into fall, the trials at Makunda increased. The devil was trying to gain a firm foothold in the colony. One week in particular was as trying as anything they had yet experienced in India. Some of the patients were rebelling against the colony rules by conducting Hindu festivals when Fred was away from the station.

Fred wrote: *"We realized how serious a thing this matter in the colony was and how far-reaching it could be, and therefore we had to call upon the Lord desperately. Although the main issue has quieted down somewhat the undercurrent is still there and we have to be very strict and yet very careful. 'Wise as serpents and harmless as doves.' The greatest comfort through it all is to know the Presence of the Lord Jesus and to know that His dear ones are faithful. We thank Him for the lessons we have learned and are learning. But please continue to pray for the situation here. How we are looking forward to the time when some of these staunch patients will bow their knees to the Lord Jesus and accept Him as their only Savior. The very thing for which they are searching can only be found in Christ, but they can't, or should I say will not, see it.*

Even this very morning the patients had me where they thought they were going to tell me a thing or two, but the Lord gave me the opportunity to tell them, simply but very frankly, that Jesus was the only One who could meet their deepest need and that He is the only One who could give them the peace for which they were seeking.

No sooner had this trouble calmed down than other things came up and I was even threatened with a doas (jungle knife), told to get going and not to come back and interfere. The bamboos that we badly needed for the patients' houses were being stolen from our own land, and I was told by the thieves not to interfere with their doings."

The same letter gave praise to the Lord that the boys were finally over a persistent fever. The missionaries were indeed "troubled on every side, yet not distressed; perplexed, but not in despair; persecuted, but not forsaken; cast down, but not destroyed."

At times the trials seemed too much and Fred or Dorothy would struggle with discouragement. Physically and emotionally they were long overdue for a furlough. And yet the ever-present Lord kept their hand to the plow.

Dorothy wrote, "*I knew, deep down inside, that we could never conscientiously walk out on it all now. We have made plans for a Bible school for the Christian patients and evangelistic meetings for the colony and surrounding villages. The devil would just love to delay our plans and see us give in to discouragement. We don't need a furlough – we need more prayer from us, as well as from the folks at home, to raise the Lord's standards against Satan and to do the work that the Lord has put in our hearts to do. The Lord wonderfully answered your prayer for us the last six months – we were very conscious of it many times and in many ways. Don't let down these next six months, rather increase your prayers. We must remember that we are dealing for the most part with non-Christians, Satan's own children, in his territory – but even more important to remember is that God is still all-powerful and He can break the chains which Satan has put on these people."*

Some spiritual victories were won. At Christmas time, at least one patient repented of his sins and gave his life to Jesus Christ. Eventually his health improved and he went to see his family up in the mountains. They also showed signs of leprosy and so he brought them back to Makunda. He was faithful in witnessing to his wife, son and daughter. Eventually the whole family was gloriously saved.

The battle between good and evil continued into the new year of 1955. While Fred was away from the station on Mission business the patients in the colony held another of their Hindu festivals in open defiance of the rules of the colony. This was a very serious matter and Fred again beseeched the home church for prayer support. He asked them to pray in the Holy Spirit and in faith for them and the work at Makunda. He urged them to pray the words of Daniel in chapter 2:20-23. "Daniel answered and said, 'Blessed be the name of God forever and ever: for wisdom and might are His: and He changeth times and seasons: He removeth kings, and setteth up kings: He giveth wisdom unto the wise, and knowledge to them that know understanding. He revealeth the deep and secret things: He knoweth what is in the darkness, and the light dwelleth with Him. I thank Thee, and praise Thee, O Thou God of my fathers, Who hast given me wisdom and might, and hast made known unto me now what we desire of Thee: for Thou hast made known unto us the King's matter."

The church members at Temple were diligent to pray earnestly and many wrote to Fred and Dorothy assuring them of this. The power of God prevailed and the victory came. The difficult situation in the colony subdued without any serious trouble.

The Makunda Baptist Church was organized on February 27, 1955 with 12 charter members, all of whom were patients in the colony. The next day an Indian evangelist from Calcutta, Mr. Sobodh Sahu, came for evangelistic meetings and really won his way into the hearts of the people. They had 150 to 200 out every night at the outdoor meetings near the dispensary. Mr. Sahu held meetings for the leprosy patients each morning and classes for the Christians each afternoon. His message was just the same simple Gospel message that the missionaries preached daily; but to hear it from one of their own people who knows what it means to come out of Hinduism or Mohammedism made all the difference in the world.

While they were preparing the bamboo and thatch-grass shelter for the outdoor meetings it was quite obvious that some of the Hindu patients were quite indifferent about helping. But from the very first night there was intense interest and many of the leprosy patients stood for two or three hours outside the fence at the dispensary listening intently.

The evangelist had been holding meetings at the Alipur station before he came to Makunda and was exceedingly tired. He was suffering from what they thought was tonsillitis; so the missionaries doctored him in between meetings. Then Friday morning Mr. Sahu broke out in chicken pox. He was a very sick man and the rest of the meetings at the colony had to be canceled.

Dorothy and Fred could not, in the natural, understand why the Lord laid Mr. Sahu aside just as the people were so interested and hungry to hear. But after those meetings they noticed a difference in the attitude of most of the patients and many became very bold in inquiring about Christian things.

March 13th Mr. Sahu was feeling much better and the Lord gave them two good meetings with him in the leprosy colony. In the afternoon they dedicated their newly built colony chapel which was built in the shape of a cross. Mr. Sahu brought a strong message on "Our Hearts the Dwelling Place of the Lord Jesus." Not only was it a time of dedication of the church; but it was a time of heart searching for everyone. The colony Christians rededicated themselves to the Lord.

The first term of service for the Waldocks had required much of them. But God had been faithful to His word and had planted His church at Makunda. There was much anticipation for the first trip back to the United States on furlough. The boys were excited about the prospect of riding on a boat and a train and seeing so much that they had never experienced before.

Dorothy described their anticipation in a prayer letter: *"The National Geographic magazine seems to be very popular in our family these days. Besides the beautiful pictures of lands and people from all over the world which fascinate the children, every type of transportation is attractively advertised therein. Whether it's a ferry or sailboat the boys run and ask, 'Is this the kind of boat we're going on to America?' And about the cars, trains and buses, 'Will we ride on one like this in America?' Yes, as far as three little boys are concerned the most talked of, dreamed of, thought of, and planned for coming event is our fast-approaching trip to America. For these little ones who have spent most of their days in the jungle seeing a few small English cars, old army jeeps, rickety buses, a tractor and trailer and a few elephants for transportation it is hard to imagine what the big cities of America will be like. I wonder if we anticipate heaven and its far greater glories and beauties with the same excitement and preparation."*

Before their furlough arrived, Dorothy gave birth to a girl, Lois Grace, on June 26, 1955 at the hospital at Alipur.

Fred went to Shillong to obtain their "No objection to return" permits. This permit was needed to facilitate their being able to return to India after furlough. While coming home on the train from Shillong, Fred's suitcase was stolen. He had been up late several nights in a row and traveling for two days. The train ahead of his was derailed and so they were held up and Fred missed the usual connection. He must have nodded off and someone took the opportunity to steal the suitcase. However, Fred couldn't help but feel that someone had either doped him or given him an injection while he was asleep. He had never in his life slept so hard on a train and the next day he had such a terrible headache. Fred not only lost his clothes in the suitcase but a stack of mission files. He did all he could to locate the papers but there was little hope of recovering them. Fred felt awful about the whole thing. Fortunately Fred's passport was not in the suitcase.

But after he heard what had happened the very next night on the train, Fred was thankful to the Lord that he was still alive. Another man was traveling with 2000 rupees along with a friend. The owner of the money went to sleep while waiting for their connecting train so he gave the money to his friend to protect. After awhile he woke up and found that some men had seized his friend and had killed him by cutting him with a knife.

Writing about the incident Fred declared, *"The Lord protects His own."*

CHAPTER EIGHT
Happy Reunions

"The Bible teaches us that on the day of rewards we shall share alike –
those who went to the battle on distant fields and those who faithfully
'stood by the stuff' at home." – Fred Waldock, September 1965

The Waldocks' journey home began in Calcutta. The streets of the
city were chaos as usual – animals, people and dirt everywhere.
But the three little boys, their ayah and their Mommie and Daddy
enjoyed a trip to the Calcutta Zoo. They boarded their ship on
August 10, 1955 with much joyful anticipation.

Fred wrote while en route to the United States, *"Yes, it is true,*
we are actually on our way home. It is hard to believe but each day
brings us further from Assam and closer to Tacoma. As we think of it,
we get triple palpitations of the heart and butterflies in our stomach. The
boys seem to be just as excited as their Mommie and Daddy. Gordie
keeps on saying, 'Daddy, when are we going to get the train?' When are
we going to see Grandma?' The other day he asked me if I had told the
driver of the ship that we wanted to catch the train.

Even with this excitement we still can't deny the fact that there is a
definite tug back to Assam. We know of the need there and of the
blindness towards the Gospel that exists. We also know of the heavy
work and responsibility that falls upon those who labor there.

We have had a very pleasant trip thus far and we are keeping our
fingers crossed that the Pacific will be smooth.

As we look over the past six and a half years since we saw you all we
can't help but praise the Lord for all His goodness and mercy to us, and
for all your faithfulness to us as has been manifested in so many ways.

Now we look forward to a time of rich spiritual blessing and fellowship together.

> *Yours in a wonderful Savior,*
> *Fred and Dorothy Waldock"*

The Waldocks were especially looking forward to seeing Fred's mother again. Fred wrote, *"How we do praise the Lord that He has seen fit to spare my mother until our return. She has had a number of heart attacks but the Lord has kept her. However you can never tell which attack will be her last. Mother lives very close to the Lord and God has used her life and testimony to the blessing of many young people. I can say without the least bit of exaggeration that Mother has been used of the Lord in the leading, under the Lord, of scores of young people to the foreign fields. It is a time of rich spiritual blessing to sit and talk to her about the things of the Lord. In these past three years since she has been sick I have not heard one word of complaint from her or from others who have been with her. They simply say that she is radiant with the joy of the Lord and lives each day one day at a time with Him. So it is going to be a real joy to see her again."*

The Waldocks arrived in San Francisco on September 15, 1955. When they arrived in Tacoma, Washington three days later at 4:30 a.m. on Sunday morning they were overwhelmed by the generosity of Temple Baptist Church. The church had rented a house for them, furnished it and even had the cupboards full of food and things all ready for breakfast! Even the beds were made. Nothing was left undone. In a note of appreciation Dorothy wrote, *"The Lord hath done great things for us whereof we are glad.' We praise the Lord for all His goodness to us and for the wonderful trip He gave us home in answer to the prayers of loved ones and friends. We were overwhelmed on the Sunday morning we arrived, as we walked into our new modern home, which was all prepared and waiting for us. This warm reception is only an indication of your love and prayers for us through the past years. We thank you from the bottom of our hearts and we are looking forward so much to visiting and fellowshipping with you. Feel free at any time of the day to drop in for a visit, we want to see you!"*

Soon after their arrival in Tacoma, Fred and Dorothy and the two younger children traveled to Three Hills, Alberta to see Fred's mother and father. Fred's mother was quite ill and they were anxious to see her again lest she should go home to be with the

Lord. David and Ken remained in Tacoma with Dorothy's mother so that they could start school.

The furlough months went quickly as Fred and Dorothy traveled from church to church sharing the needs of their people in Assam and showing slides of the work. Throughout the winter months Fred traveled extensively, sometimes without the family. He did deputation meetings in California, Idaho, Colorado and Ohio each time challenging the people with the needs of Assam.

Dorothy greatly enjoyed the times that she was able to be in their home church drinking in the word of God. In May of 1956, a revival was held at Temple Baptist Church. Dorothy wrote, *"We consider it a great privilege to be able to be here at this time and are glad the Lord worked it out for us. The messages were a real blessing and challenge to our hearts. We thank the Lord for a pastor who has such a great burden for the spiritual growth of his own people."*

In June, at the age of 34, Fred was ordained at Temple Baptist Church.

During August and September the Waldocks completed a seven-week deputation tour that included 16 states and 4 provinces covering a distance of 10,770 miles. The Lord opened many doors for them along the way and some very important contacts were made as far away as North Carolina. Up until this furlough, the Waldocks' support of $200 a month came entirely from Temple Baptist Church. Fred felt that it was necessary to raise an additional $100 a month from other sources because Temple was already planning to help with outfit and passage funds. But their paramount purpose in deputation work was to create definite and continuous prayer support for the work in Assam. Fred wrote, *"Our hearts have been encouraged by those who have been challenged and have expressed a desire to be prayer warriors for us and the work in Assam. Yet one's heart aches to see the lack of interest and indifference among most Christians today in regards to reaching the lost in foreign lands who have never had an opportunity to hear the only way of salvation through Christ Jesus. May the Lord make us all the more faithful to Him and His word each day."*

The Waldocks were much in prayer for passport and visa matters. They had problems with the renewal of Dorothy's passport but the Lord wonderfully undertook enabling them to get a valid passport in time for the preparation of their return visas. Fred wrote, *"It truly is a victory to get a visa to India these days but we rejoice to tell you that ours were granted and January 24th is the deadline for our arrival in India."*

In early September they requested prayer that they would be able to find passage to India. The matter was more urgent because of the January 24th deadline for arrival into the country. Within weeks of asking for prayer, passage was secured for December 7 on the M.S. Bawean. They eagerly began to look forward to getting back to their people in Assam, and to the plans they had of reaching out further to areas where Christ had not yet been preached.

On October 21st, Fred baptized David at Temple Baptist Church. Fred had taught the young peoples' class while they were on furlough and the young people honored them with a dinner on Friday night, November 23, 1956.

The Waldocks and the church were much in prayer regarding the journey back to the field. If the boat were more than four days late arriving in India, Dorothy and the children's visas would be invalid. The Waldocks set sail from Seattle on Saturday, December 8 and then spent several days in Vancouver, British Columbia while the ship was loaded. They left Vancouver on December 13th and began the 18-day journey across the Pacific Ocean to Hong Kong.

Dorothy started schooling the boys the first day on the ship. It gave them something to do on the long voyage. The four days before Christmas they were on the edge of a storm which rolled and pitched the ship quite hard. Eighteen-month-old Lois was sent flying a couple of times but on the whole she learned to balance herself remarkably well as the ship rocked. Dorothy and Fred reflected on God's rich promises in Scripture including: "Ye have not chosen me but I have chosen you" and "Have not I commanded thee? Be strong and of a good courage; be not afraid, neither be thou dismayed: for the Lord thy God is with thee whithersoever thou goest."

Christmas Day was sunny and comparatively calm. They decorated a small tree in one cabin and had the children's presents all ready for them to open at 6:30 a.m. The Waldocks were thankful for the dear ones at Temple who had provided a lovely Christmas and many cards and notes of encouragement.

After breakfast, Fred held a short service in which he had a wonderful opportunity to present Christ as the One who brings peace to those who personally accept Him. All the officers, passengers and some of the crew attended and many thanked Fred for it. Fred was able to witness further of the Lord to several. The chief steward had not allowed Sunday services thus far and wasn't in favor of a Christmas service either but the other passengers mentioned their desire for one to the captain and so he gave permission.

As they sailed, Fred and Dorothy continued to pray that the ship would reach Calcutta on time. One of the ship's engines broke down just as they were coming into the Manila harbor but it was repaired while the cargo was being unloaded. Then they were delayed two days in Iloilo, Philippines because of rain. But there they received word that the ship was not doing to Madras as originally intended, thus saving them three or four extra days. Right up until the last week, the captain didn't know for sure whether they would make it to Calcutta before the 24th or not because of tides on the Hooghly River going into the city. But the Lord undertook and they arrived at noon on January 22, 1957.

The Lord marvelously displayed His power with regards to customs. As Field Council Chairman, Fred had often spent weeks and months clearing baggage for other missionaries with everything having to be opened and inspected. It was almost too good to believe when the customs officer passed all their baggage duty-free that same day! They attributed their customs success to the many who were specifically praying daily for that matter.

CHAPTER NINE
The Jungle Blossoms

"God's work can never progress unless the Holy Spirit has full sway in the lives of each worker. He cannot flow through blocked channels. The problems that often confront the work are beyond human wisdom, but God is omnipotent. The future is dim. But has He not called? Has He not chosen? Has He not sent? And has He not promised? Then let us work together in this great responsibility of evangelizing the lost in Assam." – Fred Waldock, April 1954

Upon returning to Makunda, Fred and Dorothy had the joy of seeing how God had answered prayer in their absence. A number of the leprosy patients had accepted Christ and had their lives transformed by His mighty power.

One of these was Kananjao Singh, a Manipuri who was afflicted not only with leprosy but also with tuberculosis. After his conversion he had a good testimony to others confined in the TB ward and became a faithful witness for his Lord.

Jottish Bhattercherjee was another leper who came to Christ. Jottish was a college graduate and a Brahmin, the highest Hindu caste. He had come to the leprosy colony around 1951. His physical condition had been deplorable – fingers and toes were missing, there were open ulcers on his body and he was blind. His body responded to the medical treatment and his soul also responded. In early 1956 Jottish testified in a church service of his faith in Jesus Christ.

There had, however, been a tremendous patient turnover and most of these new patients had never heard the Gospel before coming to Makunda. Both Fred and Dorothy taught Sunday school classes each Sunday for the compound people and for outsiders who came, and then various classes in the colony. Fred had devotions with the patients each morning and then helped with the treatments and in giving out medicines. During the week Fred also taught two Bible school classes for the patients and one for a Muslim convert. He also went on regular evangelistic trips to Tripura State with Jim Garlow in connection with outpatient leprosy clinics. Dorothy homeschooled their three boys each morning and also taught a class for Muslim women who professed faith in Jesus. Both Fred and Dorothy did visitation among the patients and compound people. In all things they were coworkers.

In March a terrible tragedy brought a new reality to their hearts of the seriousness of their task. Their faithful Manipuri driver, who had worked for them for 5 ½ years, was trying to get the tractor out of the mud while plowing when his foot slipped off the clutch as the front end of the tractor went up in the air. The tractor went over backwards and pinned the driver between the wheel and the ground, killing him instantly. He had heard the Gospel and had received tracts but was a strict, proud Hindu and had rejected the truth. The sorrowing and wailing of his relatives was indescribable. The missionaries were helpless to comfort them concerning the dead man but they had several opportunities to tell his relatives of Christ who could give them hope of sins forgiven and eternal life. Others of the compound workers were struck by this tragedy and some came to Sunday services for the first time.

When Fred and Dorothy finally received the freight that they had sent out, they praised God for the miracle that everything had came through. From the time the things left home until the time they opened them at Makunda not one thing had been opened by anyone along the way! The only casualties after the halfway-around-the-world trip were three broken jars of fruit.

The first permanent hospital building at Makunda had been finished several years ago and they had been happy to have room for 16 patients. But the work in the colony had continued to grow and the need for more hospital wards increased as well. So the missionaries purchased a "Long Tom" - a prefabricated aluminum building over a steel super structure. They made it two and a half feet higher by setting it on brick walls. That gave them room to put in extra ventilators. This made it cooler than the old hospital building during the oppressively hot summer. The 100 by 20 feet ward provided space for 38 beds. The new ward was attached by a breezeway to the original building, which then served as an administrative, treatment and dispensary unit.

When Fred and Dorothy had come out to India in 1949, the attitude was that the white man was superior and was to be deferred to in all things. But Fred was never comfortable with the "Big White Man" image. Early on, he sought to create a truly indigenous church where the national Christians were the leaders.

In April Makunda Baptist Church had its' annual business meeting. For Fred it was a thrill to see these unlearned babes in Christ start to take hold of the things of Christ and grow in the Lord. Fred threw more of the church responsibilities upon the Indian Christians that year, albeit with some fear and trembling. It was Fred's assertion that they would never become indigenous unless the missionaries began turning over responsibilities. There was a potential pastor from among the patients that Fred sought to train to do some of the preaching and directing of the meetings with the help of the deacons and with the missionaries as advisors.

Fred wrote of a marvelous Easter service in 1957.

"Easter Sunday Evening
Dear Ones at Temple:
Hallelujah, what a Savior! This has been a blessed day here at Makunda and we want to share it with you.
We started off the day very early in the morning with a sunrise service. It was a joy and a thrill to declare the glorious truth again of the Resurrection of our Lord to the patients in the colony. Many there who had never heard of it before were amazed and you could tell they just couldn't take it all in. Just imagine if today was the very first time that you ever heard that Jesus arose from the dead and that He died on the cross to pay your sins' penalty!
After the sunrise service we hurried home and had breakfast and tried to 'brush up' a bit on our Sunday school lesson for 9:30. In the Sunday school hour we had a wonderful opportunity to give the

Resurrection story again to about 25 Moslems (besides others) who probably hadn't heard before. After that we hurried off to the hospital compound to hold our other Sunday school. The Christians met in the church. I had about 40 in the large ward and Dorothy went to the women's section. I wish we could explain in just a small way the thrill of giving the message of a Living Savior to people who have never heard, and to those who have heard who are bound by some dead religious teacher, or some heathen deity.

Directly after these classes we had a special meeting in the church with the deacons to question candidates for baptism. For the past two weeks we have been having some special times with a number of Christians who have asked for baptism.

After this meeting at the church, we came home and had dinner. Immediately after dinner I went down to the river to see if the dam was still holding the river so that we could have our baptismal service. We had prepared the dam yesterday but it broke last night or else someone wanted to catch the small fish that had been collected and broke the dam. What a joy it was to me personally to baptize nine leprous patients this afternoon. To stand by some of these dear ones in the waters of baptism is a joy. Just think for a moment of these poor benighted people – many of them have no standing at all because of their disease. They are segregated from their own society and villages – yet with a newfound joy in the Lord and they are rejoicing in Him. Some of those whom I baptized this afternoon didn't even have enough fingers to grasp my arm. One poor fellow besides having leprosy has TB and is very weak but he has asked for a long time to be baptized. We practically had to carry him into the water but you never saw a more eager fellow.

Rejoice with us, but do continue to pray. The days are getting very hot – we need your continued prayers for health so that we can continue giving out the Gospel message. Our hearts are encouraged as we think of the many at Temple who are faithful in remembering us in prayer.

Yours for souls in Assam,
Fred and Dorothy Waldock"

Fred and Dorothy wrote of the great benefit their Spiritual Life Conference had been and how the work among the patients continued to blossom. During the conference they had been reminded of that glorious truth from John chapter 15 that as followers of Christ we are called to abide as branches in the Vine and that everything we require is supplied through the Vine. All fruitfulness is a result of being in the Vine.

July 1957
"Dear Friends and Loved Ones,

'Christ wants a man through whom He can live His life,' was the truth so wonderfully presented to us by means of a taped message by a Major Thomas of England at our Spiritual Life Conference. Even though we had heard this truth before, I'm sure few of us grasped the import of it like we did when hearing these messages. God doesn't want to use our lives – He wants to live the Powerful, Resurrected Life of Christ through us! What a contrast to the defeated, carnal life that the majority of Christians live. We don't have to worry about how much we can accomplish or how well we can do it – we just surrender our lives to Him and let Him work out His Eternal Purpose through us.

This wonderful truth has brought a new attitude and approach to our work here. It is a real joy to be able to teach the patients that they don't have to try to live a new life when they believe – Christ desires to live His life through them. It has also given great encouragement to realize what the Lord can do for these leprosy patients who have a background of only dark heathenism. We can't – in ourselves – do a thing, but Christ working through us and in them can work a true miracle.

We are rejoicing these days that a number of new patients are reading the Bible and showing a real interest. Pray for their definite salvation. There is increasing interest in Bible study among the Christian patients and they are showing growing concern for the salvation of the other patients. Fred has a Bible study class during the week in the colony and attendance is increasing all the time. Even some non-Christians are coming. The questions they ask about the Word show real thought and keen desire to learn. The newly elected pastor of the colony church seems to be growing spiritually and taking hold of his responsibilities. One young fellow, who is of the High Brahmin caste, and who was formerly quite insolent and independent in his attitude, is giving wonderful evidence of 'new life in Christ' and is now happy in the work of trimming the ulcers on the patients' feet and even scrubs up the floors afterwards. This work is only fit for missionaries and low-caste people!"

The needs extended beyond Makunda – nominally Christian tribes from Manipur State requested teaching and medical treatment. The government of Manipur would not allow missionaries to reside within their borders but permission had been granted for missionaries to teach the people and to do leprosy clinic work. Also there was a need for a missionary couple in Dharmanager in Tripura State, 21 miles from Makunda. The BMM missionaries had done evangelistic work and leprosy clinics in this area. The government was not allowing Americans to establish new stations in Tripura State but because Fred was Canadian, the Field Council thought that perhaps the Waldocks could get permission to live there. They requested that the Waldocks consider Dharmanager. Although Fred and Dorothy did not yet have a real sense of call to the work in Dharmanager, they were team players and as such they were willing to go where needed. They would pray and wait on the Lord to open doors and to show His will for them.

At this time, both Dorothy and David were experiencing more health problems. It had been difficult for them to adjust to the long, humid rainy season after being home for a year. David had suffered from bronchial asthma for months and the other children endured prickly heat as they persevered with their schoolwork each day.

By the November Field Council meetings there was still no word on whether Fred and Dorothy could go to Dharmanager. However, for the time being they felt that God still had a definite ministry for them at the leprosy colony and they were happy in that.

One night when neither Fred nor Jim was at Makunda a fire started at the cookhouse. In the Providence of God, one of the nurses in dormitory #1 had not been able to sleep. It was around midnight when she noticed a bright glare outside. Dormitory #2 was right next to the cookhouse. In horror she realized that the dormitory roof was already flaring. She roused the six girls in dormitory #2 and they managed to save half their bedding and about half of their personal belongings before the fire also consumed this thatch and bamboo structure.

The women quickly got everything out of dormitory #1 and the adjacent baby house. Patients and villagers came running to help fight the fire and to keep dormitory #1 from burning. Fortunately, this dorm was built of brick and cement with a tin roof so it was not nearly as vulnerable as the other dormitory. However, the tin roof had a layer of bamboo and thatch grass on it to keep out the rain. The workers were able to soak the top layer but underneath it was tinder dry so it kept flaring up. Workers cut away the burning part as fast as they could. Even the nurses and ayahs scooped up wet dirt with their hands to throw on the fire.

The wind was blowing sparks everywhere and the fire began spreading down over the hill towards the missionaries' bungalow. Dorothy and the other women quickly got the children out of bed and took sweaters and jackets and scurried down the hill towards a safer area until the wind let up. Anxiety ran high as they waited for the wind to die down, praying fervently for God's protection for themselves, the workers fighting the fire and the mission property. After about 45 minutes, it seemed that the threat to the bungalow had passed. So they returned, bringing the untainted children and their two ayahs with them.

The men continued to fight the fire for over two hours on the roof of dormitory #1 to keep it from spreading. Finally they said it would be safe. The patients stayed on and poured water until 3:30 a.m. and watched all night to see that it was all right. The morning light was a welcome sight to the many at the station who thanked the Lord for His protection through the night and His safe keeping in the hollow of His hand.

About this time, a newly saved Christian named Promode Malakar came to Makunda from the Alipur hospital for treatment of his leprosy. As a student at Gauhati University, Promode contracted tuberculosis and went to Alipur for treatment. As a Hindu, Promode did not believe the Bible and rejected the Bible teaching that was offered at the hospital. He read through the Bengali New Testament three times in an attempt to prove it untrue. After some time his tuberculosis was arrested and he was released from the hospital. Dr. Quentin Kenoyer offered him the opportunity to learn how to become an x-ray technician. Promode stayed on at the hospital and voluntarily attended the Bible classes. Many were praying for his salvation and one day, approximately three years after arriving at Alipur, the Light broke through. Promode was saved and the change in his life was greatly apparent.

That faith was soon tested. Promode developed leprosy and was sent to Makunda. As is often the case with God, man's tragedy was really God's superior and gracious plan. Promode would have a tremendous impact on the spiritual life at Makunda for decades to come. Promode stayed true and grew in the Lord in the midst of persecution and trials. He asked to be placed in the hostel with the young boys who had leprosy. He faithfully witnessed to them, holding evening devotions and praying with them and for them.

As always at Christmas, the missionaries took the opportunities afforded them to explain to as many people as possible the blessed event of Christmas. Throughout the week they showed the Christmas story on film to various groups and proclaimed the miraculous birth of Christ, our only Savior.

In January 1958, the work in Assam lost a faithful prayer warrior – Fred's mother went home to be with the Lord. She had suffered from a serious heart condition for the last six years of her life but in her infirmity the Lord had given her a powerful prayer ministry, not only for Assam, but also for Africa where Fred's brother Hedley served and for many other fields where former students had gone. She prayed by the hour each day and remembered each missionary on Fred's field by name as well as many of the workers and patients. Several times Fred knew his own life to have been spared from danger because at that very hour she had been praying.

In early January, a heartbroken Hindu father brought his son, Bhola Nath Dey, to the leprosy colony. "I have gone to every doctor I know of and have spent all my money to get my son cured and he is just getting worse. Will you please treat him and teach him all about your Jesus too," he cried. What an opportunity! Bhola was placed in the boys' hostel where Promode lived. Bhola had completed 7th grade and could already read well so Fred and Dorothy gave him plenty of Christian books to read and also started him on a basic Bible course. He had no trouble answering all the questions but when it came to the one asking him specifically what he thought of Jesus Christ, and did he want to accept Him as His personal Savior, he left it blank.

In January they started a library for the patients and one for the workers. Realizing the power of the printed word, they also set up literature booths at the various bazaars and fairs. Fred and Dorothy spent more time in Bible classes, setting up a school for leprosy children and one for the workers.

The gospel was spreading far afield of Makunda as healed patients returned to their homes. One of the first patients to be moved to Makunda had been Keunimang. He wasn't a deformed case so he was able to work and did his part willingly and faithfully, joining with the rest of them in clearing the jungle and erecting suitable housing for the other patients. He regularly attended classes and services and one day he came to know the Lord as his Savior.

When more effective leprosy drugs were invented, his disease was arrested and in October 1956 he was discharged as an arrested case. He returned to the hills of Manipur State among his own people. He became a missionary to those around him, sharing the grace and love of God. He organized a Sunday school and by spring of 1958 there were sixteen households who had become Christians and were worshipping the Lord Jesus together in their own little village church, which they built themselves.

Fred spent much time in the villages doing leprosy survey work and giving out tracts and holding meetings wherever he went. Tablets had been invented that arrested the spread of leprosy and Fred took these to the various villages. The roads were narrow and of slick clay. Overloaded trucks were top-heavy and accidents were common. Fred routinely stopped and helped the injured. Often Fred made trips into town to pick up lepers who had been abandoned by their villages.

The jeep was equipped with loudspeakers and Fred played gospel records in the various villages and other remote areas. The people's faces would light up when they heard their own language coming from the speakers. Fred had an all-consuming desire to lead people to the Lord and establish churches.

Fred was a father who expected honesty, integrity and thoroughness from his children but who also made sure that they knew that they were loved. He was fun loving and a big tease. Both Fred and Dorothy carved out time from the busyness of ministry to spend quality time with their children. Dorothy made sure that birthdays and other special days were memorable for the children even though money was tight.

As the children grew, the problem of their schooling became more acute. Both Fred and Dorothy were engaged in the work of the ministry. From early on in the ministry in Assam, various missionaries had sent their children to Woodstock, a boarding school 1,200 miles away in Landour, Mussoorie in the state of Uttar Pradesh.

It was an excruciating decision for Fred and Dorothy but they felt that there was no way for the boys to continue their schooling in the society and culture that they were living in. The plan was that ten-year-old David and eight-year-old Kenneth would go to Woodstock in June 1958. The family traveled together to Landour. While there, Gordie was adamant that he was not going back to Makunda without his brothers. It was finally decided to enroll seven-year-old Gordie as well.

Fred and Dorothy were faithful to keep close communication with their children through letters, parcels and prayer. They wrote many letters to encourage them in particular needs and to counsel them with principles from God's word. The separation was hard and yet they drew strength from the sacrificial example of their Heavenly Father who had been separated from His own Son for them.

Sometime after Bhola had arrived, another father brought his son to Makunda. This Moslem Manipuri father fell at the Americans' feet and begged them to heal his only son, Abdul. But he strongly warned Abdul, "You take their medicine and do everything they tell you to do to get well, but don't you dare listen when they tell you about their religion. That is a Western religion and not for us. If you listen and believe it, we will kill you."

Abdul was placed in the same boys' hostel as Bhola and Promode. Bhola and Abdul became good friends and did everything together. One day Bhola and Abdul were down at the well taking their baths and washing their clothes by beating them on the cement. All at once Abdul began to shake. Bhola saw him and said, "Abdul, what is wrong? Are you sick?" Malaria fever and accompanying shakes is very common in Assam.

Abdul replied, "No, I'm afraid. What if I should die? And Jesus is not my Savior. I want to accept Him right now!"

Bhola, being a bit bigger than Abdul, took him by the shoulders and shook him and said, "Are you crazy? If you do that, your father will kill you!"

"I don't care," said Abdul, as he tore off across the field to the hostel where Promode was. Promode led him to the Lord right then. There was such a remarkable change in Abdul's life and attitude that soon Bhola and six other boys accepted the Lord.

Abdul's father did hear of it and took him home. Abdul was afraid to come out openly for the Lord but still held unto his faith.

Eventually Bhola became cured of his leprosy and went back home to finish high school and college. He became a teacher in a Christian mission school and has remained faithful to the Lord.

After Bhola returned home, his younger brother, Sambhu, also contracted leprosy and was brought to the colony in 1963. In the month of May that year, missionary Paul Versluis came to Makunda for special meetings. In one meeting the Lord spoke definitely to Sambhu. He understood that he was a sinner without salvation and without hope. He understood that Christ died for him, bearing all his sins on His body on Calvary. Sambhu realized then and there that there is no other Savior or any other way to go to heaven. The burden of his sins became so heavy. At that moment the sins that he had committed began to appear before him in his mind. After the service he knelt and confessed all his sins to God and asked Him to cleanse him and make him a new man. God heard his crying and he passed from eternal death to life! His case was arrested early so he was able to return home to Agartala, Tripura for high school and college.

In November 1958, missionary Dr. Gene Burrows and his wife arrived in India to take over the medical work at Makunda. Dr. Burrows, the son of Dr. Lilburn and Beulah Burrows, was the first of the Mid-India missionary children to return to the field for full-time service.

In late fall, the missionaries at Makunda conducted a Vacation Bible school for ten days. They registered 143 children with an average attendance of 76 each day. The children, who were from surrounding Moslem and Hindu villages, were exceptionally attentive and many of them learned at least part of the memory verses. Fred and Dorothy noticed in comparison to the year before that the children were not nearly as reticent or embarrassed in giving the answers to questions concerning heaven, hell, eternal life and Jesus as the only way of salvation.

They wrote of it to Temple Baptist Church, *"We are laying hold on the promises of God for the children who recently attended our Vacation Bible School. Do pray with us that this seed sown might truly bear fruit to His glory.*

A young lady in the colony is greatly burdened over the guilt and shame of her sins. She feels her disease is a result. Pray that she might come to Christ for forgiveness. Recently four more men in the colony have accepted Christ. Pray for their growth and strengthening.

Our (own) children will be leaving school Dec. 2 and will arrive here Dec. 5th. Pray for a safe journey for them. I needn't tell you how much we look forward to their coming. They seem to have adjusted well in school and have not been sick a day since we left them. They will be with us for nearly three months before returning for another school year."

Before the two younger boys had been off the plane half an hour, they shared how Jesus had been working in their hearts while in boarding school. Fred and Dorothy praised the Lord. The boys' matrons and teachers were true Christians and had been a real help to the boys in spiritual matters. David's teachers were not so spiritually minded and therefore his parents prayed much for him that he would be able to live for the Lord.

While the boys were home on vacation they kept up a busy pace of playing ball, riding their bikes, hunting, rafting and going with Fred on his clinics. Dorothy learned to put her children in God's hands and was not overbearing or over protective. The boys often collected orchids for their mother who loved plants and flowers. Dorothy spent most of her time trying to fill up their stomachs and altering and mending their clothes before they returned to school in February.

In the beginning of 1959, three men and two women accepted Christ but two others who had begun well had gone back to their former way of life. Satan's influence was strong in the colony to turn back those who desired to accept Christ.

Since the 1957 Field Conference, the Waldocks had been making application to the government authorities in Tripura State for permission to reside there permanently. Finally in early January 1959, the Waldocks made a trip personally to the capital,

Agartala, and the authorities assured them that a residential permit would be granted when they transferred their residence. It appeared that the Lord was opening the way for Baptist Mid-Missions to establish a more permanent work in Dharmanager.

The Waldocks were not without mixed feelings about the move. In a prayer letter to supporters they wrote: *"There is naturally a reluctance in leaving Makunda as we have been here since the beginning days and especially since returning from furlough we have felt a burden to evangelize and teach the patients more. However, we are encouraged that the need will be met in a measure by the coming of Mr. Mullick, a Bengali, who has just completed Bible school in Calcutta. He will arrive by the first of February. And as soon as Dr. and Mrs. Burrows gain a grasp of the Bengali language they, too, will be able to minister to the patients' spiritual needs. So we feel that the Lord is at last opening new doors and we are to 'Enlarge the place of thy tent...and lengthen thy cords.' There is also great anticipation as we open the work there. It is a known fact that the hill tribes, who are animists, are far more receptive to the Gospel than the Hindus and Moslems of the plains. The New Zealand Baptists are the only mission working in all of Tripura State with its population of over 700,000, except for a very small Roman Catholic work. They count their Christian community as numbering over 6,000 and they have 66 churches and 38 branch churches (of less than 10 members). Most of their work is in the midwest and southwest section of the State and very little in the northeast where Dharmanager is located. Dharmanager is the only town of any size in this end of Tripura and it in itself is a challenge with its high school and college students and business people. Dharmanager is building up fast these days because of its being on the new trans-state highway which runs from Assam to Agartala."*

The Waldocks would have to wait to move to Dharmanager until the Lord provided funds for the building of a house there. The mission already owned a piece of property in Dharmanager with a two-room bamboo hut on it but that facility would not be suitable during the heavy rains nor large enough when the boys were home from school on vacation. The plan was to split their time between Makunda and Dharmanager until a house could be built.

A Spiritual Life Conference was scheduled for April 14-17 at Makunda, which was by this time a thriving complex that included a hospital, patient wards and a chapel building in the shape of a cross. The church was designed this way so that the non-contagious people could sit on one side, male lepers in the center and women leprosy patients on the other side. The pulpit was located in the top portion of the cross. The funds for the church building had been given as a memorial to their husbands by Mrs. A. P. Borden and Mrs. Fred McManis.

Extensive cultivation of the land provided food for the colony and employment for the patients. The rice harvest in 1959 was 110 tons. Patients raised all the fresh vegetables needed to feed 250 daily. The colony livestock included 30 buffaloes used for plowing and heavy work, 150 head of cattle, 175 goats and 18 pigs. Patients were also employed as weavers to provide all the sheeting, mosquito netting, and muslin needed for the colony. Educated patients taught the illiterate how to read and write.

The missionary force at Makunda Leprosy Colony in 1959 consisted of the Waldocks, Jim and Joyce Garlow, nurses Doris Bruce and Glenola Marchel and Dr. Gene Burrows and his wife Bette. Rev. and Mrs. J.T. Midyett lived at Jaffirband and did part-time leprosy survey work.

Fred wrote in April 1959, *"We praise the Lord for His blessings on the work here. Three men recently accepted the Lord and another woman came for salvation after Sunday school class yesterday morning. The patients have asked for Bible classes from 6:30 a.m. to 7:30 a.m. each morning and again from 6 p.m. to 7 p.m. each evening. This makes a long day for some of them as right after Colony devotions at 7:45 a.m. they go to work and except for their lunch hour work until 6 p.m. and then many of them go to night school from 7:30 p.m. to 9 p.m. or later. With the temperature up to 90 or 95 degrees each day now it doesn't make it any easier. Attendance at these classes is purely voluntary but many Christians as well as non-Christians attend and are really eager to hear more. Calls are coming from different tribal peoples for Bible teaching and we are making definite plans to go regularly to a couple of these areas. They say they have become Christians but we shall be able to tell better when teaching them just where they stand."*

In preparation for moving to Dharmanager, they had the bamboo hut on the BMM property rebuilt so that they could camp down there and open up the work. Through leprosy survey and out-patient clinics they had a unique entrance into these jungle tribes. They experienced real joy sitting on the peoples' small bamboo porches or around their smoky fires playing Gospel recordings in the national language and talking of the wonderful Savior.

In July 1959 while Dorothy was in Landour with the children, 37-year-old Fred had a mild heart attack. His greatest concern was for Dorothy some 1,400 miles away. He knew how concerned she would be and all the problems she would encounter to come home alone. But in faith he committed her to their faithful God, and in that committal they both found rest. Fred sensed the nearness of the Lord during those uncertain days and praised Him and thanked Him for His Presence. 2 Corinthians 1:3-4 took on new meaning for him. "Blessed be God, even the Father of our Lord Jesus Christ, the Father of mercies, and the God of all comfort; Who comforteth us in all our tribulation, that we may be able to comfort them which are in any trouble, by the comfort wherewith we ourselves are comforted."

When Dorothy and the children got the news they were heartbroken and as Dorothy boarded the plane to Assam her thoughts drifted to how her own Dad had gone home to be with the Lord so quickly. She prayed for Fred's life to be spared for a longer ministry here on earth.

Dorothy wrote to Temple Baptist, *"When I got off the plane Thursday noon I went to Alipur to consult with Dr. Walker and was encouraged so very much by his report. He said that this attack was a warning of a narrowed coronary artery and called it coronary artery spasm without permanent heart damage. With two or three months' rest and with a diet bringing him down to 165 pounds, he will be able to resume a full work schedule with no further worry of heart trouble. He is already allowed up for meals and spends several hours each day in the office as well as doing some book work in bed, and usually there is quite a string of workers and patients coming to consult with him. He feels well but tires quickly. How we praise the Lord for giving us this warning without any permanent heart damage so that we can guard against any more serious trouble.*

Dr. Burrows and Dr. Walker are recommending that we return to Landour for two months in order for Fred to get away from the work and because Dr. Walker will be up there to supervise Fred's activity and progress. The doctors say that we should plan to go after one month."

Arthur Fetzer, the president of Baptist Mid-Missions, who had himself recently suffered a heart attack, wrote to Temple Baptist Church, *"His age and his excellent physical condition are in his favor, and with the proper treatment and carefully regulated activity for a period of some months, the damage to his heart should be remedied almost completely. Certainly we will be praying much to that end and looking to the Lord for Fred and Dorothy. Their ministry has been an exceedingly fruitful one in India, and we cannot help but feel that the Lord has further usefulness for them. He and Dorothy are needed in India, and if it is the Lord's will that they continue their ministry there, He is able to heal Fred's damaged heart so that he can continue the work that is so close to his heart."*

Fred and Dorothy returned to Landour on the first of August for the prescribed rest. They enjoyed the extra time they could spend with the boys. Their sons were doing very well in school and they had wonderful Christian teachers but Fred and Dorothy were concerned for a more spiritual and helpful boarding life for them. Fred made good progress, and even with the altitude and steep mountain paths to climb, he felt no difficulty. They praised the Lord for both physical and spiritual renewal while they were there. The Lord spoke to their hearts and challenged them to a new submission to His discipline and discipleship by way of the cross.

Fred's heart attack delayed the opening of Dharmanager. But Fred and Dorothy acknowledged that *"The 'stops' as well as the 'steps' are ordered of the Lord."* In a letter from Landour, they wrote *"Pray that God will open the doors and guide us very definitely at this time. First of all we are seeking an amiable agreement with another mission in the state. The Lord is blessing their work but they have not been able to adequately cover the northern part of the state where we would like to work."*

They returned to Makunda the third week of September to prepare for a special evangelistic service in the Colony and two weeks of Daily Vacation Bible School for the village children. They were "attempting great things for God, and expecting great things from God."

In October there were signs that something was wrong with Dorothy's health as well. On November 3 the doctors at Alipur removed a lymph node from Dorothy's neck. It developed into a rather serious case. There was a bit of a tail on the node that was attached along the wall of a rather large vessel and in the dissecting process it tore the vessel and caused a bleeder which was difficult to tie off. Dorothy lost quite a lot of blood but within days was fine except for a very sore face and neck. She stayed at Alipur for the next week as the doctors observed her condition and ran further tests. The biopsy was sent to three different places in the States for verification. The results were somewhat better than originally thought and the doctors felt certain Dorothy could be treated on the field and therefore finish out the term before going on furlough.

At the November Field Council meetings, it was determined that the Waldocks would not go to Dharmanager after all. While Fred and Dorothy were up in Landour, the New Zealand Baptist Mission had reviewed the past correspondence and wrote a rather strong letter stating that the Waldocks were coming in under different arrangements than had first been discussed. The letter influenced the thinking of the Field Council. Then with Fred's and Dorothy's sicknesses and the health problems of others on the field and furloughs coming all at once, it seemed wise to the Field Council to drop the matter of Dharmanager. The Garlows planned to go on furlough in May 1960, so Fred would be in charge of the Makunda station until their return. The Waldocks were due for furlough in January 1962.

In April 1960 Fred and Dorothy wrote,

"Dear Dr. Powell and Temple Friends,

These have been rather full weeks with the boys home from school and trying to do a few extra things with them as well as carrying on the full program of the cool months. Now they are back in school again and, except for the month we go to the hills to escape the long hot season, that is all we will see the boys for the next nine months.

Let me tell you a little of what is taking place at Makunda. This is the Lord's doing – it is marvelous before our eyes. How we praise the Lord over and over again that He so definitely led us to stay at Makunda. Ten years of laboring and sowing the seed is now beginning to bear fruit. These past months we have been thrilled by the response. Nearly every week there have been decisions for Christ. I have been holding Bible classes for believers twice a day for about two months now. The other

Sunday an invitation was given to follow the Lord in baptism and 23 responded. I wish I could have been there to enjoy the thrill of the sight, but I was away in Calcutta. The following week, the deacons, with some of the missionaries, examined the candidates and Dorothy said it was thrilling.

In the eyes of the people baptism is THE step; in other words, one is then marked as a Christian. Then the persecution starts – they have brought shame on their society and have broken from their family and have forsaken their religion, etc. I wonder how many in our churches would obey the Lord in this step if they knew that they were no longer part of their family, if they weren't allowed into their own house, if they knew that they would be beaten and yes, even more than that too.

How these facts come home to us as we teach them the meaning of walking with the Lord in full obedience, knowing all the time that it is going to cost them far more than it has ever cost us. But what a thrill to see their faces beam when they have truly experienced the new life in Christ and follow Him in obedience. Why shouldn't they beam with joy? They have been freed from the bondage of tradition, fear and sin. It is a new life, a new life in Christ Jesus.

How we thank God for the way you have stood by us during these anxious past six months. As we passed through the two medical crises our confidence was in Him and our faith was encouraged by the faithfulness of you dear ones. The indecision of our moving bore heavily upon us also, mainly due to the fact that we couldn't feel free in our spirit about it all. The burden, which we felt from Him, to stay on at Makunda to help establish these young believers and thereby multiply ourselves many times in their villages through their ministry, grew increasingly upon us. Now as we face a tremendously heavy two years before furlough we again ask you to stand by us every day.

Let me quote a paraphrase of Psalm 37:5 in closing. It may not be exactly correct but here it is, "Roll your burden on Jehovah, TRUST in Him – He worketh or He doeth the work."

> *Lovingly, your missionaries for HIS sake,*
> *Fred and Dorothy Waldock*
> *Bazaricherra, P.O., Cachar District, Assam, India"*

In addition to the administration of the leprosy colony, Fred was also the Assam Field Council president and trying to carry on his teaching ministry in the colony and the church. Dorothy, too, had many added responsibilities including acting as treasurer for the Field Council and taking over Mrs. Garlow's tasks of supervising the untainted children and cooking for the nurses and children. She also would be ordering all the literature for their colporteur work in Manipur State. This was on top of her regular work of Bible teaching and literature work for Makunda. Their prayer constantly was that the spiritual side of the work would not take second place to the many duties and responsibilities thrust upon them.

As the winter moved into summer, it became apparent that this year was very unusual. It was the driest year in Assam in over 50 years. Very little of the first crop of rice could be planted. The season for this first crop was just about finished in May and they had very little rain. Less than 5% would be cultivated. They were in a tight pinch. Fred was trusting that extra funds would continue to come in during those months so that they would be able to meet the needs.

There was a drought not only in the weather, but also in the number of missionary personnel. During the summer of 1960 six of the BMM missionaries were on furlough and six others had withdrawn from the Mission because of health and other issues. There were no replacements for them. It wasn't that there were none that felt called to India. The problem was that the Indian government was not allowing in new missionaries, except medical or technical workers. Yet the work was continually expanding.

The admonition of 2 Timothy 2:2 "And the things that thou hast heard of me among many witnesses, the same commit thou to faithful men, who shall be able to teach others also" was compelling to Fred and Dorothy. How thankful they were for two national brethren, Promode and Mihir, who felt a real burden for the new Christians in the colony. Promode accepted the task of church pastor and he and Mihir met daily with the Christians to pray and to counsel them.

In July, Fred, Dorothy and Lois went up to Landour for vacation and to spend time with the boys. Fred returned to Makunda at the end of July but Dorothy and Lois stayed on until the end of August to have some extra time with David, Kenny and Gordie.

In August, Makunda Baptist Church went through a time of purifying and the congregation learned what it meant to really live for the Lord. There was some rebellion and one member had to be dismissed but they trusted the Lord to give them a strong church that would bear witness to the surrounding community.

The future for missionaries in India was uncertain and therefore the greatest need was to train the national Christians to carry on the teaching and evangelism. The Waldocks planned a Bible school program for the fall that would train about eight of the choice, literate Christians in the colony. Promode and Mihir would help with the teaching. These eight young men, who had every chance of becoming arrested from leprosy with little or no deformity, had a desire to return to their homes with the Gospel message.

Plans for the fall also included a vacation Bible school in October and gospel teams from the colony holding meetings in various villages and bazaars and distributing and selling literature.

The first ordination service in the history of BMM's work in Assam took place at Makunda in April 1961. Two weeks prior to the missionary Spiritual Life Conference one of the church members suggested to the church leaders that the conference would afford a good opportunity to ordain Pastor Promode Malakar. Most of the ordained missionary men of the field would be attending. The church approved the plan. A letter calling an Examining Council was quickly drafted and delivered directly to each of the other four sister churches in the Fellowship of Baptist Churches of Cachar. On Tuesday afternoon, April 25, the first day of the missionary conference, the Council examined the candidate. The impressive examination was four hours long. It concerned Promode's salvation, his call to the Gospel ministry and his doctrinal belief. The examination was conducted in three languages – English, Bengali and Manipuri - so that everyone would be able to understand the proceedings. The Examining Council unanimously agreed that Promode was a suitable candidate and recommended to the church that they proceed with ordination. The ordination service was held on Thursday. The hour was late when they concluded, but no one really cared. It had been a most memorable day.

In June another lymph node on Dorothy's neck became enlarged and Dr. Kenoyer immediately removed it and sent it to the United States for evaluation. The report that came back was not favorable but there was no need for an emergency return to the States. They decided to wait until December when their regular furlough would come.

In November the new Baptist Mid-Missions president, Allan Lewis, and his wife Ann came out to India to see the field and to speak at the annual Field Council meeting at Alipur. They were a day late arriving in Calcutta but the Lord undertook and the conference was a wonderful time. The missionaries were challenged with heart-searching messages brought by Dr. Lewis. Fred commented on what a humble, gracious servant of the Lord Brother Lewis was.

Fred and Dorothy praised the Lord that they had been granted their "No Objection to Return" permits which would greatly help in getting return visas to India after furlough. The situation with visas was increasingly complex and therefore they were doubly grateful for the permits.

Literature work had greatly increased during their second term and it was this potential that laid a new ministry on Fred and Dorothy's hearts. They became burdened for a Christian Book Depot in Silchar, the largest town of the district and the government headquarters. Through Christian literature they could have an outreach to the thousands of college students in and around Silchar.

Just before the Waldocks left Makunda they received a letter from Deb Singh, a Manipuri Hindu schoolteacher who had taught many of the BMM missionaries the Manipuri language since 1948. Even though the missionaries had witnessed to him constantly in their course of study, he had remained an adamant Hindu. He had moved his family of two boys and four girls back to Manipur State in 1955, where he had inherited the family land. He took with him a copy of the newly printed Manipuri New Testament.

Now in 1961 he was writing to the missionaries to let them know that he and his eldest son, Selungba, had attended some evangelistic meetings held by Pastor Promode and other Fellowship of Baptist Churches' evangelists in Manipur State. They had accepted the Lord and wanted to come to Makunda to be baptized. Deb Singh had special training under a government program in agriculture and animal husbandry so the missionaries stationed at Makunda invited him to bring his family and come be in charge of the agricultural work and at the same time receive Bible teaching. Deb Singh accepted and brought most of his family to Makunda the following year. His second son, Sana, stayed in Manipur State to finish high school. This family would, in the years ahead, become very special to the Waldocks and their ministry in Silchar.

The Waldocks went on furlough in December 1961 looking forward to a time of rest before embracing this new challenge.

CHAPTER TEN
Home Again

"Faith is a blessed experience. How much we deprive ourselves when we try to reason out so many things." – Fred Waldock, March 1963

The journey from India to America was a wonderful adventure for the six Waldocks. From Bombay they sailed to Aden, Yemen. There they had fun trying to figure out where the children of Israel could have crossed the Red Sea, which was a mile or more wide in most places. They rode camels in Egypt. They saw the pyramids, sphinxes and ancient buildings, many of which dated back to the days of Joseph. They visited missionaries in Italy and hiked through the excavations of the city of Pompeii, which had been buried with hot ash from the eruption of Mount Vesuvius in 79 A.D. They took a quick tour through the catacombs, the Coliseum and the temples of Rome – all of which gave a dramatic picture of the life of early Christians.

From Rome they went to Switzerland where they spent three quiet days over Christmas and enjoyed the grandeur of the Alps. There was very little snow until their last day. From there, they visited Paris for one day and then went over to London. The crossing of the English Channel was truly the worst boat trip they had ever experienced. The day after they arrived, it snowed a foot – the most snow England had seen in years. They stayed there for six days with Fred's aunt and uncle and enjoyed the quietness. They managed to see Westminster Abbey, Big Ben and the outside of Buckingham Palace but it was too wet and cold to enjoy much walking around.

Their trip across the Atlantic wasn't too unpleasant although the ship had to slow down considerably due to heavy seas and they were two days late arriving in New York. Through the help of the Lord's servants, they were able to get a station wagon in Pennsylvania and headed toward Cleveland to the Home Office of Baptist Mid-Missions and the Cleveland Clinic. While the children and Fred were going through medical exams with Dr. Jon Rouch, the mission doctor, Dorothy had a thorough check-up at the Cleveland Clinic by a cancer specialist. The diagnosis of non-Hodgkin's lymphoma was confirmed but it was thought that x-ray therapy would take care of it and that Dorothy would be able to return to India. Her condition was progressing slowly and therefore could be controlled.

Fred was examined by a heart specialist who pronounced him in good condition with no heart damage. Fred and Dorothy were convinced that it was the prayers of God's people that had resulted in these good prognoses.

The trip west from Cleveland started out uneventful. They spent the weekend in Dellroy, Ohio with Fred's new relatives (his Dad had remarried) and then started out at 11 a.m. Monday for Chicago. It had snowed in the night and was still snowing when they left but the highway was clear and they soon experienced beautiful, sunny weather all the way to Chicago. The next day they made it as far as Eau Claire, Wisconsin. Wednesday morning, January 31, they started out, hoping to get to Dorothy's aunt's house in North Dakota that night.

For about 20 miles out of Eau Claire they had followed a Coca-Cola truck. Fred was hesitant to pass it because the left lane still had a covering of snow. The truck slowed down and turned into the left lane for no reason at all. Fred slowed down, too, to see what the driver was going to do. Suddenly, the Coca-Cola truck made a right turn directly in front of the Waldock's car to pass over to the merging lane coming out of Menonomie. Startled, Fred braked and swung out to the right but even so the two vehicles collided.

As the Waldocks climbed out of their crumpled vehicle, they accessed what had happened. Kenny's head had shattered the windshield but he was all right. Both Fred and Gordie had cuts on their foreheads. The back seat had broken sending suitcases flying all over David and as a result his back hurt. Dorothy and Lois seemed to be OK.

At the hospital, the cuts on Fred's and Gordie's foreheads required stitches and an x-ray was done on David's back to make sure it was all right. They were thankful that no one had been badly hurt. The car was badly rumpled and required a new windshield, fender, hood, grill, front headlights and radiator core.

They spent the first three days in a motel waiting for their car to be fixed. Then the pastor from the Conservative Baptist Church found them and arranged for them to be taken care of in homes. Lois, Fred and Dorothy were at one house and the three boys stayed with the pastor's family. Many people were friendly and kind to them. Fred spoke in Sunday school and in the evening service.

They knew that nothing happens without a reason for those who love the Lord. They thanked the Lord that it was not more serious and for the many friends and contacts they made in Menonomie. They were finally able to leave town February 9 – ten days after the accident. From there they went to Canada on business and to see Fred's father.

When they finally arrived in Tacoma on February 15 they found that Temple Baptist Church had prepared a nice comfortable home for them. The church members had spent much time and energy in painting, cleaning and repairing the house. Then they had furnished it with linens, dishes, cooking utensils and lots of good food. They praised the Lord for loved ones such as these at Temple Baptist who did so much for them.

Fred was not home long. Two weeks after arriving in Washington he left again for Indiana to speak in a conference and then to attend the Baptist Mid-Missions' conference. He was in the Midwest and in Ontario until the middle of May. The Lord gave some wonderful contacts and Fred believed that, all in all, the blessing of the Lord was evidenced. He was in scores of homes and had good opportunities to talk to people about the Lord and especially as related to missions. Many young couples opened up in conversation – some hungry, some just interested and some that Fred trusted would make a definite commitment to the Lord for His service.

Meanwhile the children enrolled in school in Tacoma and Dorothy began the treatments for cancer in April. The x-ray treatments hit Dorothy harder than she had expected. Faithful friends from Temple Baptist rallied around the family. Dorothy's longtime friend, Marion Foss, came over daily to make lunch for the children and a blender shake for Dorothy. Her throat was over-radiated and so painful that for months after the treatment she could swallow only with much difficulty. She lost 15 lbs. She couldn't speak for three weeks. Dorothy was a soldier from the word go and yet she was so sick that for a time, friends had to take care of the children. Fred knew that Dorothy wouldn't call for him to come home unless she was so sick that she couldn't move. It almost came to that but she stuck it out and so did Fred.

In May, Dorothy wrote a letter to her friends at Temple Baptist Church.

"I want to take this opportunity to express in a small measure how much I appreciate what you have done and what you have meant to me in this time of illness. I didn't really expect to be hit so hard by these x-ray treatments but the Lord knew and I praise Him for the way He has provided for every need during this time. I want to thank you for the gifts of food for the children, the entertainment for them during their spring vacation, for those who helped with the washing and ironing, for those who have called for the children to take them to various church activities and meetings, and not least, for the many lovely cards and notes to assure me of your love and prayers.

All these have been such a comfort in this time of being laid aside and I do thank you from the bottom of my heart. I would appreciate your continued prayers that my throat might be healed soon.

Several have asked about Fred. He is in his last week of meetings in London, Ontario, Canada. Then he will go to Hamilton, Ontario for his brother's graduation and ordination and then start for home May 10. I'm sure he would appreciate your prayers for the meetings this week and then for traveling mercies.

Sincerely in Christ,
Dorothy Waldock"

Dorothy continued to have trouble swallowing food into June and therefore was not able to build up her strength. Her progress was slow but day-by-day she got a little better.

Their summer schedule involved speaking at many Christian camps in California and Montana. They also had to move into another apartment in July just before beginning a month-long deputation trip.

Fred commented in an interview for the Temple Tidings newsletter, *"It's been a real busy time, and a real blessing, but our hearts and minds are burdened for India and its needs, and we feel that we should take every opportunity while home to challenge the hearts and lives of our friends back here in America to a fresh realization of the needs. The time is short – the situation is critical – we must do all we can before 'the night cometh' while the fields are ripe unto harvest."*

Nearly every week throughout the autumn was taken up with mission conferences. The Waldocks trusted the Lord that they would be a blessing to the churches they visited. They were also praying that God would raise up more than $3,000 for outfit and passage back to India. This was a major concern for them. Everywhere they went they shared their burden to see a work carried on in Silchar. Their vision included a vernacular Bible school and much literature work including translation, publication and colportage work. They also hoped to establish a Christian reading room with a book room.

In late September, Dorothy's radiologist decided to observe her swallowing to see if there was any undue obstruction. He gave her barium and observed the throat with x-ray and a fluoroscope. He was satisfied that everything was normal and that the choking difficulty that Dorothy still experienced would gradually clear up.

Their soon return to Assam came into doubt when on October 20, 1962 China attacked India along the Himalayan border. The cause of the attack was an unresolved territory dispute along the 3,225-kilometer-long Himalayan border. In remote parts of Assam, the Chinese forces advanced easily despite Indian efforts at resistance. The Chinese advanced within 200 miles to the north of where BMM operated.

The Waldocks, in faith, applied for visas. These were granted despite the unrest in India. Then on November 21, the Chinese unexpectedly declared a unilateral cease-fire.

In a prayer letter dated December 1962, the Waldocks wrote: *"The missionaries and national co-laborers are holding forth on the field under increased problems and tension. Recent news states that inflation continues to rise due to the threat of war. The movement of needed supplies to our area has been greatly curtailed. Friends, are hearts are heavy and burdened for the ministry in Assam. The opportunities are so great. At this crucial time we dare not even consider retreat."*

One Sunday Lois, Gordon and Kenneth all went forward and asked to receive baptism. They went through the required baptismal classes and were all baptized on the same day by Dr. Eugene Barnes at Temple Baptist Church.

The first part of January 1963 Fred and Dorothy felt they had to know definitely the Lord's will regarding their return to India. At the moment, things seemed dark. No one could give any answer to the future of the Chinese situation on the borders of Assam.

People in the churches were questioning the wisdom of going back to India in light of the world conditions. Some thought they were foolish to even consider going back. But the Waldocks hearts were in India and with her people.

They contacted the Indian Embassy in New York requesting an extension on their visas so that David, Kenneth and Gordie could finish the school year in the United States before going back to India. No word had been received. The Waldocks had been inquiring for some weeks about bookings on ships going from the West Coast but everything was taken through March.

The travel agents said that they had to make a decision immediately if they were to even get a booking in April or May. So Fred and Dorothy laid the matter before the Lord and asked Him to show them His will for their return by working out each of these matters. Paying for the bookings was also a concern as sufficient funds for passage had not yet come in.

During the next few days the verse "Ask and ye shall receive" came in three different devotional times and they knew this was their answer. Then word came from the Indian Embassy saying that their visas were granted with an extension that allowed the children to almost finish the school year in the States before leaving.

Fred went over to Seattle and found that there was a booking open in San Francisco. The travel agents warned that it might not stay open long. They insisted that the Waldocks give word at once. They prayed and considered other less suitable bookings and then called up the travel agents and told them to wire for this booking. The Lord undertook again and in a matter of three or four days everything was settled. They were scheduled to sail from San Francisco on the Billiton, a Dutch freighter, in May. They would be able to load their heavy freight in Seattle in April, which would save considerable expense.

They had the assurance of the Lord's will for them. He continued to prove His faithfulness by laying the financial need of the Waldocks' passage on the hearts of individuals and churches. One small rural church with an average attendance of 100 gave a birthday offering to Jesus at Christmas and designated it towards the Waldocks' passage. This same church also supplied a large amount of the family's clothing needs and also the drums to pack them in.

One dear old lady in California wrote that the Lord wanted her to give the Waldocks $500. Fred and Dorothy couldn't remember ever meeting her although she was probably in one of the meetings they had in California during their previous furlough. Friends and relatives from near and far and even strangers wrote, telling how the Lord had laid the need on their hearts and that therefore they were sending their gift. Truly the Lord was supplying their needs. "O fear the Lord, ye His saints; for there is no want to them that fear Him. The young lions do lack, and suffer hunger; but they that seek the Lord shall not want any good thing."

Temple Baptist Church held a special fund raising effort called "Over and Above Day" on March 17. The goal was $4,000. Every member of the church was asked to lay aside a special offering for the Waldocks' passage. Even the children in the congregation were busy earning money by washing dishes, working in the garden, sawing logs, dusting etc. The church saw the need for passage funds as a "family affair" because the Waldocks belonged to the church and were representing them in the needy country of India.

An extra feature of "Over and Above Day" was for people to bring in jars of home-canned foods – vegetables, fruits, jams and pickles to fill the Waldocks' pantry in India.

The church relied on the prayers of God's people to bring in the necessary funds. The church finances at the time were somewhat precarious and therefore the congregation was asked to give over and above their regular tithes and offerings to meet the Waldocks' needs. The needed $4,000 seemed like an impossibility to the church as they considered the responsibilities of their own financial program. But they knew that the Waldocks were their own responsibility, and if they were to get back to the field of India, God expected Temple Baptist to do their part. So the only recourse was to go to Him who delights to do the impossible in answer to the faith-filled prayers of His people. Wednesday, March 13 was set apart by the deacons as a day of prayer, remembering especially the Waldock Passage Fund.

"Over and Above Day" was a rousing success. The church newsletter declared, "When God is going to do something wonderful, He begins with a difficulty. If He is going to do something very wonderful, He begins with an impossibility!" The offering for the Waldock Passage Fund totaled $4,041.43

Truly it was a day of victory for the whole church. As the Waldocks greeted the people after the service it was a thrill for them to receive so many hearty handshakes accompanied with such remarks as 'Praise the Lord for the victory,' and 'What a wonderful day.' From the younger classes to the adults, expressions of praise and thanksgiving were prevalent.

Fred wrote, "*Faith is a blessed experience. How much we deprive ourselves when we try to reason out so many things. We personally felt that the victory was won at the day of prayer last Wednesday. There was a definite spirit of unity and expectation throughout each prayer session. Someone remarked after the services yesterday how impressed he was with the quiet, unpressured way in which this special offering was taken. God was in it and He had prepared the hearts of the people to meet this need. It is with renewed dedication that we as His servants return to Assam for our third term of service. It is our prayer that our lives will be 'Over and Above' what we have been for Him in the past.*"

Changes in their itinerary made it possible to sail from New Westminster, British Columbia – rather than from San Francisco. On May 3, 1963 the Waldock family and many of their friends gathered in the home of Mr. and Mrs. Robert Ellener before leaving Tacoma. Dorothy's mother, who was saying goodbye for the third time, courageously declared, "I would not have it any other way." It was no small feat to get three cars loaded to the hilt with baggage and 18 people, over the customs line into Canada. They stopped en route so that the Waldock children could have one more American hamburger. When they arrived at the border, they found the Lord had gone before them and had touched the hearts of the customs officials. All that was necessary was to answer a few simple questions, without a single bit of luggage being inspected. How they praised the Lord. They arrived at the ship and found the sailing delayed again. This gave the weary missionaries some time for relaxation.

Fred met the workmen aboard ship. All were from India and Fred found himself immediately at home with them. They packed everything away in their stateroom for the six weeks of travel. Then they had a walk around the ship before having tea. Then everyone piled into the cars again and headed for Vancouver for a wonderful trip to a park. They had dinner at a Chinese restaurant before finally returning to the ship. In the stateroom they had a blessed time of prayer and worship with the Lord, ending with hands held tight and tears held back singing, "Blest Be the Tie That Binds." Goodbyes came next with David saying, "See you in two years" and Fred saying, "See you in 1969, Lord willing."

When they finally set sail they had a beautiful trip up the Canadian coast with sunny weather. The Lord gave them another missionary family of like faith for fellowship along the way. They praised Him for His abundant goodness to them. Their route took them north of the Aleutians in Alaska and into the Bering Sea and then down the east coast of Russia's Kamchatka Peninsula and then along the coast of Japan. The route was designed to save 800 miles to Hong Kong. It was the best ocean voyage yet, with no bad weather at all. They enjoyed wonderful rest during those days.

The field of Assam desired to broadcast Christian radio in the Bengali language to the 18 million Bengali-speaking Indians. The Far Eastern Broadcasting Company in Manila offered to beam the broadcasts daily to India if someone would supply the tapes. The Kenoyers had started making the tapes before they left for furlough and had asked the Waldocks to continue the tape ministry in addition to developing the work in Silchar. En route they experienced God's miraculous answers to prayer for this work. The Waldocks were to purchase considerable technical equipment in Hong Kong. They arrived there on a Saturday at noon and had only one half day to complete the purchases. The Lord had it all worked out. They contacted a missionary of the Far Eastern Broadcasting Company. He and his engineer each got on a telephone and made contacts with reputable shops and after just two hours they had a lineup of all that the Waldocks needed at prices far better than they could have bargained for. Within four hours it was all at his office. By that same evening, Fred had it on the ship – equipment that would have cost at least double in the States.

Other equipment - a professional tape recorder and mixer - had already been purchased for the India field by BMM missionaries in Japan and was to be sent to the Waldocks. A letter from Japan to the Far Eastern Broadcasting Company in Hong Kong stated, "We hope to get it to Manila by the 28th of May to meet the Waldocks." That was the day the Waldocks were to arrive in Manila. The ship's original orders were to be in Manila for only four hours. To make the transfer even more difficult there was a dock strike in progress! How was Fred to find these two parcels from Japan in such a short amount of time and get them onto the ship when the gates were picketed? Assuming, that is, that the parcels arrived in Manila on time.

God's answer was that the ship received orders to wait for cargo to be loaded in the harbor which resulted in two days in Manila. While still in the harbor, Fred received a letter from the agent stating: "Two parcels lying alongside Pier 9 (the destination of their ship). See Mr. M for custom procedures." Within ten minutes from the time the Waldocks left the ship to look for the parcels, they had them on board. Mr. M was sitting at his desk unoccupied. He identified the parcels, initialed them, wrote a pass and Fred took them on the ship.

The story of how the equipment got to Manila was also reason for praise. The Mid-Missions missionary in Japan contacted the Far Eastern Broadcasting Company representative there. One of them knew an Army pilot. He was due to fly to the Manila base on the 28th. He took the parcels with him at no charge. On his declaration at Manila customs he listed "two pieces undeclared," resulting in being met by the military police who drove him to Customs – quite a long distance from the base – free of charge. This enabled him to turn the packages over to Customs, without duty, to hold for the Waldocks.

Due to the extra day in Manila, Fred was able to spend a good part of the day at the Far Eastern Broadcasting Company studios getting firsthand knowledge from the top man in electronics on the technical side of setting up a studio. He also received many suggestions for effective programming and recording. What a blessing from God!

CHAPTER ELEVEN
From the Jungle to the City

"We seek only His leading that the work may be of Him and blessed by Him." – Fred Waldock, summer 1964

The Waldocks arrived in Calcutta June 25, 1963 but no berths were available for the ship so they tied up in the river. Although it made it difficult to get their things ashore, it did save days of work because everything was cleared through customs from the ship without having to take everything into the Custom House. They were completely cleared with everything off the ship by 3 pm on the 26th.

The Lord wonderfully undertook. They had to pay about $750 duty but that included all the equipment they had brought from Hong Kong for the radio ministry. Considering everything, Fred felt that was not too bad. Things had become very scarce in India and they felt they would be glad for what they had brought out.

Encouraging news from their colleagues in Assam was waiting for them in Calcutta. The Field Council had been able to rent suitable housing in Silchar for the Waldocks! The apartment was new and right in the center of town. Dorothy and Fred had been much in prayer about this need because they desired to get right into the work in Silchar upon their arrival in India. "And it shall come to pass, that before they call I will answer and while they are yet speaking I will hear." (Isaiah 65:24)

Since their arrival date in Calcutta was so uncertain, making reservations for the train journey to Landour had not been possible. Usually the train was completely booked for at least ten days in advance but the Lord answered prayer again and reservations were secured for June 27. The conductor told Fred that the 27th was the only day that they were not completely booked. *"Truly God doth all things well,"* wrote Fred.

Dorothy took the boys to school while Fred remained in Calcutta to attend to matters of business there. Dorothy stayed up in Landour for five days, getting the children situated and ready for the next five months of boarding. After Dorothy returned to Calcutta, they went to Assam together arriving there on July 11. They were looking to the Lord for a fruitful and effective term. They praised God for bringing them back to India. "Faithful is He that calleth you, who also will do it."

A legal snag kept them from occupying the new apartment in Silchar for several months. It was a long, hot summer and both of them felt dragged out by the heat. In early September they were finally able to move into their small "penthouse" built over a warehouse. They found that they had lots of adjustments to make in living in town after having spent so many years at Makunda.

Fred started a Bible class and Dorothy was hoping for ministry among the children who came to play with Lois, and with their mothers. Their new ministry would be focused on literature and ministering to college students.

Fred and Dorothy would be in charge of all the literature booths in the coming year – not only in Silchar but also two other bookrooms in Manipur State.

They had no leads on a place to rent for a bookroom in Silchar. However, they felt definitely led of the Lord to order a very large stock of literature so as to be ready for the winter months when they would have camps, literature booths and other opportunities to sell literature. They felt that this was the Lord's time to begin this strategic work.

Fred was asked to speak at a little gathering of Christians at the railway station in Silchar. The group was composed of Rongmei Nagas, sweepers on the trains. These people, who did the dirtiest of work, were looked down upon by other tribes. A young couple was trying to hold the group together. The Waldocks had known the wife, Martha, since she had been a fourth grader and the Waldocks had lived in Silchar for a couple of months before taking their first year language exams in Calcutta in 1950.

Martha and her husband, Gaipuchong, were living in the railway quarters and he was a maintenance man on the trains. They had Bible classes for the children and were meeting in a small bamboo shack in the midst of the railway colony for church services. One rainy Sunday afternoon during the monsoon season, Fred and Dorothy picked their way carefully through the muddy mess toward the church. Pigs of all shapes and sizes were wallowing in the mud. Naked little children ran in and out of the houses. Fred thought, "How can a person live like this, and how can they begin to worship in such a place?"

The air reeked with the odor of homemade rice beer and open sewage drains. The service had barely started when a bunch of pigs started to fight and squeal, almost entering the church building. The mothers had come to worship but their children kept running in and out.

Fred was sitting on a bench near the lattice-like bamboo window while another man preached. Hearing a commotion outside, he glanced out the window to see a man bring a bamboo club down on the skull of a sucking piglet amid the squealing and grunting of the old sow who, with the rest of the litter, scampered through the mud and slime trying to escape from the intruder. The barefoot man calmly picked up the piglet by its snout and slouched off to his little bamboo shack to prepare for the feast.

During the message one of the villagers, who was completely drunk, stood just in front of the door yelling and making a general nuisance of himself. He threw mud at all who interfered with him. At times Fred could not hear the speaker. As he sat there, he was terribly bothered and deeply concerned. He looked at that little gathering of believers who had come to worship and a scrap of Scripture flashed in his mind, "and such were some of you." Oh, the marvels of the grace of God! These very believers had previously been like those outside. They worked as sweepers at the rail station doing all the dirtiest jobs imaginable. They had made and drunk rice beer. Now by God's marvelous grace, they were saved and were holding a communion service in the very center of their village. Some of these believers, although still employed by the railroad, had cleaned up themselves and their homes. Their lives were changed!

But life was very hard for these Christians. Most of the men attending the services still made illegal rice beer to augment their incomes. Many children and teenagers were growing up in this environment. But faithful ones like Martha were giving their best to teach them.

The field council had been searching for three years for a suitable site for a Christian bookroom and reading room in Silchar without success. But the Lord's timing is always right! In October, one month after moving into Silchar and the very week that the first shipment of literature arrived, a new building on the main road of good construction and adequate frontage was offered to them at $40 a month rent. The building even had a large room on the upper story suitable for living quarters for a manager. Within a relatively short amount of time, the Lord provided the necessary $1,000 for the advance payment. The final papers were drawn up in November. Enough money came in to pay for all the literature that they had ordered plus enough left over to start purchasing the necessary furniture. This would be the first and only Christian book room in the town of over 80,000 people and would supply all of Cachar District.

That same month they went up to Shillong, the capital of Assam, for an eight-day camp. They praised the Lord for the opportunity to minister to college students at this camp. Shillong, about 150 miles north of Silchar, is in the hills at an elevation of 4,000 feet. The location provided a wonderful respite from the heat of the summer and was invigorating to Fred and Dorothy. The rainy season was supposed to be over but for the first two days of the camp it rained heavily. Most of the young men were in tents and they finally had to shift to the small meeting room where they were literally packed in like sardines, sleeping side by side on the floor. They filled their plates between drips from the leaking tarpaulins used to cover the outdoor dining room and then hurried to some corner of the veranda for shelter to eat their delicious curry and rice. Yet, the spirits remained high and Fred and Dorothy never heard one word of complaint from the 51 campers.

Fred had a Bible study hour each morning using 1 John. It was a time of heart-searching for them all. The evening Gospel meetings were a unique blessing. After the invitation and benediction some of these keen students would go outside and talk with their unsaved classmates and invite them to accept the Lord. Many came to be saved. Others yielded to the Lord for a life of separation from worldliness and of close fellowship with Jesus. There were students gathered this way each night. With each needy soul there were at least two who came with him to encourage him and pray for him. Fred hadn't seen such active, personal soul winning for a long time. The whole camp was such a thrill to Fred and Dorothy and such an encouragement to them as they anticipated further work among the students in Silchar.

They were much in prayer for a national coworker to manage the bookroom. They knew that the Lord had the right man for the ministry. They were also much in prayer for facilities for a meeting hall, student center, and, Lord willing, a Bengali Bible School. The only meeting place they had at this point was their 11-by-13 foot living room. They had as many as 20 packed into that small space. A large bungalow-style building with three other smaller buildings and over an acre of land was up for immediate sale in the center of Silchar. Fred challenged the churches in America with William Carey's words: "Attempt great things for God – expect great things from God."

In December Fred wrote of plans to lease an old Anglican church building in town for Sunday services. This large building had been unused for years and it was in need of considerable repair.

Christmas was a wonderful time of opportunity to share the gospel of Jesus Christ. Fred gave the message at a special Christmas function in connection with the army camp just outside of Silchar. There was close to 500 present. Fred was encouraged that they were becoming better known in Silchar. He believed that the Lord was going to give them a fruitful ministry there.

When their three older sons came home from boarding school, the "penthouse" was full to overflowing but they managed just the same. The family was looking forward to expansion – Dorothy was pregnant with her fifth child, due in May. They praised the Lord in January when they were able to secure enlarged quarters in the house where they were living.

The bookroom finally opened in February 1964. They praised the Lord for the good dedication ceremony. They had an opportunity to tell businessmen and other people in Silchar what their purpose was and this was well received. Fred and Dorothy believed they were off to a good start with the possibility of a solid outreach for the Lord. Martha begged Fred to let her bring the Rongmei young people to the classes in Silchar. When Fred agreed she personally escorted the young people each Sunday and helped with the teaching in Rongmei for the little ones. The older ones listened in Bengali.

God provided two young men to come and work full-time in the bookroom in Silchar. Ajit, a former tuberculosis patient, had been saved about two years before at the hospital in Alipur and this was his first experience in full-time Christian work. Ajit had helped in the meetings at the hospital and had led several patients to the Lord. Although Ajit felt that his relatives and friends might be opposed to his Christian work, he was willing to follow the Lord. Mihir, who had worked with the Waldocks at Makunda for several years, also came to help with the bookroom. The timing of their arrival was definitely of the Lord as it was time for the Waldocks to go up to Landour for vacation and for the birth of the baby.

Fred would only be able to stay there with the family for a couple of weeks but Dorothy planned to stay for several months. Caryl Louise Waldock entered the world at 11:07 pm on May 23, 1964. Dorothy had an easy delivery and both she and the baby were fine. In a cable to Temple Baptist Church the Waldocks referred to Psalm 9:1-2, "I will give thanks to the Lord with all my heart; I will tell of all your wonders. I will be glad and exult in You; I will sing praise to Your name, O Most High." The other children were completely carried away by Caryl, an adorable red-haired little baby. Most of them had been hoping it would be a girl, especially nearly nine-year-old Lois.

Several months later the Waldocks were again looking for help for the bookroom. Ajit felt led to Bible school and Mihir was having a much wider ministry with opportunities to minister for a week or more in different villages and churches.

That summer Fred and Dorothy felt that the Lord had more doors to open in Silchar for the coming dry season. Fred wrote, *"We seek only His leading that the work may be of Him and blessed by Him."*

By November 1964 the Waldocks realized that their finances were in serious trouble. The extra funds that they had brought out to the field from furlough were depleted and their monthly support was not keeping pace with the expenditures. They calculated their monthly need at $800 per month and yet receipts of gifts averaged only about $635 per month. They asked their praying friends to make this a matter of earnest intercession.

"Now we are faced with the possibility of curtailing the ministry which is just getting started in this city and we don't feel this would be honoring to the Lord who has promised to supply all our need according to His riches in glory in Christ Jesus. Curtail? Retreat? How? Where? And why? In these last days we must not think of retreat – we must advance. Therefore won't you accept this prayer challenge and help lift this burden which is actually your part. We don't want to curtail the work because this is the reason for our being here. The sales from literature are being turned back into more purchases to build up the stock; even so we have a few outstanding bills as we bought a large quantity of certain items to obtain a greater discount. For the bookroom to be even more effective we need another $1,000 capital for stock. As it is now, we quickly sell out of good sellers and aren't able to purchase more in any quantity until there are sufficient sales to finance it. Orders take at least six weeks to reach us even if ordered from Calcutta.

We have found a genuine born-again Christian Lushai student who will be taking his BA examination in February. He is anxious to come and do translation work in Lushai. This is a great need as over 90% of the Lushais claim to be Christians but a very low percentage are born again, so much teaching is needed. More than 50% of our literature outreach is to this tribe. Thus far we haven't seen the way clear to hire this man as a coworker with us. His salary would be about $50 a month. May we ask you to join us in special prayer for these needs and the future of the work?

Hudson Taylor found it true that 'God's work done in God's way would not lack God's supply.' Join us in prayer as we search our hearts and lives and consider the work. We desire that we might be only fit instruments in God's hands to reach out to these needy souls."

About this time the Waldocks became acquainted with two young men who would become answers to their prayers for national coworkers. Hranga, the Lushai student, was able to start doing translation work into his native language in December and he also worked at the Christian Literature Depot. He had wonderful opportunities to talk to the many Lushai who came into the bookroom.

A Manipuri college student named Gobin Singh also came into their lives. Gobin came from a strict Hindu home. One Sunday afternoon in March 1965, Gobin was in Fred's Bible class. Fred was proclaiming the Good News of the Messiah from the book of Acts. That day was a glorious one in Gobin's life when he simply opened his heart and accepted the Lord Jesus Christ as his personal Savior. He testified, "I know that it is all because of God's great love and grace that He could stoop to save a wretched sinner like me."

Since the church at Silchar was not yet organized, Gobin was baptized at Makunda Baptist Church. When Gobin took this open stand for Christ, his father was enraged and disowned him. He took away all his books, blankets and support for going to college and told him never to come home again. In answer to the persecution he faced, the Lord filled Gobin's heart and life with wonderful joy. Fred and Dorothy invited him to stay in the upper story of the bookroom and work part-time to finish his studies.

Gobin later wrote a tract of his experience called "A Changed Life." He wrote, "*I, too, was looking for joy, peace and satisfaction. My background of orthodox religious devotion and restriction brought no peace to my troubled heart. I was born in a Manipuri Hindu family. My parents were strict Baisnabites. Touching any unclean thing or eating any unclean food was a great sin. I remember having to wash myself because I touched an egg. But I never thought about God seriously. Rather, I was taught that I myself was God. My father used to say, 'Realize your own self.' According to this faith, the knower and the known are one and to realize this is salvation. I was a self-righteous young man and I was just satisfied with the religion of my parents. But a day came in my life when my little world was shattered to pieces. My dear mother left this world suddenly. I was completely broken up. But God meant it all for my good. It was a great turning point in my life.*

For many days after my mother's death I had no peace of mind, always thinking about my departed mother whom I loved so much. I started thinking that this world is nothing but an illusion. What profit was it to study and earn money to live in this world? Questions crowded my mind. What is life? What is death? What is God and who is God? One day I made up my mind to renounce this world and live in some Ashram and spend the rest of my life in serving humanity and seeking salvation.

Then I became a very religious person. I spent many hours reading the Bhagavad-Gita and other Hindu holy books. Every morning I would meditate and chant the thousand names of Krishna and fast to find peace of mind and salvation. In Bhagavad-Gita I found that I had to attain salvation through yoga so I followed the path of yoga of action and I again joined college for study. But soon I found myself in the stream of the world. After a few days I started doing the things which I once had hated. I started going to cinema and was doing questionable things with the wrong crowds. I was lying, cheating, using filthy language, and cursing and swearing. But I never realized my true condition that I was spiritually blind.

While I was studying in college, I was staying in a hostel. Some Christians used to come to our hostel to teach the good news of salvation from the Holy Bible. Finally, I got interested in the Holy Bible and one day I purchased a New Testament in my own language (Manipuri) and started reading it. Through hearing and reading the word of God I came to realize that I was a sinner and living far away from God. I also came to realize that the Lord Jesus Christ is the incarnated Eternal Son of God who came to this earth about two thousand years ago to sacrifice His own body to pay the penalty for my sins and for the sins of the whole world.

But I was in a great struggle to know how to accept the Lord as my personal Savior for the remission of my sins. I started thinking what my family and people would say if I accepted the Lord Jesus Christ. But the Spirit of God was continually working in my heart day by day. I was greatly moved when one day a servant of God told me, 'For what shall it profit a man, if he shall gain the whole world, and lose his own soul? Or what shall a man give in exchange for his soul?' (Mark 8:36-37). That was a glorious day in my life, when I simply opened my heart and accepted the Lord Jesus Christ as my personal Savior."

The spring and summer of 1965 brought several milestones for the Waldock family. David graduated from Woodstock High School. When the new school year started in July, Lois joined Ken and Gordie at Woodstock for the first time. Fred, Dorothy, David and Cari returned to Silchar. The hardest part for Lois was leaving her little sister but Lois greatly enjoyed the activities with other girls her age so she fit in well at boarding school. David flew back to the United States for college. He entered Seattle Pacific College in August.

An undeclared war between India and Pakistan broke out in August 1965. Pakistan continued to challenge India's claim to the predominately Moslem state of Kashmir. Assam, separated from the rest of India by East Pakistan, was quite unsettled. Even though their material needs were great, Fred advised Temple Baptist Church to not send them any packages. He also wrote to the Home Office of Baptist Mid-Missions to inform them of the situation.

"September 11, 1965
Dear Brother Fetzer,
You are well aware of the conflict between Pakistan and India. Up until recently it has been on the Western side but in the news today it is reported that paratroopers have been dropped into Assam and air raids have been reported over airfields in the eastern sector of West Bengal and Assam. There have always been a number of troops on the East Pakistan border and on the Assam and West Bengal borders, but since this recent conflict these have been greatly fortified. And it is not impossible that this will spread to this area also. Much will depend on U Thant's talks with the two leaders. But in a broadcast this morning it stated that the talks with the Pakistan leaders seem to have been a failure. U Thant goes to Delhi today.

Yesterday morning five American Peace Corps volunteers dropped in on us from Tripura State where they had been working. They received orders from the Peace Corps directors in Delhi to leave Tripura and proceed to Alipur and await further instructions. It was good that they stopped here first. I was able to report their arrival to the authorities and it took me most of the day to get permits for them.

Paul Versluis had received a telegram from the American Embassy asking us to give them all the assistance that we could. They are out at Alipur now. They have no idea what to do next and can only wait. As you know, Tripura State is only six miles from Makunda. They were in Agartala, which is about 100 miles further up the state.

With developments in the news this morning we just could receive orders to move and especially if it gets worse. Where they will tell us to go is a question to us, as Calcutta is certainly no better off. Most all of the cities are on 'blackout'. We have been on 'blackout' in Silchar for two nights now and the order stands until further notice. They might ask us to go to South India but we haven't heard anything of conditions down there. It probably isn't affected as both West and East Pakistan are well in the north of the subcontinent.

I don't feel that there is need to worry unless for some reason there developed some feelings against foreigners. There is no sign of rioting. The people are very subdued. One of the greatest concerns is the line of communication being disrupted. Well, I think this will do for now as there just isn't much more to report.

Yours in His hands,

Fred Waldock"

"September 1965

Dear loved ones at Temple,

'GO...and LO I am with you always.' With this precious promise and coupled with many other like precious promises such as Joshua 1:9, what is there to fear? We do praise the Lord for the consciousness of His presence during these days. We are perfectly safe even though we have been given notice about two weeks ago that we are to consider ourselves as being in the first stage of evacuation. This simply means that we are alerted to the possibilities. Stage two is for women and children to leave and all non-essential personnel. Stage three is final evacuation. We are well aware of the possibilities that may develop but there is no need to worry. You probably get the same news we do and probably even sooner and in more detail. How we have appreciated our little radio this term.

Other than being on 'blackout' and a few restrictions, we are carrying on the same. We had three good services yesterday. This is certainly an opportunity to awaken people to the message of hope we have in Christ. The Lord is blessing His word. We are still making plans for holding the special meetings in October from the 11th to 22nd.

Dr. Kenoyer returned from Landour today and reports that the children are fine and school is carrying on as usual. It is hard to be separated so far from them during these days of tension but again we praise God for the rest of heart and peace of mind that He gives.

Today was the first plane from Calcutta in a week. It comes via a much longer circuitous route but it brings us mail. There is word of a plane tomorrow so I want to get this mailed tonight. I hope it is not too delayed in reaching you. We do covet your continued prayers during these days; not only for our safety but that the Word of God will penetrate the hearts of these people and that the doors for missions will not close in this land.

Yours, rejoicing in our Victorious Savior, Fred and Dorothy Waldock"

A ceasefire between Pakistan and India was put in effect in late September. That put the work in Assam in a more stable position for the moment. However, the food situation was so bad in October that Fred and Dorothy suggested that instead of sending Christmas cards, the people in the United States could use the money that they would spend on a Christmas card sent airmail and buy a soup mix packet and send that by ordinary mail. If sent in October it would reach them by Christmas.

Even with the ceasefire agreement there was a continual military build-up on the borders around them. It made Fred and Dorothy constantly appraise their work to try to determine just how much would be continued if they had to leave. They felt the Literature Depot could be carried on and therefore they sought to build up the stock and prepare the workers for the future. By this time, both Hranga and Gobin were working in the Literature Depot and rejoicing with the opportunities they had to witness for Christ.

Fred began having special Bible studies with them two days a week to instruct them in the deeper things of the Christian life. Fred and Dorothy had no fear since they were in the Lord's hands, but they did sense a greater urgency to do His work while it was still possible.

The weekly Bible class drew young men representing fourteen different tribes from the hills. Many came from Christian villages but so few really knew the Lord personally. Fred and Dorothy prayed for the Lord's working in many hearts during those troubled times.

The situation between India and Pakistan remained tense until the Soviets helped mediate between the two countries. They negotiated a troop withdrawal agreement, which was signed on January 10, 1966 in Tashkent, USSR. A few hours after signing the agreement Indian Prime Minister Lal Bahadur Shastri died of a heart attack. Former Prime Minister Nehru's daughter, Indira Gandhi, was chosen as the new Prime Minister.

"We have lived from crisis to crisis these last 18 months in India what with the sudden death of two Prime Ministers, an undeclared war, tension on the borders, epidemics, internal rebel attacks, famine, high prices and general unrest. However, at the moment things are fairly quiet and we are trusting the Lord that we might go ahead with our work with new drive and diligence to reach the many unsaved and nominal Christians here in Silchar," wrote Dorothy in a letter to friends at Temple Baptist Church.

Packages from the home front had finally arrived after four months in transit. The Waldocks were so very glad to receive them. Dorothy was especially thankful to have the extra food and goodies on hand for the time when the children were home on vacation from boarding school.

After three years of negotiating, they finally leased the Anglican Church building and started services there in February 1966. They repaired and whitewashed the inside but had to leave the outside until more funds were available. Their desire was to establish a strong national church in Silchar. A large military air force and armed police force were now stationed in Silchar. A number of these men were from the Church of South India so they were glad to have a service in English to attend. However, most of them were only nominal Christians and therefore Fred and Dorothy sensed a real burden to see them accept the Lord as their personal Savior. A group of government veterinary students also came to the services. They were very responsive and contributed much to the meetings.

Dr. and Mrs. Fetzer, from the BMM Home Office, arrived in Assam for a visit in March. The Fetzers experienced firsthand the tensions due to food riots in Calcutta and to an uprising by rebel tribal peoples demanding independence in the area. Lushai tribals had been the best customers at the Book Depot but now their movement in and out of Cachar District was very much restricted. This cut the Book Depot business by 75%.

While Dr. Fetzer was in Assam it was decided that Fred should help part-time at the Alipur station, as Paul and Genella

Versluis were due for furlough leaving Dr. Kenoyer the only man to supervise the station work as well as the hospital.

Fred was out at Alipur four or five days a week doing administration and often felt really pressed but had faith that the Lord would give him grace and strength. Fred and Dorothy, although saddened by the lack of time to develop the Silchar work, tried to walk in the Lord's leading and trusted Him to work out His plan for their lives. Dorothy attempted to go out to Alipur two days a week for Bible classes with the nurses and to help with the bookkeeping. Despite the demands on Fred's time at Alipur, the attendance at the morning service in Silchar was increasing for which they praised the Lord.

During March two majors came to the service as well as seven servicemen who had been stationed in Silchar. Three of the soldiers were Christians and the others were Catholics, Hindus and nominal Christians. Fred and Dorothy praised the Lord for the opportunities He gave them to witness.

The first part of May 1966 one of the Naga tribal students, who had been regularly attending the services, drowned in a pond at the school while taking his bath. He left his parents, a young wife and five-month-old baby back in his village. How thankful Fred and Dorothy were that, although he came from a non-Christian family and village, he had found the Lord since coming to Silchar and had been eager to go home on his short Christmas vacation and witness to his family.

Also in May, Hranga took seriously ill and was on the critical list for some weeks. He recovered but had to spend several months in bed.

At the end of the month, Dorothy and Cari traveled alone to Mussoorie and had a very difficult trip. The area was experiencing extreme drought. Famine and heat stroke had claimed many victims. Fred joined them there in mid-June.

It had been unusually dry in Assam as well, and the farmers were anxiously awaiting the early rains to get their rice crops planted. But when the rains came they brought flooding and destruction. Almost continuous rains for a month and a half put most of their district in Assam underwater by mid-June, leaving thousands homeless and without food. The floods started to recede in mid-July but transportation by road and rail was still cut off so there was a severe food crisis for many weeks. The army airlifted in rice to the district but it was not enough. The first rice crop had been completely destroyed.

The Waldocks returned to Silchar and Alipur in mid-July. It was difficult for the children to return to boarding. With so many tensions in India, they felt insecure being so far away from their parents. There were problems in the school regarding food for the children and satisfactory supervisors for the hostels. It was a heavy burden on Fred and Dorothy's hearts and they asked Temple Baptist Church to be in special prayer for Ken, Gordie and Lois.

Food and fuel were scarce in Assam and the Waldocks were experiencing real need. The Home Office of Baptist Mid-Missions sent a list of needed items to the Waldocks' supporting churches.

The flood situation continued to be serious. Since the Waldocks had been channels for distribution of relief foods for a number of years in the past, they were given a sum of money to purchase rice and brown flour to distribute. They surveyed a number of villages in their immediate area and started distribution. They were given notice that they would receive a load of cracked wheat direct from the ship when it arrived from the States. This was approximately 35,000 pounds so they had even more responsibility added to their already overcrowded schedules. The government officials gave Fred complete freedom in the distribution. They only asked him to submit a report of the villages and the numbers served. They could do evangelism right along with the distribution and were trusting and praying that it would open doors into these villages in the future.

Conditions were tense in the area in August with food shortages and high prices. The majority of the people were not able to purchase needed rice and vegetables as prices had tripled. Dorothy and Fred wondered what the future held in regard to their work there. In six different towns in Assam during the first week of August students demonstrated and rioted. A number were killed by the police.

Fred tried for two days to get across the river to go to Alipur but all three ferryboats were out of commission. This was also causing protest. He finally set out by rickshaw on August 11.

In response to all the difficulties and uncertainties they faced, Dorothy wrote, *"We look for our redemption drawing nigh. Luke 21:38."* She was determined that her focus would not be on the temporal but on the eternal.

Very heavy rains continued. The rail line was out again and the rivers were up to flood stage. Every week there were hunger and high price demonstrations – but so far none violent in their district.

Fred continued to spend four days a week out at Alipur administering the hospital and coming back to Silchar to pastor the church the remainder of the week. Fred and Dorothy were so burdened for those coming to the church services. They asked for much prayer for the working of the Holy Spirit to bring many people to true conversion.

By this time, Sana Singh, the second son of Deb Singh, was living in Silchar and attending college. Sana had come to know the Lord at Makunda several years before when he was 17 ½ years old. He had arrived at the colony in January 1964. There, for the first time, he had heard a clear presentation of man's fallen condition and his need for salvation. He realized that he needed to be born again and yet for a time he delayed accepting Christ because he considered himself good enough to get to heaven. But the Holy Spirit continued to work in his heart and he began to be concerned about his sins. The burden became heavier and heavier until the Lord won out and on February 8, 1964, he had fallen down on his knees and confessed his sins to the Lord Jesus Christ and received Jesus as his personal Savior.

While in college Sana worked part-time in the bookroom and was helpful in the work in many ways.

Just before Christmas 1966 the Waldocks returned to Makunda for a Christmas feast and welcome party for new missionaries. This was the first time for them to be back at Makunda as a family since their return from furlough in 1963. Later on in the week they joined the Alipur missionaries for Christmas dinner and then Saturday and Sunday they spent in Silchar. They invited about 15 students and others for Christmas dinner Sunday afternoon – chicken and pork curries with plenty of rice. The following language groups were represented: Hmar, Lushai, Manipuri, Khasi, Ao, Munda, Malayalam and Tamil. It reminded Dorothy of the chorus; 'Some from every tribe and nation will be there.' John and Cora Wilkens, missionaries stationed at Binnakandi, also came and John showed Christian films in church that night.

Fred had came down with a heavy chest cold after the Makunda trip so he was glad for someone else to take one service on Sunday. Ken led the evening service and read Scripture in between the films. His parents were so proud when he did such a fine job with poise and confidence.

In early 1967 both Fred and Dorothy felt the strain of so many responsibilities. In addition to their ministries at Silchar and Alipur both were very busy with Field Council duties. They both felt that unless the Lord gave special strength and wisdom they would not be able to carry out many of their assignments in a thorough way.

In March, word was received that visa applications for two new BMM missionary nurses for Assam had been rejected by the Indian government. It was becoming increasingly clear that new missionaries, especially those headed for Assam, were not seen as desirable by the government. The BMM missionaries were much in prayer about this because they desperately needed more help. They were all overworked.

The government policy was that no visa would be granted for a person who would be doing a job that an Indian could do. The fact that Assam was a restricted area and bordering on more than one troubled region further complicated the matter.

Four years of living in unsettled conditions along with the continual pressure of work in a different climate had taken a toll on nerves, minds and bodies and both Fred and Dorothy were ready for relief. Although they would be eligible for furlough in the summer of 1967, under the circumstances they just didn't see how they could go with the field being so short staffed.

After months of waiting before the Lord, and with approval of both the BMM Home Office and the Field Council, the Waldocks felt it was the Lord's will for Dorothy and Cari to accompany Ken back to the United States for college at the end of July.

Both Fred's father and Dorothy's mother had been in poor health, so Dorothy reluctantly consented to go for a break for three and a half months and see those loved ones and also get a thorough medical checkup. Their regular furlough as a family would be delayed until the summer of 1969 when Gordon would graduate from high school.

In May, the Indian government reconsidered the visa applications of the two missionary nurses after receiving favorable recommendations from local officials in Assam. The missionaries were hopeful that God would indeed move the hearts of the government officials to grant the visas.

At the end of May the family arrived in Landour for vacation. Gobin and Hranga were left in charge of the work in Silchar. Fred wanted to take Ken and Gordon on a special trip to Kashmir but he had not been able to make travel reservations ahead of time. Then when it was clear that he could go, there were no seats available. The boys were disappointed. The next morning Fred said to Ken, "Well, lad, how about us going to Kashmir?" Ken asked, "How will we get there?" Fred's answer was: "We'll hitchhike!" The three of them had a great adventure. Because he was the older man, Fred was allowed to ride in the cab of a truck while Ken and Gordon perched on top of the load. It took them two full days and a night to get to Kashmir. On the way back, with the temperature around 110 degrees, Ken developed dysentery and was sick with a fever. So Fred pleaded with the officials at the train station and managed to get them all seats. The next morning Ken woke up perfectly well.

Temple Baptist Church in Tacoma, WA took a special offering for Dorothy's and Ken's traveling expenses. The church newsletter reminded the congregation: *"In last Sunday's Sunday school lesson we found that the Philippians sent three or four presents to a suffering and much needful servant of God, and from that moment they could reckon that every need of theirs would be supplied. What tremendous returns come as recompense to us for such small acts of giving on our part. God refuses to be in debt to any man. He always repays with interest. How wonderful to reckon on God for this! According to our faith, it will be to us."* The church ended up sending $1,000 to the BMM Home Office for the Waldocks' airline tickets.

By the end of June, word had reached Fred that the nurses' visas had again been denied. Fred wrote in a letter to Brother Fetzer at the Home Office,

"This is a real blow to us and we don't know what is going to happen. Let us hold on for some time before we do anything right now. We need to be much in prayer. I'm frankly concerned about our whole ministry. We are going to have to do some hard thinking and lots of waiting before the Lord seeking His perfect will for the future of our ministry. We need guidance and wisdom from above."

The first week of July Fred received a telegram from his stepmother telling him that his father was having surgery for a vein blockage and asking him to come home. By this time, all three of the senior Waldock's sons were serving on the foreign field.

Fred, being the oldest son, felt a real responsibility to go to his father. Obviously his father's condition was critical or his stepmother Ruby would never have considered calling him. After praying about it, Fred felt he couldn't leave his heavy responsibilities in Assam. The present mission treasurer had just undergone major surgery and would have to stay for x-ray therapy for another six weeks. She had turned over her work to Fred, besides his many other duties as field president and his ministries in Alipur and Silchar.

There were other grave reasons why it was not possible for Fred to leave at that time. He was under great pressure to produce for the Indian government within a very limited time, detailed reports on all the BMM work and finances and assets.

A number of missionaries from other agencies had been refused 'No Objection to Return' permits and others who had obtained these permits before proceeding on furlough had still been refused visas for returning. With such a critical shortage of male missionaries and especially with the future so uncertain, Fred didn't feel he could risk leaving at that time and then not be able to get back into Assam.

Dorothy received her 'No Objection to Return' permit and trusted that since half of the family was still in India she would be able to get a return visa. Fred's heart was torn to go to his father but his duty was clear and Fred chose to remain at his post. Dorothy wrote, *"The Lord knows the future – we don't. But we need to number our days and apply ourselves to leaving a witness to carry on when we go. We are indeed grateful for your praying, friends, and count heavily on your intercession in these days of tension and uncertainty."*

Fred was able to join the family in Landour to watch Ken graduate from high school on July 14, 1967. Dorothy, Ken and Cari traveled home via Bangkok, Hong Kong, Tokyo, Honolulu and finally into Seattle. Three other high school boys and Mrs. Burrows also went with them. While in Honolulu they visited Pearl Harbor. The USS Arizona War Memorial had been completed in 1962. Thus Dorothy was able to visit the place where her brother Albert had given his life in the service of his country 26 years earlier.

After arriving in Tacoma, Dorothy spent a week at Camp Glendawn for their family camp. This enabled her to see many pastors and friends that she wouldn't otherwise have had time to see. It was good to be home but her heart and thoughts were constantly with the needs and problems of India.

On the 18th of August the newspaper carried the following headline: **"Missionaries' visas not to be extended."** The article went on to say, "The Home Ministry, it is learnt, has recently taken a decision to see that all foreign Christian missionaries leave India after the expiry of their visas. All the States concerned have been told that the visas of foreign missionaries would not be extended any more. They would thus depart as and when their visas expire. There are, at the moment, about 5,200 foreign missionaries in the country, of whom 1,105 are from commonwealth countries other than India. Indian missionaries, it is noted, have been pleading for some time past that they themselves could carry on the work of all Christian missions in India."

Dorothy wrote Dr. Fetzer at the BMM Home Office, *"Many things run through my mind concerning all of this. No doubt you will hear from Fred right away. Fred's residential permit expires May 6, 1968. I strongly feel that even if it is for 6 or 7 months, I should try to get my visa and return. There is much I can do to help clear up the Silchar work, turn over the files, et cetera that have to do with the Literature Depot and to sell our own property while Fred helps at Alipur and the other larger stations…*

I have been in the University of Washington Hospital since Wednesday the 25th. They took me in as an outpatient first but I wasn't a bit satisfied. Then that afternoon they admitted me into the hospital and they have given me the most thorough going over I have ever had in my life. I am just home for the weekend and have to go in again Sunday afternoon. A specialist on the esophagus is coming to the hospital on Monday to check my throat – at no extra cost. Then they want to biopsy a small node. They don't think it is too significant but want to be sure. I asked for the weekend out of the hospital to get Ken off to college. He will be leaving on Tuesday afternoon driving down with a family from our church and I was afraid I wouldn't be out in time to get his things together."

Over the weekend Dorothy received a letter from Fred telling her that there had been no official confirmation of the newspaper headlines. That was good news, but the missionaries knew that something was brewing and accordingly they were much in prayer.

In mid-September Dorothy had minor surgery on her throat. They thought they would find scar tissue obstructing the esophagus but during the surgery the doctors discovered a constricted esophagus which they tried to dilate. Dorothy had to go in for another try a week later. The dilation procedure was particularly uncomfortable but she persevered. Dorothy asked for prayer that there would be lasting results from the dilation. All the tests for a return of cancer came back negative.

In October Dorothy received her return visa for India! Dorothy traveled to the Treasure Valley in Idaho in the latter part of October. The Idaho churches had been canning foods in tins for her to ship back to India. Dorothy and Cari planned on leaving Tacoma for California on October 31. While in California, Dorothy had several speaking engagements including a missions conference at Los Angles Baptist College where Kenneth was a freshman.

Several BMM missionaries were laid aside because of illness in November and Dorothy was anxious to return and help Fred with the tremendous load on him. The trip from Los Angeles to Calcutta was quite good although Dorothy and Cari were confused on their sleeping schedules and wide-awake at 3:30 a.m. in their room in Hong Kong. The only rough part of the trip was just half an hour out of Calcutta and Dorothy couldn't help musing, "Is this indicative of the months ahead?" Every time the plane landed three-year-old Cari hugged her mother and jumped up and down with excitement thinking she would at last see her beloved daddy. Then from Bangkok to Calcutta she finally settled down into a deep sleep and the stewardess had to carry her off the plane. Fred was on the tarmac to meet them. It was the only airport that Dorothy had ever seen that allowed visitors out on the tarmac to meet the incoming plane before the passengers cleared health authorities and customs. His little girlie was too sleepy to jump up and down but she was quite content to snuggle close in his arms.

They flew up to Silchar the following day and were greeted with wreaths and songs by some of the students. The whole house had been decorated with colored papers and flowers and Herka, their kitchen boy, served tea and hot cinnamon buns. It was so good to be back!

On Sunday they welcomed the new veterinary students – twenty-four in all. Most of them were from the American Baptist Mission work in the hills. The Waldocks asked for prayer for a real working of the Spirit among them as the word of God was taught. Most of them from the hill areas were Christian in name only.

That week they met together with the national Christians and waited much on the Lord for the future of the work in Assam. There were many indications that they would not be allowed to stay there many more years and they felt the need to prepare the national Christians to take over the work. Some of their Indian brethren were not willing to accept this view – they wanted to carry on the same as previously and that made it difficult to turn over more responsibility.

There was a happy reunion on December 2, 1967 when Gordie and Lois came home from boarding school. Their parents feared for their coming through Calcutta because of riots but the Lord calmed the storm just at the time that they came through.

On Christmas Eve they had quite a crowd for church in Silchar. Even though he was struggling with the flu, Fred preached Christmas morning. At the 10 a.m. service quite a number of young fellows from town who had never been to church before came to the service.

The last morning of 1967, Fred preached his heart out, pleading with all to be sure of their salvation before 1967 passed into history. Dorothy and others were earnestly praying for the Spirit to work in hearts and show the nominal Christians their need of a vital, personal experience with the Lord. Their hearts were so burdened for these so-called Christians who lived under the delusion that their Christian name and church membership were sufficient guarantee of acceptance with God.

Sana Singh had left Silchar to join the military but his sister Urirei had come for college. She lived on the outskirts of Silchar but rode her bicycle in for college and services. Later though, Urirei's father sensed that Gobin and Urirei were becoming too much interested in each other, which is just not acceptable in India, and pulled Urirei out of college. She instead completed nurses training at Makunda and became a very fine nurse at the Makunda Leprosy Hospital and also a valuable worker in the Makunda Baptist Church and Sunday school.

As they wrote of their expectations for 1968 Fred and Dorothy declared, *"The future is as bright as the promises of God – in spite of the fact that we live under dark and threatening clouds."*

The visa situation still hung over their heads. Two high government officials had verbally told Fred that the Central Government policy was that all missionaries would be phased out of Assam within the next two years. Doctors and nurses might be given a little longer to find Indian replacements for their work. However, Fred and Dorothy had not yet received any official notice.

The Waldocks wanted to send Gobin to Bible College in June to prepare him for ministry in Silchar. Hranga also wanted to take leave of his work in the bookroom to complete his college course. These two young men had been the mainstay of the literature work both in the bookroom and in translation work for two and a half years. Fred and Dorothy wondered how they could let them both go. They asked for prayer for the replacements of the Lord's choosing.

The early part of the year was their busiest season with the annual Conference of the Fellowship of Baptist Churches, three fairs in which they sponsored Christian Literature booths, special evangelistic meetings and Bible camps. They asked prayer for a real revival among the Christians and for the raising up of more national workers.

By March both Herka and Hranga had left. Dorothy wrote, *"We have a definite prayer request in regards to the bookroom. The lease on the building expires this fall. We have heard that they do not want to give us another term of lease – perhaps due to pressure by the Hindu neighborhood – we can't know for sure. This is one ministry we want to leave in good working condition should we have to leave. Do pray that the Lord's will might be done in either keeping this building, which is an ideal location, or getting another one. We want to be assured of a permanent testimony here in town.*

We still live under a cloud of uncertainties. The latest order though is that we now have to apply for our yearly residential permits 97 days in advance of the expiration date rather than the usual 15 days. Then each individual case will be thoroughly investigated and passed here and then in Shillong and then it goes to Delhi for final judgment. They are following through on their policy to phase out missionaries by the end of two years. Fred's permit expires on May 6th so be praying. We don't have any technical qualifications to make us essential in their opinion! We live a day at a time and ask the Lord to keep us steadfast in the work He has called us to until we have to leave."

Fred's dad continued to be poor health and it seemed as if he could go to heaven at any time. After much prayer, Fred determined that he ought to go to his dad for a short visit. If he could get a 'No Objection to Return' permit, he planned to leave right after the Spiritual Life Conference April 27 – May 3 and stay in North America for a month. The Home Office gave approval for this plan.

Fred arrived in the USA in early May and stopped in Tacoma to see David before rushing on to Three Hills, Alberta to be with his dad. His two other brothers had also come home from the mission field. While Fred was in North America, Dorothy and Cari went up to Landour to be with Gordon and Lois.

Fred wrote of his time with his father, *"It was so good of the Lord to allow me this opportunity to come home at this time. It has meant so much to Dad and Ruby (my stepmother) and it has been a real blessing to me to just be with them and to see and hear their testimony of faith in the Lord. Further we three brothers have been together for the first time in almost 20 years. All of us serve on the foreign mission field."*

Fred returned from Three Hills to Tacoma and preached at Temple Baptist Church on June 9. His message was a challenge and touched hearts tremendously. From Tacoma he flew to Cleveland, Ohio to confer with the Home Office in regards to the situation on the field. From there he flew to India. It was quite a change to step out of the beautiful Pan Am airplane in New Delhi at 5 a.m. on Sunday morning and within a few hours be seated in a hot and dirty Indian bus. It was only a 150-mile trip to Landour but it took eight hours over dusty hot plains in the heat of the day. After spending three days with Dorothy and the children in Landour, Fred returned to Alipur on June 20. The Kenoyers were scheduled to leave for furlough on June 25.

Fred's father went home to be with the Lord on July 8, 1968. Dorothy and Cari joined Fred in Alipur at the end of July. They still kept their apartment in town but they spent a considerable amount of time at Alipur, going into Silchar on Sundays for services and as necessary for the supervising of the literature work. They sensed a real need of prayer as they carried a double load in the absence of the Kenoyers.

With the Kenoyers gone from Alipur, the patient load dropped drastically and Fred had real difficulty keeping the hospital going with so little income. He did not want to reduce the staff because when the doctor returned the hospital would be overflowing again. The stress was taking its toll but furlough was just around the corner.

Their March prayer letter written from Alipur revealed their mixed feelings about furlough, *"Just 90 more days...that may seem a long time to you – but so short to us. This weighed on us heavily this morning as we ticked off the unfinished tasks – so many goals and aspirations still uncompleted, so many decisions to be made about packing and turning over our work...We admit we are anxious to get home to be together as a family again for a short while but we are equally as anxious to see this ministry go on in the best way possible to continue to reach souls for the Lord."*

They desired to see the organization of the church in Silchar and the registration of all the Christian Literature Houses – an important step in nationalizing the ministry. They also wanted to find a competent bookkeeper and accountant for the Alipur hospital and station. They had been doing this work for the past three years and had not yet found someone to take this responsibility.

They asked for prayer concerning their 'No Objection to Return' permits that they applied for in March. The granting of these would mean the difference between packing for furlough and packing to leave Assam permanently.

Dorothy's health problems flared up again and Dr. Burrows at first thought he would have to remove two nodes but then decided it could wait until the Waldocks returned to the USA.

They did not hear about their permits for some time. Finally the Deputy Commissioner for Cachar district took it upon himself to send a special message to Shillong to discover the reason for the delay. There had been some extra inquiries and it was evidently being questioned. When at last the Deputy Commissioner got word on a Friday night, he sent out a driver to Alipur with a special officer to let them know that the 'No Object to Return' permits had been granted! Praise the Lord!

Fred and Dorothy left Alipur on June 11 in order to get to Landour in time for Gordie's graduation. From there, the family planned to go to Kathmandu, Nepal before returning to the United States.

As they had the first two furloughs, Temple Baptist Church gave them a very nice welcome home. The Waldocks walked into a spotlessly clean house with the refrigerator and cupboards filled with food. The beds were all made and there was everything that they needed to get started. It was good to be home in the care of such good friends in the Lord. The past six and a half years had been possible only through God's sustaining grace. "Faithful is He that calleth you who also will do it."

CHAPTER TWELVE
Years of Uncertainty

"Yes, there are many problems to be faced but praise God we don't have to face them in our own strength and wisdom. If we would just lean more heavily on Him." - Fred Waldock, May 1971

One of the first priorities after arriving in Tacoma was scheduling a medical checkup at the University of Washington for Dorothy. Until Fred was certain of Dorothy's condition, he was unwilling to schedule any deputation meetings outside of the immediate area. He wrote, *"Last furlough's experience was enough and I don't want that to happen again. Of course, none of us knew what all she was going through or was going to go through."*

They had quite a bit of support to raise. During the past term some support had dropped off and they needed to pick up some more this furlough. Besides that, they wanted to try and raise enough money to purchase land and erect a building for a permanent bookroom ministry. Fred felt that if they could leave the field with a bookroom adequately stocked and on their own property it would be a tremendous help in nationalizing that particular ministry. Fred had only been able to renew the lease on the bookroom until the fall of 1970 and that only with much persuasion.

The financial situation in the Pacific Northwest was tight as the major employer in the area – Boeing – was laying off people. But Fred was sure that *"the Lord still has those whom He can touch and who love Him enough to sacrifice some of the extras of life to see His work go on."*

It took some time before they could get into the University of Washington Hospital. They finally managed to contact one of the doctors who had seen Dorothy two years previously and he made an appointment for them to come to see him at the clinic. When the doctor finally saw her, he made immediate arrangements to admit her to the hospital. That was about the only way they could get her in the hospital without going through all that long clinical procedure again. Beds were difficult to get and that added to the delay. Once Dorothy was admitted things started to roll but even then it took about a week to get all the preliminaries taken care of before they would do the biopsy.

It was ten days after the biopsy that they were given the diagnosis. The doctors said that the lymphoma condition had increased. They were quite definite that they had found a small mass of enlarged nodes on the media sternum. At the university they took at least 20 x-rays of that area alone as well as a few other areas that showed some involvement. After consultation with specialists, the doctors decided to put Dorothy on chemotherapy pills for at least a year. She would need to have blood checkups every two weeks. The doctor was careful not to give Fred and Dorothy a false confidence. Fred told the doctor that they had given their lives to the Lord. He had worked miracles in this situation in the past and their lives were in His hand to do just whatever He willed. The doctor appreciated their frankness and said it made it easier. Fred believed the doctor was being honest when he said that there was a very good reason to believe that this treatment would be effective. Fred and Dorothy trusted that there wouldn't be too many side effects.

Specialists also looked at her throat. Again they felt that they could correct the trouble, so they gave her general anesthesia. But after the examination they decided that nothing could be done but dilation again.

The dilations started in mid-August. The doctors were surprised that the esophagus had shrunk so much since the last treatment. These dilations were very painful and with all of the other medical problems involved it was rather taxing on Dorothy.

After four years of being apart, the Waldocks relished a wonderful summer together as a family. In August they enjoyed an extended family reunion with Fred's brothers. For the first time in 20 years, Fred's furlough and Hedley's furlough from Ethiopia coincided. Their younger brother Ray and his family came down from Canada and the families had a happy time getting acquainted.

In the fall, Ken and Gordie went to Los Angeles Baptist College. David continued at the University of Washington.

In September it was determined that the lymphoma condition in the nodes had decreased about 30%. Fred wrote, "*We certainly praise the Lord for this and are trusting Him that the treatment will continue to be effective. She is also continuing with the throat dilations. They have been very painful and difficult but progress is being made. However, the laryngitis problem has them stumped. She first had trouble with this before we left India and it hasn't cleared up since. We have been told to keep her from talking as much as possible. The doctor said she was to go away where she could get lots of sun and not talk for about a week. So we even tried that and I actually 'dumped' her off in a motel for five days and then went back and picked her up. It didn't help one little bit; in fact, I think it made it worse. So just yesterday the ENT men saw her again and reported that with the exception of a very slight reddening on one side of the larynx they can find absolutely nothing further. They declare it will eventually clear up. This is a bit discouraging especially when she has a number of women's meetings that she would like to take.*"

The medical care required about two trips a week to Seattle and the University of Washington Hospital. In October Dorothy's condition was about the same. She was troubled with laryngitis most of the time and nothing had helped so far. The throat dilations were progressing very slowly. The doctors did not think that they would be able to dilate the throat to the level that they were able to do two years previously. This, too, was discouraging.

However, good reports were coming from the work in Silchar. New Bible classes had been started in two areas near town among nominal Christians. A Bible class for the nurses at the government hospital was also underway. The officials at the Indian Airlines office gave permission to place a tract rack in an area where hundreds of people passed through daily. Permission was also granted to distribute tracts in one of the large military camps near Silchar.

The Indian government had by then worked out a schedule for when missionaries would be required to leave Restricted Areas. The Waldocks received word that they would be required to leave Assam permanently in the summer of 1973. The two doctors with Baptist Mid-Missions would be the last to leave in 1974.

In December, Dorothy's laryngitis was much improved and the cancer was responding well to chemotherapy. Fred left home at the end of January for an extended time of deputation. He was on the road from January to the beginning of May.

Fred and Dorothy received their pins for 20 years of service at the Baptist Mid-Missions Triannual conference March 16, 1970. After the conference, Dorothy visited her sister in Ottawa and Fred resumed deputation in North Carolina, Florida, Texas and other states. By the end of April Dorothy had been cleared medically to return to the field, although she continued to take medication to make sure that everything was cleared up.

Fred and Dorothy were rejoicing in the spring of 1970 that the Lord was increasing opportunities for witness in Assam by both nationals and missionaries. A new literature depot was being opened in Shillong, the capitol of Assam.

Evangelistic campaigns were held during the dry season in the major cities of Assam, Manipur and Tripura with many wonderful results. Fred and Dorothy especially rejoiced at the news that the parents and sisters of Bhola and Sambhu Dey had accepted the Lord. Bhola had been one of the boys who had accepted the Lord at Makunda in 1959. Now he was a teacher. Sambhu had come to Christ in 1963 also at Makunda.

Some Baptist Mid-Missions' missionaries along with Brother Jordan Khan, an Indian evangelist, had gone to Agartala for an evangelistic campaign. Both Bhola and Sambhu had worked hard to prepare for these meetings in their hometown. Sambhu met the missionaries at the campsite and said with a deep sigh, "I wish my father would turn to the Lord this time during these gospel meetings."

After the fifth day of the meetings, there was a day off so Brother Khan and Brother Deb Singh went to pay a visit to Bhola's house. His father, Debendra Chandra Dey, welcomed them into his home. Bhola's father had been seeking the truth and reading the Bible quite often and was earnestly seeking for peace. As Brother Khan shared with him, the Spirit of God spoke to his heart and he repented of his sins and was saved. Three of his daughters also received the Lord that same evening. Only one remained unsaved in the home – Bhola's mother. The next afternoon Brother Khan returned to speak with her again. She gave many reasons for resisting, and felt no need to believe in Jesus to be saved. She firmly believed her guru could save her. It was time to go for the evening gospel meeting and it seemed the talk had ended in failure. Before leaving, however, the Lord led Brother Khan to show her the verse, 'I am the way, the truth and the life, no man cometh unto the Father, but by me.' (John 14:6). Brother Khan asked her, "Did the Lord tell a lie?" The word of God, like a two-edged sword, pierced her heart. Then and there she confessed and received the Lord Jesus Christ as her Savior! What had started a dozen years before with the salvation of the boy Bhola eventually found root in the entire family. Praise God!

Fred and Dorothy applied for their return visas to India in May 1970. But before they returned to the field they participated in David's wedding and sent Ken and Gordon back to college. Lois returned to India July 1 for her freshmen year in Woodstock High School. Fred, Dorothy and Caryl left for India on September 15 for their fourth term. They arrived in India in the early hours of the morning. The day after their arrival in Silchar they drove the 70 miles to Makunda for a special conference. They had to plod through the rain and slippery mud for the last mile to the leprosy colony because a vehicle had slipped off the road and blocked the way.

A Young People's camp was clear evidence that they were back in India. It was almost impossible to use the movie projector because of the millions of bugs that were attracted to the light. Perspiration ran down their legs and arms as they taught. They slept on the floor with the campers. The camp classes were in three different languages. The daily camp diet consisted of only rice, lentils and a small portion of curried squash.

The Baptist Mid-Missions missionaries were offered a good American printing press from a Christian publishing agent in New Delhi. Fred planned to go to Delhi in early November to finalize the purchase, learn how to set it up and arrange for shipping it to Assam.

They asked for prayer for a new site for the bookroom. The owner of the present bookroom site insisted that they move. They had nothing in view but knew that the Lord was able to provide as they prayed.

Fred was well pleased with the printing press. The Lord wonderfully answered prayer. The owner was not in a position to release the press outright for a couple of months because his new larger press hadn't yet arrived. Fred hoped to send a young man burdened for the printing ministry to New Delhi to be trained. It would be good for him to learn on the very machine they were getting.

Fred asked for continued prayer for Dorothy's health. She was having a hard time keeping her white blood cell count above the danger line. The cancer medication that she was on seemed to be causing the problems. Dorothy was not supposed to go off the drug yet, but they felt they might have to. Fred wrote on November 13, *"These are days when we need to depend upon the Lord as never before."*

Fred was concerned about what they might have to pay for customs when the things that they had shipped arrived. He did not expect an easy time. The process of clearing their things through customs was, indeed, an ordeal. Fred was stuck down in Calcutta for almost three weeks. The Lord answered prayer despite the fact that the rules had changed drastically. They had a good appraiser and an officer who was sympathetic. But they still had to pay fines on a few things as well as 100% duty on everything. On December 10 Indian Airline's pilots went on strike and that lasted until December 29. Very few flights were arranged through charter services and as a result Fred couldn't get back to Silchar until December 26. He regretted missing all the Christmas activities as they always tried to make it a very special day in which to present the true meaning of Christmas.

The axe began to fall in regards to Baptist Mid-Missions missionaries' visas in 1970. Helen Sension was planning for furlough and applied for a 'No Objection to Return' permit. It was granted but an accompanying letter demanded, "...Upon return to India you will shift from the Restricted/Protected and

Tribal areas." From further information that Fred received while in Calcutta, he was sure that it wouldn't be long until others of the missionaries would be asked to leave. Fred was concerned that they were not ready.

Dr. Kenoyer and Marleah received an extension until July 2, 1971 with the following note added, "As directed by the government you are hereby requested to make necessary arrangements to shift yourself outside Restricted/Protected/Tribal areas by the 2nd of July 1971." Other Mid-Missions personnel received similar notes.

Fred wrote to Mid-Missions on January 19, 1971, "*We will need much prayer these next months. We need to be directed by the Holy Spirit for every step we take.*"

The local people around Alipur submitted many petitions to the government regarding the Kenoyers. This proved to be effective as the notice to the Kenoyers was annulled.

In February Fred still had not been able to reach an agreement with the owner of the building in which the Christian Literature House was located. The lease had expired before furlough. Since the first agreement the landlord had raised the rent by 50% and still he was asking for more. By April 1, 1971 the bookrooms would be operated as an association. The association would still need subsidy for some time but Fred's hope was that they would be able to be self-supporting before the missionaries would have to leave.

Fred wrote, "*We praise the Lord for answered prayer concerning the recent election here in India. It turned out much better than most anticipated. As far as missionaries are concerned I believe it couldn't be much better under the existing circumstances. Only time will tell if it will relieve some of the restrictions. In our effort to fully indigenize, there are areas where we are going to have to make more progress. Now that we have started to receive our notices to leave Protected, Tribal and Restricted areas, they may carry right through with it. Even if they do give further extensions of time, it's definite that we won't be able to get new recruits. Therefore, it is essential that we get all the work on a basis that our nationals can carry it. We praise the Lord for some of the able nationals that He has given us but they are so few, we need many more. Pray with us that God will raise them up.*"

On March 26, 1971 leaders of East Pakistan declared their independence from West Pakistan and formed the new nation of Bangladesh, the land of the Bengalis. East Pakistani refugees poured over the border into India. By May, Fred reported that there were already 50,000 East Pakistan refugees in Cachar District already. The District Commissioner called Fred in on a couple of meetings. Fred wished they could help them more. They were able to send them a good supply of clothes. Baptist Mid-Missions had just begun the World Relief Fund and Fred asked if some of those funds could be designated to help East Pakistan refugees.

Fred went to Shillong to see officials concerning the status of missionaries in Assam. He was able to see in writing that the orders to leave for the Kenoyers and Doris Bruce had been cancelled and that they could apply for an extension of their residential permits in the regular way. He was also assured that the Burrows who were serving at Makunda would not be asked to leave. The good news pertained mostly to medical personnel, however. When Fred asked about other pending residential permits, the answers were vague. The official stressed that they needed to keep Indianizing the work.

Fred wrote, *"Yes, there are many problems to be faced but praise God we don't have to face them in our own strength and wisdom. If we would just lean more heavily on Him. May the Lord help us and may we experience His divine intervention."*

Fred sent Gobin, the manager of the Christian Literature House in Silchar, to Delhi for over two months to take training on the printing press. They still did not have a building for the press yet and neither did they have a contract finalized for the present Christian Literature House in Silchar. The owner did not want to continue renting to them but really could not evict them. Fred was looking for something else but it was very difficult.

Dorothy continued to have health problems. Fred wrote on May 5, 1971, *"We have to watch her white blood count constantly. It fluctuates very quickly. Some nodes have appeared, as we had to decrease the prescription due to the white count. However, recently by the help of steroids again she is able to maintain a higher dosage of the prescription and we trust that this will cause the nodes to melt away again. She does real well if she gets her rest and I keep after her for that.*

She still dilates her throat herself each morning and that has solved the throat problem."

Despite the medical problems, Dorothy continued to be vitally involved in the ministry. Arthur Fetzer from the Baptist Mid-Missions headquarters wrote to Fred, *"Certainly Dorothy is a brave person, Fred, and you have every reason to be proud of her. When I think of her going through that ordeal of dilation of her throat every morning and still remaining on the field and keeping active, I have to rank her as one of our real missionary heroes. Tell her that we are surely praying much for her and trusting the Lord will grant relief."*

Fred took Dorothy and Caryl to a women's camp in May. They had a good but busy week. About 65 women gathered with about 30 babies – most of them below the age of 3 and one just a few months old. Dorothy spoke during the general assembly hour in the morning on the role of mothers in the church. She taught Nehemiah in the evening. Dorothy spoke in Bengali and one of the women from Silchar translated into Naga. Sometimes the messages were translated into yet another language.

It was really quite an experience - forty women with their babies sleeping on the floor all in one house. Caryl and Dorothy put their sleeping pads down on the floor in the kitchen so they had a little more privacy and room to keep books and camp things.

They had lots of rain that month but only one afternoon did it rain during camp. The days were very hot but the nights were fairly cool for that time of year. One particular scene stayed in Dorothy's mind. The second night one of the groups from a village church asked if they could sing a special number. Dorothy had forgotten to call on them until after the lesson so she called on them then. Six women got up – four of them had babies tightly and very neatly strapped to their backs sound asleep as they sang.

It was encouraging to Fred and Dorothy to see young men that they had nurtured now involved with the ministry on a broader scale. Bhola and Sambhu Dey and Selungba and Sana Singh were elected to the governing board of the Makunda Christian Medical-Agricultural Joint Seva Mandel in May 1971.

The refugee problem was very serious. Fred talked with the Deputy Commissioner in late May and he said they would be very grateful if Baptist Mid-Missions could help. The commissioner mentioned that they were in desperate need of 5,000 mosquito nets. Each net could be made at approximately Rs. 7.50 ($1.00). That would exhaust the $5,000 of relief funds that had been sent. And this would only be the start. In Bengal, Assam and Maghalaya they said that there were over 4 million refugees and thousands more coming in daily. India was very concerned why so little help was coming from abroad. The borders were very tense and unless the situation improved there could be another India-Pakistan conflict.

Fred wrote to the Baptist Mid-Missions Home Office, *"The situation is pathetic and such a tremendous task. I don't know how the Government is going to be able to cope with it. There are over 300,000 children in the Calcutta area who are on the verge of death due to malnutrition. This will increase as food becomes shorter. There is supposed to be a field hospital near Makunda. Jim reports that besides a few iron beds they have nothing else. The doctors don't even have a stethoscope or hardly any medicine. If people at home could even remotely visualize the situation they would certainly send more aid. With some of the money that you sent [World Relief funds] we are going to make a few wooden beds and supply some necessary equipment and medicine. Besides that the camps are greatly in need of mosquito nets, soap, wells, cooking utensils, sanitary chemicals, clothing – in fact, just about everything that is necessary just to exist. I hope that as you publicize the World Relief Fund at home that you will be able to send us at least another $20,000. There are now close to 7 million refugees."*

The local authorities are very grateful for this assistance. Mr. Garlow is working with a camp near Makunda and I am working with a couple of camps near Silchar. The urgent need right now is to help them equip their field hospitals so we are both helping with these needs. We are supplying beds, mattresses, linens, cupboards, chairs and tables, some medical instruments and clothing."

Fred felt tremendous pressure to "Indianize" the works of Baptist Mid-Missions in Assam. They did not know when they might be asked to leave and turn over the ministries to their Indian brothers. Much still remained to be done to ensure that the Lord's work would continue should the missionaries be forced out. Fred felt the pressure not only from the Indian government but also from Brother Fetzer at the Home Office. In October 1971 Fred wrote, *"I have felt all along and still do feel very strongly that we are just not Indianizing fast enough. It is amazing that we are still here*

*with the growing political tension on the border right now and with this
entire Bangladesh and refugee problem, which is indeed colossal. It
certainly isn't out of the realm of possibility that we would all be asked to
leave in a minute's notice, and we are absolutely not ready."*

By October Fred had managed to get the lease on the
bookroom renewed for another three years. The owner was very
reluctant to do it but Fred was glad that they were more or less
secure for another three years. In order to renew the lease on the
present building they had to pay 75% of the rent for the entire
three years in advance. This came to $1,000.

December 16, 1971 Fred wrote to the Home Office staff, *"I
know you are much concerned over the situation in our part of the world.
We certainly don't know what is going to happen but things don't look
too good right now. We were getting quite used to the jets flying
overhead and also the sound of heavy artillery but the action has calmed
somewhat the last day or two. As I am writing this, the loudspeakers are
announcing Mrs. Gandhi's message to the nation that Pakistan has
surrendered in East Pakistan and that Bangladesh has been liberated.
These are momentous days over here."*

The Waldocks' Christmas letter of 1971 praised the Lord that
they had completed the first year of this term in spite of many
tensions and uncertainties and that they had received permits to
stay another year. They reported that Silchar Baptist Church
would soon be a reality. Classes were being held preparatory for
organizing the church. Fred and Dorothy trusted the Lord for a
strong nucleus of believers as charter members.

The press and most of the auxiliary equipment was on its way
to Silchar. This made the need for a bookroom and press location
all the more urgent. Fred had checked into a number of
possibilities but due to local opposition and owners desiring
dishonest transactions to evade taxes et cetera they hadn't been
led to accept anything.

On January 23, 1972 Fred celebrated his 50th birthday. Not
long afterwards Lois returned to Woodstock taking eight-year-old
Caryl with her for the first time.

With the beginning of 1972, the Indian government was not at
all favorable to Americans. All Restricted Areas Permits now had
to be granted from Delhi. This included renewals as far as Fred
could tell. It had been their experience that Delhi had been very

reluctant to give such permits. Fred felt that this recent policy was just further evidence that their days of being able to minister in Assam were numbered.

That spring the missionaries had quite a shock when "Quit India" notices were served on Bette Burrows, Joyce Garlow and Olive Brittain. It was the quit <u>India</u> order that surprised them. They had been aware that the quit Assam order would eventually come. But this development put things in an even more serious light. It could mean that all of them would be out of India by the end of 1972. Fred didn't think it would be quite that serious, but it was certainly time for accelerated action in getting all the properties and ministries in Indian trusts so that they could be carried on by competent Indian Christians.

In April the Indian government reversed itself and granted Olive Brittain a "No Objection to Return Permit" but did not promise that she would be able to return to Assam. Still, it looked like she would be allowed to return to India after her furlough and that was indeed good news. It seemed as though the officials were rather capricious in their granting and refusing of N.O.R. permits. It was impossible for the missionaries to predict what would happen next.

April 20, Fred received the news that Jim Garlow's trip to Shillong to inquire about the other "Quit India" notices bore fruit. All the orders were rescinded! Fred pushed ahead with the nationalizing of the work despite the favorable change. He wrote to Brother Fetzer, *"To me the greater faith is to believe that God can so work on our behalf, with all of these many difficulties which face us on every hand, that the work will continue to propagate and grow under the leadership of our own national brethren."*

The Spiritual Life Conference for 1972 was very good. The Spiritual Life part of the conference was a special blessing. They used only their own personnel. They were thrilled and truly blessed by the messages that their national brothers brought. Fred sensed that there were signs of real spiritual growth. It was an encouragement to him and others.

The business part lasted two days. They were long and tiring sessions. They started at 8 a.m. and stopped at 10 p.m. with only an hour off for lunch and supper. That week was the hottest that they had had for a long time. As president of the Field Council,

Fred was adamant that more concentrated effort was needed in turning ministries over to national leadership. Some perhaps thought that Fred was depressed and discouraged or that he lacked faith. But, in reality, Fred was simply greatly burdened that the Field Council was not moving fast enough under the circumstances. His burden was to turn over all responsibility to the nationals <u>now</u> while the missionaries were still there, so that the nationals could feel the load and make decisions while the missionaries were still there to work alongside them.

At the conference much discussion centered on beginning a Bible school program. The missionaries felt that they were long overdue in establishing an advanced training program. Over the past few years they had held a number of short-term Bible schools – a week or two of concentrated Bible study. These had been helpful but didn't fully meet the need. With so many churches without pastors, it was critical that they have theological training for potential leaders.

Fred was of the conviction that they shouldn't start anything new as missionaries at this stage. Fred felt it was wiser to let the nationals feel the responsibilities that they would have to carry first and then let them make those decisions. He was 100% for a Bible school or Bible college but he couldn't go along with pushing to get one started before the missionaries left. Fred wrote, *"The burden is upon many of our nationals' hearts even now and I firmly believe that God can lead them and provide the means for them to start a Bible school even after we leave."*

In September, Fred and Dorothy received tremendous news. They wrote this note of praise, *"As we come to the end of our second year of this term we have much for which to praise the Lord: this was supposedly the year scheduled by the government for the departure of the Waldocks. Praise the Lord, our permits have been recently renewed until September 1973."*

But all was not well. India was considering stopping or greatly reducing the flow of foreign funds for the support of foreigners and their work. This issue would be coming before parliament in the coming month. The rumor going around was that if the bill passed that it would mean that all foreign funds for missionaries and their work would be immediately stopped. Fred wrote, *"This has been going on for a long time. All this shows us how shaky our position is right now."*

Although Brother Gilbert, the new Foreign Secretary for India, had planned to come to be at the Field Conference meeting, at the 11th hour permission was denied for a Restricted Areas permit and so the whole plan had to be scrapped. As soon as Fred received definite word that permits could not be issued for Silchar, which was 7:30 p.m. Friday October 20, he put in a phone call to Cleveland hoping that it would go through during office hours. This was Fred's first attempt at an international telephone call.

He kept the phone by his bed that night but they were not even able to get beyond Calcutta. Saturday morning very early Fred rebooked the call to Dr. Fetzer's personal telephone hoping to catch him in the early evening. But the call didn't go through until 4:30 a.m. Cleveland time. He was very sorry that the call went through at such an unearthly hour but was glad that they had been able to get word to Brother Gilbert before he boarded the plane.

This would be Lois' last winter with them and Fred and Dorothy had promised to show her Darjeeling before she left India. So instead of the girls coming with the regular school party by train to Calcutta and then flying up to Silchar, they came with another family. Fred and Dorothy met them and took them up to Darjeeling. The scenery was beautiful and the snowed-capped Himalayas were out in all their grandeur. It had been 20 years since Fred and Dorothy had done their Bengali language studies there. Fred and Dorothy considered Darjeeling one of the most beautiful places in India.

In their Christmas letter for 1972 the Waldocks wrote, *"Even here in our immediate locality we have experienced only tension and one crisis after another for the last ten years. Four times in this period our mission has formulated plans for evacuation due to wars with China and Pakistan and local uprisings. Just now we are seeing mounting agitation in our district and actual physical violence over language and regional demands for autonomy."*

The rest of Assam wanted Assamese to be declared the official language but most of the people in Cachar district spoke

Bengali. At times the agitation shut down government offices and disrupted communication lines.

Finally the Silchar Baptist Church was ready to be officially organized. Several of the Rongmei believers from the railway station wanted to join. At first, Fred and Dorothy wondered how that would affect their being able to reach out to other people groups who looked down on the Naga sweepers. But they gradually adjusted their thinking in their minds and hearts.

On December 28 and 30, they had the final organizational meetings of the church in Silchar. On Saturday night, December 30, 1972 the Silchar Baptist Church came into being. Praise the Lord! It had been a long struggle but God had answered prayer.

Fred felt they were off to a good start. What a joy it was to fellowship together around the Lord's Table on New Year's Eve for the first time as a church. New Year's Day they took the whole church family in the back of a big truck and in two mission vehicles for a picnic along a beautiful river near the foothills. It was a tremendously happy occasion for their Sunday school children who seldom got out of Silchar or had opportunity to ride in any kind of vehicle. They sang all the way! There were close to 100 who came. They enjoyed delicious chicken curry and rice, which was cooked by the banks of the river.

The missionaries made another attempt at getting Brother Gilbert to India for consultation with the Field Council. Fred wrote, *"If the Lord wants you to come to Assam He will grant the permit. Daniel 2:21 'Let us wait upon the Lord and trust in Him.'"*

The power of Jehovah overruled stubborn Indian officials. Fred met Dr. and Mrs. Gilbert in Delhi on February 26, 1973. The Gilberts had come from Tel Aviv on an all-night flight. After a couple hours of sleep in the YMCA guesthouse, they rode six hours in a taxi to Landour where the missionary children gave them a royal welcome. During their visit in Landour, located at 7,500 feet above sea level, a very heavy snow fell and the temperatures plummeted. Unfortunately, they only had two small wood burning stoves to ward off the cold in the guesthouse.

From there, Fred and the Gilberts returned to Delhi and then went on to Bangalore in South India. After an initial refusal, permits were issued for the Gilberts to come to Assam. "This is the Lord's doing; it is marvelous in our eyes." The Field

Conference with Dr. and Mrs. Gilbert was very profitable and Fred felt much relief that their plans for Indianizing the work seemed to be on track with what was acceptable to the Home Council. He wrote, *"There was a very good spirit during the conference business sessions. As we faced up to the major issues, which have plagued us, or had us stumped for months, it was wonderful seeing the way the Lord opened a way before us. In this whole Indianization program we felt as though we were on our way down a dark tunnel and were having trouble seeing the light. How thankful we are now that we have essentially been going the right direction all the time."*

The Silchar Baptist Church was averaging over 100 in Sunday school and they were praying for a full-time pastor. Fred and the workers in the bookroom were sharing the responsibility for the services. They had seven Sunday school classes in four different languages.

Further restrictions were implemented in the spring of 1973 restricting travel by missionaries between districts. They were not allowed to go anywhere without a permit issued by the authority in the place that they wished to go and that permit could only be granted after government approval. Fred wrote, *"The devil certainly continues his attacks but praise the Lord he is a defeated foe. We need to be constantly on the watch and in prayer to meet his subtle and open attacks."*

Dr. Burrows was scheduled to have a hernia repair on April 12. As Fred was driving him to Alipur from Makunda, he casually showed him a mole on his leg that had been growing. Dr. Burrows advised Fred to have the mole removed immediately. So on the same day as Dr. Burrows' surgery, Dr. Kenoyer removed the mole from Fred's right leg just above the knee. The doctor took out a fairly good-sized specimen and sent it to Vellore and Ludhiana for diagnosis. However, after the doctor had dissected it he was somewhat relieved because it didn't look as bad as he originally thought. If the mole were malignant, Dr. Kenoyer would send Fred back to the United States immediately for surgery. Fred wrote, *"The Lord has given real peace and we are trusting Him. As Dorothy and I have been talking it over we feel that she and Lois will still come home as planned (to take Lois to college and for Dorothy to get a medical checkup). I just hope it won't take too long to get a 'No Objection to Return' permit."*

Fred walked too much too soon after the surgery and developed a slight infection so he was put on bed rest for several days. On April 23, they received the results of the biopsy from each place. The pathology report from Vellore was that it was benign but they requested a larger sample. The report from Ludhiana was that the mole was malignant. Dr. Kenoyer ordered a specimen sent to the Walter Reid Hospital in the United States. He often sent borderline cases there for confirmation.

Fred was reluctant to leave India at this time with the many responsibilities and pressures in regard to the Trust, nationalization program, registration and selling of two stations – Jaffirband and Binnakandi. A new finance act required reports to be submitted by July 1, 1973. If the Trust were not registered by then, they would not be able to receive funds from abroad.

Just in case a trip to the United States would be required, Fred applied for and was granted a return visa. He wrote, *"It is awfully tempting to go home with Dorothy and Lois for one month. I'd like to find out if there is anything that could be done to fix this condition in my hand. It is now almost impossible to write at all. But with so many things pending right now I'm not allowing myself to consider it."*

In June the biopsy report came back while the family was in Landour: malignant melanoma. Dr. Kenoyer said that the treatment of choice was excision of the lesion in 60% of the cases. He wrote to the Mayo Clinic and the Cleveland Clinic for advice.

June 22, 1973 Lois graduated from Woodstock High School with a 3.7 grade point average – the highest in her class. They praised the Lord for His goodness. Fred and Lois left for Silchar the following day. Dorothy remained in Landour to be near Caryl in boarding school. She would meet Fred and Lois in Delhi on July 7.

Dorothy and Lois would leave from Delhi and visit various relatives en route to Tacoma. Caryl would remain in boarding school and Fred would return to Silchar to handle the very important work of fulfilling the Indian government's requirements for Trusts.

The advice that came back from the various doctors was not conclusive and Fred felt that after the paperwork for this financial act was complete then he would be free to return to the States for further treatment. He set his sights on returning to the US in mid-

August. They had received an extension of the deadline for applications until August 15.

After arriving in the United States, Dorothy and Lois stayed at the missionary apartment in the basement of Temple Baptist Church with Gordie. The wedding of Ken and Mary on August 4, 1973 at her home church in Everett was a happy time.

The Home Office of Baptist Mid-Missions felt that it was too risky for Fred to remain in India without further treatment for his skin cancer. So Fred pulled Caryl out of school and they headed home to Tacoma. They missed Ken's wedding by just three days. Fred went to the hospital the day after he arrived in Tacoma. The specialist in charge of this particular carcinoma was on vacation and did not return until the 20th. On the 22nd Fred had a complete medical exam.

The doctors determined further surgery was necessary to do a wider incision near the site of the mole, a skin graft and a node dissection in the groin. Fred was scheduled for surgery on September 4. The doctors estimated an 8 – 10 day hospital stay. Fred wrote, *"I'm confident the Lord is going to undertake. We need to pray that there won't be any complications."* They also checked out his hand but the doctors were doubtful they could do anything about it.

After the surgery the doctors were confident that the surgery had been necessary because they found malignancy in some of the nodes in the groin. Fred called Brother Fetzer at the Home Office while still in the hospital.

The Home Office had been praying a great deal for Fred and were relieved that he came through the operation in good shape with every indication that there would be no further problems. The Home Office staff expressed their admiration of Fred and Dorothy for their steadfastness in a difficult ministry despite serious medical problems.

Dorothy's report was very good. They took her off the chemotherapy medicine, which was a great relief as it had been such a problem to keep her blood counts where they needed to be. She was experiencing much soreness in her throat and hoarseness. This time the Lord gave them one of the top doctors in the field and he found the reason for her trouble. She had ulcerated granulations on both sides of her larynx. She underwent surgery to remove the granulations on September 13. Per doctor's orders, she was not allowed to talk for two weeks after the surgery.

The doctors would not let Fred return to India until at least five weeks after his surgery. The two weeks of silence were up on September 25. Fred quipped, *"Tomorrow we both go for checkups. Dorothy will then talk to me, I hope! Two weeks of silence is a <u>long</u> time when in the same house and together all the time."*

Brother Gilbert wrote September 28: *"Dear Fred and Dorothy, 'Lord, I am not worthy that thou shouldest come under my roof; but speak the word only, and my servant shall be healed.' (Matthew 8:8) Truly it would seem that the Lord has intervened for both of you in a very wonderful way and we are joining with you and raising our hearts in praise to our God for the manner in which He has brought both of you through this difficult time. I am sure that two weeks of silence must have been difficult for Dorothy and I can well imagine that she had a great deal stored up to say when she was able to talk again. The manner in which you folks have taken these difficult days has surely been an inspiration to all of us. We trust that God will continue the good work that He has started."*

After they had healed sufficiently they spoke at several churches and the Lord blessed. One couple, the Sandgrens, came up to them after a service at the end of September and said that they were going to send $1,000 for the work in Silchar. Praise the Lord. Grace Baptist Tabernacle of Lynden, Washington also gave $1,000. In early October Fred, Dorothy and Caryl were able to travel down to Southern California and Los Angles Baptist College to visit with the rest of the family.

On October 21 Fred preached at Temple Baptist Church and shared the challenges of the work in Assam, India. After the evening service an informal reception was held at the church in their honor. An offering was taken for the expense of getting them back to India. The Lord's people gave $1,300. The Temple Tidings recorded the following, *"Well do we remember the first time they went out as missionaries. David was a baby and their paths were untried and their service a prospect of faith. Never have we known a more sacrificial and earnest pair of missionaries. They have served well. Their going back this time is a 'miracle of grace' because they came home on health furloughs and they did not know what the future held for them. God in His mercy made it possible for them to return."*

On the way to the East Coast they stopped in Grand Rapids to visit Hranga Khiangte and his wife and the Edwin Divakars, Indian nationals who were taking advanced theological training at Grand Rapids Seminary. They also stopped at the BMM Home Office in Cleveland and Fred's brother's home in New Jersey before departing October 29 for India. They took off in a heavy rainstorm. After the first one and a half hours of turbulence the trip was uneventful until they couldn't land in London because of dense fog. They flew instead to Frankfurt, Germany. Wednesday morning they arrived in Delhi and took Caryl up to boarding school. Even though she had been out of classes since August she had managed to keep up nicely and was even a little ahead of her classmates.

The Lord had blessed the work in Silchar while the Waldocks had been away. A veterinary doctor, his wife and two girls were saved as well as others. The church went ahead with the Daily Vacation Bible School and it was a wonderful experience for them. Their first baptism as a new church was held in a large river at the edge of town where hundreds of people were watching from the banks and bridge. One boy who was baptized was formerly high caste Hindu and many knew him. What a testimony!

They were still praying for property for a bookroom and press. They had become convinced that even if they found a good place for the bookroom (other than the one place that they wanted so much) they would need to buy the Anglican church property that they were presently leasing.

Fred and Dorothy were dismayed in mid-February to discover two suspicious-looking raised areas near the site of his operation. Dr. Burrows did a biopsy and sent the specimens to the University of Washington for evaluation. Dorothy celebrated her 50th birthday on February 23, 1974.

The push to nationalize the ministry and to register everything under Indian trusts gained momentum in early spring as the Indian government established a deadline of June 30, 1974 for the completion of the work. Fred wrote, "We are really going to have to keep our nose to the grindstone these next three and a half months. The government has set some deadlines, which is good for us. I felt the Lord wonderfully led in my trip to Landour and New Delhi. My visit with this Mr. Banerjee has been so helpful. It has given us a *confidence, which we sorely needed. On the basis of some of the things that he told me we now realize that we are going to have to make many changes and very hurriedly to be able to comply with government requirements."*

On March 10, Fred received confirmation of an even more impossible deadline – Sunday, March 31, 1974! Unless all foreign-held immovable property was registered in a local trust by that date it would become the possession of the Reserve Bank of India. The missionaries committed it all to the Lord again and made an all-out effort to complete the work.

Fred wrote, *"There is so much detail and little points to be sure about in finalizing all this. If we meet this deadline it will be a miracle."*

A week before the deadline Fred wrote, *"We can certainly praise the Lord for the help of Mr. Banerjee. Now we have just this week left. We have everything outlined as to what to do. But as the local lawyers are not too well versed in this sort of thing, they are somewhat hesitant to act purely on the suggestions of Mr. Banerjee. We are praying for patience and sanctified tact. Our local lawyer has kindly agreed to make out the required schedule of properties according to the acceptable legal manner. This would be a terribly tedious and difficult process for us as the deeds, et cetera for everything are written in very poor Bengali script. We just pray that he will have it done within two days as we then have two more steps (we hope not more) before we can file it for registration."*

To heighten the suspense even further, Fred needed a current Power of Attorney document from the Home Office in Cleveland. It was on its way, but would it get there in time to meet the deadline? The Power of Attorney had to be legally registered before it was effective in India and that required paying fees through the Government Treasury, which would also take time.

There were so many details that Fred really doubted if they could possibly do it. But the Lord marvelously undertook. Certain documents had to be finalized and registered in Gauhati (the capital of Assam), but travel to Shillong and Gauhati required a permit. Usually it took weeks to gain this permit. Fred received his in three days. The Registrar of Societies was very helpful and this document was signed on March 23rd an hour and a half before Jim Garlow had to leave Gauhati by air for Silchar with the document. Fred went on to Delhi with all the necessary papers and a lot of questions to again confer with Mr. Banerjee and to work on the draft for the legal transfer of the property to trust.

They were really concerned about the Power of Attorney. Then Jim remembered that he had an old Power of Attorney, which was registered during the time that Baptist Mid-Missions had changed its name (from the General Council of Cooperating Baptist Missions of North America, Inc. to simply Baptist Mid-Missions) in 1952. Jim was able to find it and even the words "transfer to a trust" was on it! They jubilantly praised the Lord. So instead of Fred being the Transferor and Jim the Transferee, they simply changed "seats" and executed the document accordingly. Fred's Power of Attorney arrived the same afternoon they registered the deed. They couldn't have made it much closer as it was finally signed at 4:00 p.m. on March 29, 1974. The next day was a Saturday so they would have had only three hours left in which to get it done. It was a 63-page document and included a listing of all the buildings and details of the land.

As they were going up the street to the court to present the papers for registration, Fred mentioned to those who were with him that this was the day that he had been looking forward to for the past ten years. As he thought back over the past five weeks since he had contacted Mr. Banerjee in Delhi all he could say was, "This is the Lord's doing; it is marvelous in our eyes." (Psalm 118:23)

After the work was completed it was with great satisfaction and tremendous relief that Fred sent the following cable to the Home Office: "Praise the Lord all registrations completed on time. Waldock." All of Baptist Mid-Missions immovable property in India was now registered under a local registered trust! Praise the Lord!

There would be more government procedures to deal with – including a Finance Act that was sure to create many more headaches – but for now, the Lord had won the victory.

CHAPTER THIRTEEN
Preparing a Legacy

"We'll praise Him for all that is past, and trust Him for all that's to come." - Fred Waldock, April 1974

During the time when all the registration work was going on, a large lump developed on Fred's leg below the knee. When Dr. Burrows first saw it he thought it was a clot in a small vein, but two weeks later he felt it definitely had to come out. By the time he removed it in early April, it required ten stitches to close the incision. It didn't look good. They sent it the same day to the doctors at the University of Washington for evaluation. The specimens sent earlier had been received but the pathology report had not come in yet. Fred expected it within a few days. He felt it was likely that the doctors would want him to return to the University of Washington for further evaluation. He was feeling rather tired lately with the hot spell and the long hours spent on the registration.

Fred and Dorothy wrote to Temple Baptist Church on April 12, 1974: *"I'm sure you can understand what all is going through our heads and hearts at this time and yet there is a peace that only the Lord can give. 'How great is the God we adore – our faithful and unchangeable Friend...We'll praise Him for all that is past, and trust Him for all that's to come."*

With the thought of having to return to the United States for cancer treatments looming in the back of his mind, Fred confided in his Indian brethren that he would be greatly disappointed if he had to go without finalizing the property for the bookroom and press. The present building was in bad need of repair and with the rainy season coming on, they feared for the inventory stored there. The missionaries and national brethren increased their prayer effort and there was much concern. Fred, however, had been out at Alipur since April 8 and could do nothing about it.

Then Monday morning Fred received word from a contractor friend about two places, both of which were suitable for a bookroom and press and were readily available! He hoped to start negotiations on one or the other that week. Praise the Lord! Both sites had buildings already on them that could be renovated to suit their needs. If the price quoted for either of the sites was the final price, Fred felt that he had enough on hand to pay for it out right and to make all the necessary renovations.

Fred also felt that the Lord would have them keep the church property but they lacked the funds to buy this on top of the bookroom.

It was with great joy that they received a cable from the pathologists in the United States that the mass removed from Fred's leg was a thrombosed venous aneurysm and not cancer. The doctor did want Fred to return to the United States for a previously scheduled checkup in July.

On Tuesday, May 7 as Fred was preparing for prayer meeting, the Lord clearly gave a passage of Scripture as a promise to Fred. "Have I not commanded thee? Be strong and of a good courage; be not afraid, neither be thou dismayed; for the Lord thy God is with thee withersoever thou goest...Command the people...Prepare you...for within three days ye shall pass over this Jordan, to go in to possess the land, which the Lord your God giveth you to possess it."

On the Thursday following the prayer meeting – *the third day* – Fred's contractor friend took him to meet with the owner of one of the properties. After the title was examined by the lawyer and found to be clear, the customary discussion regarding price et cetera took place. A document to pay earnest money was drawn up. This was a legal document, which required the owner to vacate the land within four months, after which the buyer would pay the full balance of the purchase price and take possession!

For ten very long years they had been praying, looking and saving for suitable property to purchase for a bookroom and press ministry. At times they were discouraged. But only this year did they have enough money to make complete payment for any property. Most sellers demanded the full price at the time of sale.

On this piece of property there were three fairly good buildings. The front building had 24 feet of frontage but six feet of that had already been leased to another bookstore. The owner had tried to persuade the other bookstore owner to relinquish his lease but he refused. The Waldocks were trusting the Lord to make him willing to leave according to the promise of Joshua 3:10 "Hereby ye shall know that the living God is among you, and that He will without fail drive out from before you the Canaanites."

In the meantime, they still would have as much frontage as their present bookroom. The front building was two-storied so some of the bookroom workers could live upstairs. The building in back was also two-storied and could be used for offices downstairs and living quarters upstairs. A third building could be used for the press and for living quarters for one family. All of the buildings would need reinforcing and remodeling but that would be much cheaper and faster than building all new buildings especially since building supplies were so expensive and difficult to get.

The area around the property was a very busy bazaar area about half a mile down the road from their present location. The area was building up fast with many new shops and Fred and Dorothy considered it a very advantageous location.

May was also a month of much unrest in India. Unemployment was high. Accusations of government corruption intensified. A nationwide rail strike was in force as of May 9. The post office and telegraph went on strike on May 11. No parcels or registered or insured mails were moving. For a week there was no mail, telegram or telephone service. There were threats of strikes on many levels and throughout the nation. On May 15 there was an all-India strike in sympathy with the rail strike. Everything, including all transportation (even rickshaw drivers) stopped. Prices were unbelievably high. Gas soared to $1.90 a gallon and food doubled and tripled in price and became much more difficult to get. Fred and Dorothy were not going hungry. There was still rice in their area and as long as they didn't want too much variety, it was OK.

Then, to the shock of the world, India exploded its first nuclear device on May 18, 1974 bringing India into an elite group of nations with nuclear capabilities.

Brother Gilbert arrived in India on May 27 and had good meetings with the missionaries before proceeding on to survey Bangladesh – a new field for Baptist Mid-Missions. They reviewed the government requirements that they were now faced with. It was all very complicated and there were some serious concerns regarding new financial policies that the missionaries would need to be in compliance with. Yet Dorothy wrote, *"But the work is still the Lord's and we look to Him to preserve that which is in His plan and purpose to carry on His ministry of reaching lost souls."* They also discussed the opening of a Bible college – the Northeast India Baptist Bible College. Originally the plan had been to open the college in Shillong; but others wanted it in the Cachar District. After much deliberation it was thought that the Cachar District, and perhaps Silchar, would be the best location. The Divakars, who were completing their training in the United States, would head up this new work.

Dorothy went to be with Caryl in Landour at the end of May. In mid-June Fred joined them for a week before flying to the United States. He flew to New York City and stayed with Hedley in New Jersey for a few days. Gordon, who was traveling with the Los Angeles Baptist College singing group "Reflections," was to be in New Jersey at about that time so Fred hoped to catch up with his youngest son there. From New Jersey he flew to Clearwater, FL to see his stepmother Ruby and to report to a supporting church. On his way to Tacoma he did a very quick stop over in Cleveland.

When Fred arrived in Tacoma, Monday night July 1 he was met by David and Mary and his little granddaughter Jennifer, Ken and his Mary and Lois. Lois would spend the summer living with her dad in the missionary apartment at Temple Baptist Church. She was delighted with the prospect and hoped that he would be able to stay the entire summer before returning to India.

It was with some fear and trepidation that Fred left the church for the University of Washington Hospital. The doctors gave him a complete checkup including a number of blood tests and x-rays as well as a head to toe examination. Fred returned from the hospital grinning from ear to ear. His doctors told him that clinically speaking his condition was good and clear of any indications of malignancy. After a long year of uncertainty, Fred and the good people at Temple Baptist Church certainly felt that the Lord had intervened in this situation. Praise the Lord!

Fred wrote the Home Office on July 11, *"The Lord is good and greatly to be praised. You will rejoice with me that the doctor has given me a clean bill of health. Barring anything that might turn up in the lab tests, I am completely cleared from any signs of metastasis whatsoever. The doctor feels that it is most unlikely that the lab test will show anything. Thank you for your prayers and concern for my health problem and now you can join with me in praising the Lord for answered prayer."*

Although Fred had planned to remain in Tacoma with his family until September, a developing crisis on the field required him to return much sooner. It was decided on July 15 that he would need to go back early for the good of the missionary team in India. One of the missionary men had become despondent and incapable of making decisions. Fred was needed to step into the gap. It was a difficult and disappointing time for Lois, Gordon, Ken and David to see their father return to India so quickly but they knew that he would have stayed if it had not been so vital.

Fred left Tacoma on August 6 and stopped over in Grand Rapids to deal with some matters regarding the future Bible college. He then went on to Cleveland and was able to spend the night of the 7th there as well as the morning of the 8th before going on to New York and then on to India.

Fred's trip back was a rather long ordeal. He had an 18-hour layover in Brussels as a connecting flight was delayed. So he missed the flight in Bombay for Delhi. He sat up all night in the airport. Indian Airlines was heavily booked but he managed to get a flight the next day. He went up to Landour for a couple of days before going to Calcutta by train. It was hot and sultry.

Poor Dorothy in Silchar couldn't figure out what happened to him! Fred finally got through to her by telephone on August 10. He was in Calcutta for a number of days completing business before finally arriving home on August 20. Bless her heart; Dorothy was at the airport to meet him. A nasty virus hit Fred rather hard and he was in bed with a fever, chills, nausea and headache. A nice way to arrive home to his wife!

Fred did what he could to provide leadership for the missionary team in dealing with the many problems before them. The situation improved and worsened in turns. There was much discussion about the Bible college as well.

Although the Waldocks were due for a furlough in the summer of 1975, with the way things were going, it seemed likely that they would not be able to take furlough then. It occurred to Fred that it would be a real help to the field if Lois could come out to India under Baptist Mid-Missions' Missionary Apprenticeship Program (MAP). Lois was in her sophomore year at Los Angeles Baptist College. She was very interested in missions and was looking to the Lord for His direction for her life. Her parents were anxious for her to investigate the Lord's leading. No new missionaries had been granted visas to come to India since 1966, but because Lois was a dependent it was likely that a permit could be secured for her.

The Waldock's Christmas letter for 1974 included the following: *"The world conditions certainly haven't been improving during this last year of 1974 but our fellowship with Him and our dependence upon Him become more satisfying and precious as we look away from the increasing sin and problems of the world and look to our 'Emmanuel – God with us.' Since our last prayer letter some more changes have been made in our plans for the bookroom property. This was necessitated by the withdrawing of plans to open a Bible college in Shillong. Now it has been proposed to start the Bible college here in Silchar. At the same time, we were given notice that our lease on the Anglican Church property will terminate March 1975, as they desire to sell the property. Since this land would be adequate for the Bible college facilities and also for the bookroom-press ministry if necessary, it was felt best to relinquish the property we told you about in our previous prayer letter and purchase the church property, as we do not have funds enough for both.*

We have not informed the owner of the first property yet and keep hoping and praying that eventually the Lord will give us both, as the church property is out of the business district and not the best location for the bookroom. The Bishop has reduced the original price quoted on the church property from $30,000 to $23,000 and will be coming December 18 to draw up the sale deed.

It is difficult for us to understand these changes when we felt so sure of the Lord's leading in regards to the first property but we only wait on Him to work out His will for every aspect of the ministry here for His glory. The work and the plan are His – we are only His servants."

February 15, 1975 Fred took the missionary kids up to Landour by train. It seemed that the holiday time had gone far too rapidly. Eleven-year old Caryl seemed to be growing up so quickly. Fred was taking them all the way by train because the airline no longer allowed student rates. Also hoodlums on the main line out of Calcutta were becoming an increasing problem. Going up last year, the ruffians had tried every way possible to get into the students' coach including throwing stones and breaking windows. And on the way down in November there had been a free-for-all in the very coach that the school party was in. The authorities said that they could do nothing about it. So for those reasons, Fred was escorting them by train all the way from Silchar. They would arrive in Landour the morning of the 19th. Fred hoped to be back in Silchar by February 24, the day after Dorothy's birthday.

In March, Fred and Dorothy wrote a letter to their supporters informing them that Lois had been accepted for the Missionary Apprenticeship Program for service in India that summer and inviting them to be part of her support and prayer team. What a joy and encouragement it would be to have Lois with them for the summer. There was more than enough work to keep her busy. The new Northeast India Baptist Bible College planned to open in August. There would be class notes to type and duplicate. The Bible college also had a library that needed to be set up. The Silchar Baptist Church was waiting for help in starting clubs for boys and girls using the AWANA material.

Fred and Dorothy were also before the Lord in regards to another of their offspring. Ken and Mary were in the process of applying to Baptist Mid-Missions for missionary service in either India or Peru. Fred wrote to Ken and Mary on April 4, 1975, *"In some of my recent letters, I have made reference to how wonderful it would be if the Lord should open the door and bring you out here to help us in the Bible college. It is not necessary for me to even suggest to you how advantageous this would be from a natural standpoint. We must not rely on carnal reasoning but we must seek the perfect will of God.*

I want to suggest what might be a possible approach as we consider this and seek the Lord's will. We realize, only too well, how discouraging it is for a candidate to try and raise his support for India, which is almost a closed door to new missionaries. Recently we have heard of a few new ones who have come out. The thought came to me that if the Lord so leads you, why not apply to the mission as candidates for both India and Peru? I feel this would be very commendable. We have had a number who have applied to India and because visas were not granted have gone to other fields.

Another reason for presenting this challenge is that our situation is somewhat changed now. We are now operating under Indian Registered Societies. Say for instance, if the Northeast India Baptist Bible College, which is an integral part of Baptist Mid-Missions Trustees India, should make an application for you to come out as teachers in the college – it gives a different category to the application. I think it is a possibility and it could be investigated.

I am not, at this stage, going to try and suggest all the possibilities and advantages. The question right now is simply – is this the will of the Lord for you? Does He want you to even pursue it? That has to be uppermost and foremost in our hearts and minds at this point. So I lay before you both to pray about it. You can be sure that we are praying for you.

Desiring only the Lord's perfect will for your lives.
All our love and prayers."

The Spiritual Life Conference at Makunda that spring was a great blessing. People came from quite far away to participate. Thirty came from the Simte tribe. Some walked three days before meeting at a central place and then they rented a bus and traveled two more days before reaching Silchar. On the following day, they and others from around Silchar loaded onto a train for the 10-½ hour trip to Makunda. Many expressed how great a blessing the conference was to them. The missionaries felt that definite results were going to be forthcoming from this conference.

On Tuesday, April 15 they held the groundbreaking ceremony for the Bible college and bookroom although construction could not begin immediately. There was a difficulty in getting cement. The Indian government had frozen cement sales for a year so that they could export more of it for much needed foreign currency. There was some cement available on the domestic market but at very high prices. Fred hoped to get a permit for 300 bags of cement to be purchased in Meghalaya. Fred would have to arrange transportation of the cement and it would cost more that way, but how could they wait? Even after getting a permit it would take a long time to transport it, as another permit from the Assam government would be needed.

The Lord cleared the way for Lois to come out to India on the MAP. Her plane was to arrive in Delhi on May 30 but her parents almost didn't make it there to pick her up. They were scheduled to leave Silchar by air to Gauhati on May 27. Due to storms, the plane didn't arrive. Everything was booked for the next day but they did get plane reservations to Calcutta for the 29th. That morning it rained very hard but the plane finally came in and they reached Calcutta with just an hour before the Delhi flight. Even at that short notice, they were able to get seats on the flight to Delhi. Shortly after they reached Delhi, the airport was closed due to heavy dust storms. All planes were diverted elsewhere. By morning it had cleared up and Lois' plane arrived without difficulty. She was excited to be home in India again and her parents also rejoiced in the reunion.

They praised the Lord for the wonderful way that He had provided the funds for her MAP. It was a great encouragement to Fred and Dorothy as they noticed gifts from people they hadn't heard from in years. Evidently, these people were faithfully remembering the Waldocks in prayer. Lois, also, was thrilled for the way that the Lord had answered prayer.

The three of them traveled from Delhi to Landour to see Caryl at Woodstock. One of the main functions of the year was happening at that time and Caryl was counting on her parents and sister being there. The family was in Landour together for about two weeks. Then Fred and Lois headed back to Silchar, as there was much work to attend to. Dorothy stayed in Landour until Caryl's summer break was over in the middle of July.

Ken Waldock graduated from Northwest Baptist Seminary in Tacoma in June and he and Mary were accepted by Baptist Mid-Missions at the July Triannual conference in Toledo, OH. They were part of the largest candidate class in the history of Baptist Mid-Missions. They were counting on India as their field until the door closed. Both Ken and Mary considered Peru as sort of a compromise. But they had real peace concerning coming to Assam.

In Silchar, it was a hot and sultry. Often Fred rose very early in the morning in order to do correspondence before the real heat of the day. On one particular morning in August, he had been sweating profusely for the past hour and it was only 5:30 a.m. August was tremendously hot especially if the monsoons subsided for a time.

More trouble was ahead for India. In June 1975 Indira Gandhi was convicted of corrupt practices during the 1971 election. Rather than lose her political position, she declared a national state of emergency and centralized power in her own hands. Fred wrote of the state of emergency in a letter that would be carried out of the country, *"In light of the recent developments over here you might expect that I will be able to clue you in on what is happening. Actually, I think you folks stateside can inform us. The press is almost completely suppressed. All India Radio says nothing and the newspapers hardly mention anything. Our information comes from Voice of America and other foreign news broadcasts. It has been rumored that we are not to listen to foreign news broadcasts. It is reported that someone was arrested for listening to BBC. All of the opposition leaders have been arrested and there is complete silence. Now with the recent amendment to the constitution it appears that the whole issue concerning Mrs. Gandhi will be cancelled. Some say that she has sold out to communism or socialism, as they like to term it. How long will the state of emergency last? That's a good question. Some feel it can't be withdrawn because she has gone too far...In some ways the emergency is good. Prices have lowered and are supposed to be fixed. On all essential commodities shopkeepers have to display their present stock and price list every day. There is a crackdown on corruption.*

Brother Gilbert you must be careful how you refer to any part of this letter, and please inform the others with whom you may share this information that they write nothing. Under the emergency one can be arrested without a warrant and without even a trial and can be detained for at least one year. Even mere suspicion is enough. So please make no reference in your letters to the situation. The intelligence branch is everywhere. You never know who is who. This is in no way to alarm you. We are experiencing no hardship. We have not been curtailed to any great extent in our ministries."

This national state of emergency lasted for a year and a half until Indira Gandhi was voted out of office during a general election in early 1977.

The plans for the Northeast India Baptist Bible College were not coming together as well as they had hoped. The first proposed building on the church compound had yet to be started. The first of several delays was getting permits for cement. The cement was finally delivered in the middle of June – the beginning of the monsoon rains. The church property was in a low spot so it would be waterlogged much of the time until the end of the rainy season in October.

The first two students of the Northeast India Baptist Bible College began their studies in August at Alipur, where the principal of the college, Edwin Divakar was temporarily living until the college buildings could be built in Silchar. Mr. Divakar had been trained in the United States and was well qualified to head up the program but the frequent delays and changes were discouraging him greatly. Nor was he used to the heat of the Cachar District.

Fred and Dorothy, as well as the other missionaries, were keenly disappointed in October when Brother Divakar gave his resignation as principal. The program had barely gotten off the ground and now they would have to start again.

The week of October 20 they held a Daily Vacation Bible School during the Hindu holidays as the schools were closed. There was rejoicing on earth and in heaven when five youth were saved through the D.V.B.S. Three of them were high school girls for whom Fred and Dorothy had been especially praying for the past two years. Four of the five who were saved came from non-Christian homes and had more hindrance than encouragement for Christian growth.

Thursday evening, October 23, 1975 a severe pain developed in Fred's calf; he couldn't bear to even step down on his foot. It was the same leg that had been operated on two years previously. Fred and Dorothy suspected a blood clot and so treated accordingly until they could get word to Dr. Kenoyer. The phone line was out of order, so Dorothy sent a messenger. Fred had a difficult night with pain, fever and nausea. Dorothy sent a second runner the next morning. It was almost noon before Quentin came with the ambulance and took Fred out to Alipur.

The diagnosis was an acute thrombo-phlebitis - a blood clot in the vein of his leg. Fred was put on antibiotics and anticoagulants. Dr. Kenoyer felt he would be all right but refused to let Fred out of bed until the swelling and fever were completely gone. Fred's temperature had been as high as 102 degrees. His leg was very swollen and discolored. Fred was in the hospital for 12 days of which the first 10 days he was completely confined to bed. After the first 4-5 days his fever subsided and he felt much better. He took anticoagulant medication even after leaving the hospital. His leg was wrapped with ace bandages from the foot to almost his hip and on top of that he had to wear support hose.

Brother Gilbert wrote from Cleveland, *"To say that all of us have been much concerned over the word that you are in the hospital with acute thrombo-phlebitis would be an understatement of the year. We have been mightily concerned and want you to know that we have been upholding you in prayer daily and during the day as the Lord would bring you to our mind. May God continue to make His power evident in your lives from day to day."*

In November the Field Council voted a furlough for the Waldocks. They had already been in India for five years and due to Fred's health problems it was determined that they needed to go home for a rest early in 1976. The group also voted to temporarily close the Bible college effective October 31st. With the Divakars gone there simply were not enough teachers to staff it at the present. They believed the Lord would undertake for the Bible college in His own unique way. They wanted to be tuned into Him as He revealed His will to them. Ephesians 5:17 declares, "Wherefore be ye not unwise, but understanding what the will of the Lord is." It was hoped that Hranga, who would complete his studies in Grand Rapids soon, would return to work in the Bible college in the summer of 1976.

The restrictions on permits to Assam continued. The missionaries had difficulty securing permits for the children to come home for the three-month winter break on November 29.

They needed to be out of their present bookroom by January and so it was imperative that work on the new bookroom go forth quickly.

After two unseasonable spells of rain that lasted 3-4 days, they finally entered into the winter season. It was so invigorating that it made Fred feel like working instead of having to push himself to get anything done. Once the rains were finally over on November 12, they were able to start construction.

In their annual Christmas prayer letter Fred and Dorothy wrote, *"For us, this has been a difficult year in many ways but through each trial the Lord has brought special peace, strength and new hope."*

Construction on the bookroom building was progressing nicely at the start of 1976. The tight restrictions on cement seemed to have lifted. They placed an order for 60 tons and it appeared as though they would get it.

Fred and Dorothy received their "No Objection to Return" permits and left for their fourth furlough on February 9, leaving Silchar Baptist Church in the hands of its national Indian pastor. To break up the long flight home, they did overnight stops in Hong Kong, Tokyo and Hawaii and arrived in Tacoma, February 18. All of their grown children and many friends were at Sea-Tac airport to meet them.

After a few days at home, the Waldocks wrote the following note to their dear friends at Temple Baptist Church, *"'Blessed be the Lord who daily loadeth us with benefits.' (Psalm 68:19) How grateful we are for a home church that has stood so faithfully behind us in vital interest, support and prayer backing down through our 27 years of service in India. And now your welcome home to us in the provision of the apartment, where we can find times of refreshing and fellowship with family and friends; your abundant help in stocking our cupboards and renewing our wardrobes, as well as your lovely reception for us last Sunday night. All (these things) warmed our hearts tremendously and we wish to thank you and the Lord for your love and care for us. We needed this year of furlough and already the Lord has begun to meet our needs through you. We look forward to more warm fellowship with new friends as well as old in the days ahead. Our grateful thanks in Christ, Fred, Dorothy and Caryl Waldock."*

Fred wrote to Brother Gilbert on March 9, 1976 *"It has been great to be with all of the family again. The Lord has been so good to us in so many ways. He has given us a wonderful family. We are so thrilled to see the keen interest in Ken and Mary and their desire to get to the field just as soon as possible. Even though they are in full-time teaching jobs this year in a Christian school they are able to do some deputation work and their support is coming in for which they are greatly encouraged. I have written the field concerning the possibility of applying for visas for them as house parents for Claremont. They would have plenty of opportunity for language study at the same time. We need to pray earnestly concerning their visas."*

In March they began the process of their medical checkups. They praised the Lord that Dorothy's lymphoma condition was unchanged. She had been off all medications since 1973, so this news was indeed great and wonderful. Fred had no further evidence of melanoma. The doctor was concerned about the thrombo-phlebitis bout that had occurred in October and considered restricting the driving that Fred could do. But Fred and Dorothy praised the Lord for His goodness and looked forward to His blessing upon this furlough.

Fred did deputation work in Montana in late March and early April. Dorothy joined him in Montana in early April for a Women's Regional Missionary meeting. Then they and Ken and Mary went up to Canada for the Worldwide Missions Conference at Prairie Bible Institute. This was the first Spring Conference that Fred had been able to attend since his graduation from Prairie in 1947. The conference was very good and they enjoyed it immensely. The emphasis on foreign missions was great. BMM was given a good spot in the Thursday afternoon service. A representative from the BMM Home Office, Fred and Ken were all given time to speak.

The Prairie Tabernacle congregation, who had sent periodic gifts through the years and often prayed for the Waldocks, invited Fred to preach in the morning service on Sunday. Fred estimated that there must have been over 1,500 in attendance.

Sunday evening they spoke at Crossfield Baptist Church. This also was a blessed memory for Fred as his parents moved from Crossfield in 1932. His dad and mother had been much involved in organizing that church. They had a wonderful time and praised the Lord for it.

They visited churches in the Northwest through June. It was also a time of great joy for their family as they celebrated several milestones. Lois was "capped" in the nursing program. Ken and Mary's first child, a son Nathaniel Scott, was born on June 15.

Then Fred had the joy of performing the wedding ceremony for Gordon and Joan Cowan July 3. After the wedding they traveled to Cleveland for the July Triannual Conference of Baptist Mid-Missions where BMM President Allen Lewis presented them with their 25-year service pins. While they were back East they visited supporting churches and friends.

That summer the new bookroom/press building was finally completed and the Christian Literature House moved in. The press was unpacked after six years and was set up in its new permanent quarters. Funds were still needed to complete the second floor, which would be used for living quarters for the manager and his family and for office space for the Christian Literature House Society. Praise to God, the Northeast India Baptist Bible College started its first term in August with twenty-one carefully chosen students! Hranga, who had returned from theological studies in the United States, was part of the faculty.

In mid-September, the road-weary Waldocks returned to Tacoma. They had logged 10,985 miles in eight weeks. They felt that they might have picked up some support in at least two of the churches they had been in.

They participated in three missionary conferences back to back in the fall ending in the Boise, Idaho area. These churches were especially dear to Fred and Dorothy because of all the years that they had partnered with them for India. Promode came to the United States for study that fall and was able to be with Fred and Dorothy from Dec. 17-23. Fred arranged for Promode to be in several meetings with him. His ministry was a great blessing and Fred was thankful for the few meetings that he had been able to arrange at Christmastime when churches had so many other special events planned.

There was reason for further rejoicing that year as Dorothy's eldest living brother, Fred, and his wife came to know the Lord as Savior. The faithful prayers of Dorothy's 92-year-old mother had finally been answered!

Fred wrote at the end of December 1976, "*As we greatly rejoice in what the Lord has done and is doing in the work out there over the past few years, yet we are deeply burdened for the immediate. Our hearts cry out 'O Lord, give us a few more years in Assam yet.' It seems, at least in the natural, that much more could be more or less crystallized with a continuing work if we had a few more years to get the Bible college functioning well and a more effective literature ministry operating. Since the ultimatum given by the Indian government in 1967, the Lord has been so gracious to us and has kept us there this long but I feel somewhat like praying the prayer of Abraham when he prayed over Sodom and Gomorrah."*

The Waldocks' visas to return to India arrived the week of February 14! How they praised the Lord. Fred wrote, *"With such a turmoil in that land we prayed that some high official wouldn't get the idea to cancel the validity of the NOR procedure. We prayed much about our return. It will be very interesting to find out the result of the India election March 16th. This could be extremely important."*

As Fred and Dorothy did deputation they shared with the churches their future goals: *"Even though we were told that all missionaries would be phased out of our area by 1973, we continue to get yearly renewal of our residential permits. However, indications are that missionaries will not be allowed to stay much longer in Assam. We would like to set up an offset press for the nationals to run. So many tribes have no literature in their own languages. There are translators at work in at least eight different languages in our area right now. We will be working in the new Bible college, local church and in the general evangelistic and Bible teaching ministry of the Fellowship of Baptist Churches as long as the Lord keeps the doors open."*

It was Fred and Dorothy's desire to see Silchar Baptist Church as a model and training ground for the students at the Bible college as they received their academic preparation to go back to their own villages. Many students coming out of other Bible colleges and seminaries had no idea of the polity and practices of a true Baptist church even though it was taught in their classes because they hadn't seen it modeled in the churches that they had been attending.

There was a serious turn of events later that spring. Dr. Quentin and Marleah Kenoyer received notice that they were to leave Assam by June 29, 1977! Marleah had to leave India for medical treatment without receiving a "No Objection to Return" permit. Appeals had been successful in overturning the order six years earlier, but would they work this time? Would the Waldocks get their residential permits when they returned? Only God knew. Fred and Dorothy continued to pray and continued to prepare themselves to return to India. However, they had many questions. Should they take Caryl back with them? If the Burrows went on furlough in June and with Kenoyers gone that would leave Caryl alone. At this point, they didn't want to send her into boarding school under those circumstances.

Their departure was delayed until June 10. Lack of definite news from the field was their greatest difficulty. Christians and other local nationals had been petitioning the government to allow the Kenoyers to stay. All were hoping and praying much that with a newly elected government, the policy would be changed. They had been scheduled to leave Tuesday, June 7 but Fred's passport and visa were delayed. The passport arrived that day but after they had already rebooked the flights for Friday evening. It turned out to be a good thing, however, because Dorothy wasn't feeling well – probably just the flu. She was in bed most of Tuesday and still felt rough on Thursday.

They praised the Lord for a good but busy furlough. They had visited 89 churches and spoken more than 200 times, driving some 46,000 miles! They were leaving behind a host of praying friends and relatives, three happily married sons, Lois in her last year of nursing at Pacific Lutheran University and three lovely grandchildren.

They left Tacoma on Friday and flew to Hawaii where they spent the weekend with the Versluises, former coworkers in India who were now pastoring a mission church in Hawaii. Fred felt that this was of the Lord, as this young growing church was keenly interested in the work in India and indicated that they wanted to help with support for the literature work and press.

From Hawaii they flew to Hong Kong, stayed there a day and then flew on to Delhi. After they arrived Fred started the process of getting his passport renewed even though it did not expire for four months. He wanted to have a valid passport when he reached Assam so that there would be no excuse for not registering him for one year. The next day they left Delhi by bus for the 150-mile trip to Landour to take Caryl back to school where she would start the 8th grade on July 26. The bus ride took eight hours. Sunday night they took the night "deluxe" bus back to Delhi. It was a little faster but what a neck-jerking, head-jarring ride. They got the last two reservations and had to sit on the back seat – no reclining and no place to stretch your legs for six agonizing hours. They got to Delhi at 4 a.m., slept a couple of hours and then Fred picked up his passport and took care of some other business. Tuesday morning they flew to Calcutta. Dorothy did not enjoy congested and filthy Calcutta. The Assam House would not issue a permit direct for Silchar so they had to go via Gauhati but there was no trouble. They arrived home in Silchar on the 23rd – two weeks after leaving Tacoma. The very first night the church had a welcome service for them, followed by a business meeting until 9:45 p.m. They ate their supper afterwards. Boy, were they tired!

Unpacking and setting up housekeeping was equally exhausting as the temperatures were up to 95 degrees and the humidity was about 95% as well. They had a continual sauna. Within the week, they were registered and had all permits valid for one year. Praise the Lord! However, it did not look too favorable for a renewal for the following year. The devil sent many discouragements their way but gradually they saw the Lord's direction as to what their work should be for the year. They asked for continual prayer. On one hand, they were thankful for the uncertainty of their future in Assam because they felt it would push them further and faster in their goal to put the leadership of all of their ministries into the hands of the Christian nationals just as soon as possible.

Despite many Indian nationals' pleas, the Kenoyers were only given a one-month extension. They would need to be out of Assam by July 29, 1977. Fred was convinced that the days of missionaries in Assam were truly numbered. He wrote on July 1, *"I certainly feel we have been warned again and that all out efforts on total Indianization is of utmost importance. I further feel that we are not to get involved in anything new or even that which has been pending should not be pursued unless totally undertaken by the nationals."*

While in the Assam capital, they saw it in writing that the Waldocks were scheduled to be told to leave during 1977. Dorothy wrote, *"That does not trouble us so much – we know the Lord has His plan for us no matter how long or short a time we are here. Our greatest concern is for our nationals."*

Both Fred and Dorothy resumed teaching Sunday school classes. Fred also helped with the classes in the Northeast India Baptist Bible College and Dorothy led the Bible lesson for the women's group and helped with the young people on Saturdays and with Daily Vacation Bible School. The church was doing well with its new pastor. They were running over 130 in Sunday school. The big problem was space for Sunday school classes in four languages. Dorothy's class met under a tree – which was fine as long as it didn't rain.

Ken and Mary were in the Summer Institute of Linguistics course that summer and had almost all their financial support. In July the India Field Council took official action to ask the Home Office to apply for visas for Ken and Mary as houseparents for the MK hostel in Landour. With the departure of the Kenoyers looming and the other uncertainties, it was out of the question to request visas for Assam for Ken and Mary. It would not work for them to apply for South India either as the mission did not yet have a resident work down there. Fred wrote in a letter to Lois on July 24, *"We trust that after they get here we might be able to place them in an active church planting ministry. We need to pray much that they will get their visas. It would be a terrific victory if they did."*

Fred continued, *"This is Uncle Q's and Faith's (the Kenoyer's youngest daughter) last Sunday. They are due to leave Friday. It doesn't look like any extension will come through. It takes time to pack and get all of his clearances. We are working on those things now. Even if he is only given a one-month extension now I don't feel he will take it. He might stay for a few days but I don't think he will apply further. It will be quite a traumatic experience when he finally leaves."*

No extension came through and the Kenoyers left Assam after 27 years of missionary service. Dr. Kenoyer eventually became the Medical Director for Baptist Mid-Missions and also resumed private practice.

It was wonderful how the Lord undertook for the Waldocks' freight. They had sent four steel drums containing mostly tins of vegetables and other foods that people in the States had provided. They were loaded on a ship the same day that Fred took them to the docks. Fred had intended to take two fiberboard drums with things they would need immediately by airfreight. But when Fred went to book them and found out how much it would cost he decided to ship those by boat as well. The shipping agent said that the two fiberboard drums would have to go on a different ship as the first one had already left. But both shiploads would have to be transshipped en route to Calcutta. The Waldocks got word that the steel drums had been transshipped in Japan. Then later they were informed that the two fiberboard drums were transshipped in Singapore on to the very same ship as the other freight – therefore enabling Fred to clear all the freight at once! Ruth and Mary Burrows, children of coworkers, were leaving India for college at just the same time as Fred's freight was to arrive in Calcutta, so Fred was able to help the girls get all the necessary paperwork in order and see them off in Calcutta. In Customs they opened every little item in the girls' luggage – probably looking for drugs. They took it well but were glad that Uncle Fred was there to give moral support.

The ship was due in Calcutta on the 12th but got hung up in Bangladesh and didn't get to Calcutta until the 20th. It was a long, hot wait. But Fred was able to get all his papers in order before the ship came in and the Lord provided a very helpful, considerate Customs officer who told him how to classify everything. Then he found out about a law saying that foreigners are permitted to bring in foodstuffs duty free so that meant that all those items of food were duty free! Fred finally ended up paying on a few toiletries and linens – total bill $17. Thank you Lord. Fred and Dorothy were greatly relieved to get it all through and in only three months' time.

The Waldocks began their teaching responsibilities in the Northeast India Baptist Bible College August 30. The Bible school had 35 full-time students representing 11 different language groups. Dorothy taught Bible Geography to second year students and worked in the Bible college library. Fred taught Genesis to the first year students and Doctrine to the second year students.

They had a full calendar for fall. The Silchar Baptist Church annual meeting was a time of rejoicing. Sixty people had been saved through the church outreach in the previous year and 16 members had been added to the church.

At the Youth Camp during the week of October 17 eight young people were saved and during D.V.B.S. 13 children came to know the Lord as their Savior. More than 20 of the 95 children that attended the daily Bible school were from non-Christian homes.

During this time, Fred and Dorothy were discouraged about the way some things were being handled. They desired to do things decently and in order before the Lord and when others chose to go their own way it put much stress on Fred as Field Council president. Fred was by nature a servant. He never lorded his position as Field Council president over the other missionaries nor did he use heavy-handed tactics. He was in all respects a Christian gentleman. He detested conflict but when it was a matter of conviction, Fred felt compelled to speak out. He depended much on the Lord to work out the various disagreements.

The letterpress was kept busy printing booklets and tracts in a variety of languages. The press was too small to keep up with the demand, though, and Fred continued to try and locate an affordable offset press or an automatic letterpress. He anticipated the coming cool, dry season when many teams would be out selling and distributing literature. When the Bible college students went on Christmas break many planned to take literature back with them to their tribes. Two teams were slated to spend part of their vacation selling literature in two hill-tribe areas where there are many nominal Christians.

Fred traveled to Bangalore, South India to meet with the Indian national under BMM – Charles John. Together they looked at a ministry opportunity in Tumkur that Charles' sister had founded. His sister, Mrs. Mary Anchan, was looking for someone to take over the work of the Rural India Medical Mission as she was not well enough nor did she have the financial resources to run it herself. Charles was, at the time, very interested in taking up the work there in this growing city 46 miles northwest of Bangalore. Fred felt it would be a good place to become established in South India for very little expense. The BMM women missionaries who were on loan to Berean Bible College were also interested in a ministry change. They had started a Sunday school ministry in an area called Wilson Gardens but the director of the college strongly opposed it. If the women broke with the college there would be opportunity to continue the Wilson Gardens ministry from Tumkur. They would need the mind of the Lord in this matter.

Friday, January 20, 1978 was a day of rejoicing. At noon a telegram came from the Baptist Mid-Missions' Home Office telling the news that Ken and Mary's visas had been granted! Fred and Dorothy made so much happy noise over it that the telegram deliverer came back and rang the gate bell again. He asked, "You got good news, Sahib?" Fred knew what he wanted but he beamingly replied, "Yes, very good news." So the man said, "Then I want some tea!" How could Fred refuse him a tip with that news!

The very next day Lois and Gordie called with the news that Dorothy's mother had passed away. She would have been 94 in May. Even though she was in a nursing home she had amazing strength for her age. When Fred, Dorothy and Caryl had left the US last June she didn't complain. But since December 23 she had fallen three times. On the last one she had broken her hip and her elbow and had split her forehead open. They did surgery on her hip and put in two pins. She came through the surgery beautifully with no complications and was bright and alert after that. That had been the last report from Lois on January 12. And then she simply passed away on the 20th. She had longed to go for so long and kept telling Dorothy, "I don't think I will be here much longer." Dorothy's three brothers and father were awaiting her in glory. Dorothy wrote, *She was a wonderful mother and I owe my Christian experience and life much to her teaching and guidance and prayers.*

Also on Saturday Caryl was experiencing constant pain in the region of the appendix. This continued for three days. Late Sunday night when the Fellowship of Baptist Churches conference was over, Fred sent a note out to Makunda with Promode for Dr. Burrows giving a layman's view of the symptoms. Monday was Fred's 56th birthday but the celebration was tempered by concern for Caryl. Tuesday morning at 3:15 a.m. Dr. Burrows arrived at the Waldocks' front gate. Fred and Dorothy really didn't expect him to come that night but they were grateful that he had come so quickly. Dr. Burrows examined Caryl and felt he should operate. It was some job trying to find a taxi at that time of the morning. The old Silchar jeep was under repair and the Wagoneer was giving too much trouble to even try to take it to Alipur. But Fred was able to find a taxi and they left for Alipur immediately.

Surgery was started at 5:45 a.m. Instead of a hot appendix it turned out to be a large cyst the size of a goose egg. A biopsy was done. Dr. Burrows thought it was benign but sent a specimen to Ludhiana for a report. Caryl was a very good patient even though the spinal ran out before they were finished. Dorothy stayed out at Alipur with Caryl while Fred and Dr. Burrows returned to Silchar. Dr. Burrows then headed right back to Makunda. Fred was so thankful for missionary doctors at hand who were so willing to help in times like these.

Tuesday Fred had two classes to teach but only took one of them and then sat down to write the family through a letter to Lois, the nurse of the family. Fred and Dorothy's thoughts were on the family that day as it was the day of the funeral of Dorothy's mother. What an emotional five days it had been!

"Blessed be the God and Father of our Lord Jesus Christ, the Father of mercies and God of all comfort, who comforts us in all our tribulation, that we may be able to comfort those who are in any trouble, with the comfort with which we ourselves are comforted by God. For as the sufferings of Christ abound in us, so our consolation also abounds through Christ." (2 Corinthians 1:3-5)

Mid-February Fred wrote to the Home Office and commented again on the visas received by Ken and Mary, "*We are so thrilled and full of praise to the Lord for granting the visas for Ken and Mary. This is truly all of Him. So often it seems necessary to make repeated contacts with the government through this official and that man with 'pull' or influence; but this time we just felt from the beginning that we would leave it entirely in the Lord's hands. After 12 years to again get a new recruit for the India field (that is other than an Indian) is really something. We are praying that this will be a tremendous stimulus to the churches who have been challenged to pray. I hope, too, that it will put some 'go' into some of the young people. Just today as we were praying at the table we were thinking of them as they would most possibly be visiting some of their churches. What a thrill it must be for them to tell of the miracle that the Lord has performed. He is still on the throne.*"

In March, the Waldocks were again feeling a pinch financially. They wrote on March 10, "*We ourselves have been viewing with alarm the decline of the American dollar against the Indian rupee, and the steady increase in prices. In the midst of this concern the Lord has encouraged our hearts with news from several of our churches that they have increased our monthly support. The Lord is good. He has promised to supply our every need and we praise Him. When the prospects were bleak, David encouraged himself in the Lord. (1 Samuel 30:6) May we learn to do that, too, day by day. He is right with us in every trying circumstance and feels it along with us.*

We have submitted our applications for renewal of our Residential Permits for another year. You will perhaps remember our telling you that our names were on the list for leaving Assam in 1977. Our present permits were granted until June 15, 1978. Pray with us for the Lord's wonder-working power according to His will for us."

Brother Gilbert came out to India to meet with Fred and the rest of the Field Council in Shillong on March 30. They were able to arrange accommodations for all of them at the Welsh Presbyterian Hospital Guest House. No special permit was required for Dr. Gilbert because Shillong itself is open to tourists as it is a lovely hill station. Six out of seven of the Assam missionaries were able to get there as well as seven of the key national workers to represent each of the societies. It was a treat for the missionaries and nationals to get out of the heat and away from the pressures and interruptions of the work.

Dr. Gilbert ministered to them from the Word first thing each morning. The Lord led him to the right passages to fit their particular needs at that time and Fred felt that this meditation in the Word was a blessed preface to their discussions each day. Dr. Gilbert counseled with the missionaries alone before the nationals arrived, then with the nationals and missionaries together and then perhaps set a new precedent in that he counseled with the nationals as a group alone as well as with many of them individually – all with the missionaries' consent. Dr. Gilbert's days were long – from early morning to late at night. Yet he remarked that the attitude of the nationals was only that of graciousness and sweetness. Since they wanted to work together with the nationals in carrying out the Lord's work in Assam, it was good to know their difficulties and Fred felt that that awareness would only deepen as they worked together. Not all the problems could be resolved – especially those concerning finances if and when missionaries would have to leave. But at least now the national coworkers had a greater understanding of BMM policy and knew fully their responsibility, as the missionaries had always been, to look to the Lord for the future.

On April 6, 1978 Fred had the thrill of a lifetime in meeting his son Ken, born in India, now returning as a missionary with his wife and two-year-old son Nathan 29 years to the month of Fred and Dorothy's own arrival. Fred took them up to Landour where they began serving as houseparents in the BMM hostel and began studying the Hindi language. It was a time to praise the Lord.

As had been the case in January, sad news followed on the heels of happy news. On the evening of April 27, 1978 at about 8:30 p.m. a police constable came to the house with the official government notice written to Dorothy. "Reference your extension application to stay in India beyond 15.6.78, I am directed to inform you that the Government have regretted their inability to allow you to stay in Assam as your stay in Assam is over due. You are therefore requested to shift yourself to a place outside Assam within period of thirty days on receipt of this notice with intimation to this office about your departure."

Fred was out at Alipur at the Fundamental Baptist Conference when this notice came. The following day the Waldocks wrote their prayer warriors in the States.

"April 28, 1978
Dear Praying Friends,
This morning we read in our devotions, 'In <u>everything</u> give thanks for this is the will of God in Christ Jesus concerning you.' (1 Thessalonians 5:18)

Time has run out for us in Assam. We applied for our new Residential Permits, which expire June 15th. The answer came last evening. 'You are requested to leave <u>Assam</u> within 30 days of this date (April 27th). The Government cannot renew your permits; your stay in Assam is overdue.'

We have been aware of the Government's program to gradually reduce missionary personnel in this restricted, sensitive area and have tried to plan toward that day. Just the same, now that the order has fallen on us, it is naturally 'shaking'. When you consider that we have lived in Assam and have been totally involved with the people and work here for 29 years, and living in this particular house in Silchar for the last 15 years, you will realize that it is no easy matter to completely clear out in 30 days. Not only all our personal things to arrange for but all the mission files have to be sorted and worked over. With Dr. and Mrs. Burrows going on furlough in June it leaves only the Garlows and one missionary nurse to work along with the nationals. The burden will be heavy on the Garlows especially. We were both scheduled to teach in the new trimester of the Bible college which starts next week.

Even though we leave Assam we hope to get located somewhere in India where we can continue to augment the work here with help in literature production and Bible lessons. Our need for work funds will naturally increase as we continue to support the general work of the mission, press, and Bible training ministry here, as well as get established in another area. At present we have no definite leading of the Lord as to where we should locate. We ask for special prayer at this time that the Lord will lead in a very definite way to show us His place of service for us. We feel this is so very important. When we leave here we will probably go to Landour, Mussoorie, to spend Caryl's vacation time with her as originally planned.

'Faithful is He that calleth you, who also will do it.' (1 Thessalonians 5:24)

Yours in His continued faithfulness,
Fred and Dorothy Waldock"

On April 29, Fred wrote to Brother Gilbert in Cleveland.

"Dear Brother Gilbert,
...So far I've only been able to tell a few of the nationals and it really seemed to hit them hard.

You ask, what will you do? Honestly, Dr. Gilbert, we have absolutely no leading as to the next step. To start somewhere else in India would take much needed finances from the work here. We are making it a very definite matter of prayer. As you can imagine there is MUCH to do. Just this past week we had our 29th anniversary in India. To sort out everything, dispose of things, pack what we will need elsewhere; et cetera will take all of the time left and then some. What to do? Just TRUST. Please do hold us up in prayer. It is going to be so hard to leave these dear ones with whom we have served for these many years, especially at a time such as this when there are still too many things dangling in our indigenous program. It is so good that you were able to come out, Dr. Gilbert, as you have a more up-to-date picture of the actual situation now.

The Daily Light readings have been so good lately. Today's text opened with, 'In everything give thanks for this is the will of God in Christ Jesus concerning you.' We are seeking His will for the next step. We covet your prayers.

Yours trusting in Him who is faithful,

Fred and Dorothy Waldock"

Monday morning, May 1, Fred went to Dispur, the capital, to determine if anything could be done to reverse the decision. He got nowhere. The officials there let him know it was final. When they said that the schedule for removing missionaries was made, Fred asked concerning the others but the officials refused to give this information except to say that all the missionaries would eventually be out of Assam. The officials were not impolite but it was very plain to see that there was no hope for reversal. Fred took the night train back to Silchar and arrived there just before noon.

Fred sent a cable to the Home Office. "WALDOCKS ORDERED TO LEAVE ASSAM BY MAY TWENTYSIXTH STOP AFTER FIFTEENETH SEND MAIL TO LANDOUR – FRED"

Fred and Dorothy wasted no time in starting the packing and sorting. But, in reality, there was no time to waste. The three and a half weeks that remained would go by quickly. Fred wrote, *"How situations can change in a moment's notice these days. Makes one think of what it is going to be like when that trumpet sounds and we shall all be caught up together to meet the Lord in the air. What a day that will be!"*

Things were in a whirl and Fred hoped for a semblance of order soon. Just a year ago they were in the same fix – packing to return to India. Now Fred found himself trying to jam the same things back into the same drums, suitcases and what not but to "destination unknown." It was quite a feeling.

Although the trip to Dispur did not result in an extension, the Lord had His own way of giving the Waldocks a little more time in Silchar. Fred's notice wasn't delivered until two weeks after Dorothy's – even though they had applied for their renewals at the same time. Therefore Fred's departure date was June 9th.

They requested permission for Dorothy to stay until that date as well.

The Waldocks gave serious consideration to beginning again in Tumkur. Although Charles John had determined that he was not interested in taking over his sister's work, Mrs. Anchan was still hoping that Baptist Mid-Missions might assume the work. The medical work consisted of 3 ½ acres of land, one small building and very good x-ray and lab equipment from the American Medical Association. BMM would need to assume the liabilities of about $2,000 but the rest would be given free. It did not seem that there was an evangelical church in the town of 100,000 people. It was a fast-growing area with several colleges and industries. More English was spoken in that area and that would be a help for Fred and Dorothy. There was a great opportunity for literature work, Bible classes, Sunday school and church ministries, where all of the expatriate missionaries from Assam could fit in.

On May 23, the Field Council made a motion authorizing Fred and Dorothy to meet again with Mrs. Anchan concerning taking over R.I.M.M. Fred wrote a letter that day telling Mrs. Anchan about their situation and interest in the work. Mrs. Anchan sent a telegram to Fred on May 24: "If interested in RIMM give answer immediately." Fred replied to Mrs. Anchan's telegram telling her that he would leave Assam June 9, go to Calcutta and then on to Landour before coming back to visit Tumkur.

The pastor of Silchar Baptist Church asked Fred to preach the Sunday mornings before their departure. At first Fred, said no because he felt that he would be too busy packing to prepare messages but he later changed his mind and agreed to take the pulpit for several Sundays. On May 7, 1978 he preached sharing with his Indian brethren the issues of his heart.

"I'll admit I was feeling much disturbed and perplexed about having to leave. This has been a matter we have thought about and talked about much but when it comes right down to leaving – it is hard. April 24th we started our 30th year in India, all of it in Cachar District. Much goes through our minds. Packing and leaving – who likes to do that, especially for the last time? Where will we go? The Lord only knows that right now.

What about the work here? So few to do it and so much to do. Opportunities are abundant. The devil again tried to discourage and depress me. Suddenly a message I had heard some time ago popped into my mind. It encouraged my heart greatly and I want to share those thoughts with you this morning.

There is a word in the English language which means the end of things; no other recourse; no hope; hopeless; to give up hope. That word is DESPAIR.

When I got back from Dispur a brother called me and asked, 'How did it go? I replied, 'No hope.'

Yes, it is a word in the English dictionary BUT it is not in God's vocabulary. A change in circumstances should not bring despair. It should not bring about a state of hopelessness. We may think that such a situation must change or that the order must be reversed or we're finished. God may or may not desire to have the circumstance changed or the 'quit Assam' order rescinded. But still there should not be despair.

The world says that where there is life there is hope. The Bible teaches that in our spiritual lives, where there is <u>death</u> there is hope. John 12:24: 'Most assuredly, I say to you, unless a grain of wheat falls into the ground and dies, it remains alone; but if it dies, it produces much grain.'

Death to our own selfishness.

Death to our own plans.

Death to our own ideas.

Death to our own determination.

Death to self.

Yes, death to all these and more – spells hope and life out of death. When these things prevail and when the work responsibility that God has given me becomes <u>my</u> work, etc. and suddenly the circumstances change drastically then despair comes in and gets us down. And we say, 'What's the use?'

The question is, whose program is it? Whose program are we in? Despair with us, yes, but not with God.

EVEN NOW. [John 11:1-6, 11-22] Is this not a hopeless situation? Lazarus dead and in the grave four days. Martha said, 'Lord if you had just been here sooner my brother would not have died' – but now it is too late. We have like circumstances, a sick loved one, or some dear friend who has passed away – and we say, it is too late now. From man's view that is true but not God's. What is the problem? We want God to do what <u>we</u> want Him to do. But He does not always choose to do what we *want Him to do. If He doesn't then we say: 'it is too late now' and our hopes are dashed to the ground.*

Peter denied the Lord. Was that the last for Peter when he denied the Lord at such a time? How could the Lord forgive him? Was Peter beyond restoration? No, EVEN NOW Peter can be restored. Isn't that hope for you, backslider, defeated Christian?

John 11:4 is the secret. 'Not unto death, but for the glory of God.' For God's Son to the glorified. <u>Any circumstance can bring glory to God.</u> Yes, even 'Quit orders' can bring glory to Him. Your situation, my situation, is not out of God's reach, or out of His power to bring glory to His Son. EVEN NOW.

EVEN THERE [Psalm 139:7-12]

Despair? Not with God. God never comes to the end of things. Joseph in prison in Egypt. Sold by his brothers, in prison for 13 years...not much hope now. This is the end of him. But the Scripture says God exalted him to be the head of the prison. God is training him in discipleship and in leadership. God is preparing him for the years to come. So EVEN THERE God was able in His power to undertake. [Genesis 50:19-20]

Daniel in the lion's den. We would say if only we can keep Daniel out of the lion's pit then it will be at least hopeful. If God doesn't do something soon, then it will be too late. So the lid is open and Daniel is thrown in and the lid is closed – that is it. But EVEN THERE God is present in power. What is your EVEN THERE? Is it really worse than the lion's den? EVEN THERE.

And there is Jonah. He is in the fish's belly for his own deeds. This is different than Daniel. Jonah was rebellious and disobedient. What a horrible situation. Seaweed choking the life out of him in the fish's belly. Jonah 2:2 says, 'I cried and the Lord heard me.' EVEN THERE. Is your state worse off that that? All Jonah had to do was repent – turn about face and God made the fish sick.

No matter where – in prison, lion's den, belly of a fish, Cachar District or wherever. EVEN THERE God is able to work. EVEN THERE He is preparing His men to bring glory to His name.

EVEN SO [Matthew 11:25-26] God never comes to the place of despair. There comes a time when all we can say is EVEN SO. It may be painful and we may have no answer. [Philippians 1:20] Paul said that in all things God will be glorified. Whether by life or by death. No matter what the circumstances – if God will only work out His purposes, then EVEN SO Lord, do it. [Daniel 3:16-18] But if not, God can deliver and He may this time but EVEN SO we will not bow down and worship your gods. Even in such circumstances, it is not beyond God's power.

Three little expressions – EVEN NOW! EVEN THERE! EVEN SO!

There is no time too late for God. No place too far for God. No circumstances too extreme for God. This sickness, this difficulty, this situation is not unto death but unto the Glory of God. Do we believe that? God really is in control of things. EVEN NOW, EVEN THERE, and EVEN SO. There is no time, no place and no circumstance that is beyond the loving care of God. Casting all your care upon Him, for He careth for you."

The nationals were very strong in trying to persuade the Baptist Mid-Missions Trust India committee to approach the authorities for an extension for Fred and Dorothy. Fred had told the other missionaries that if they felt that applying for an extension for the Waldocks would bring about a more speedy investigation of those still remaining, then Fred did not want an application made. But after he returned from the capital, it seemed that the officials had it all laid out and that when the time came each one would get his notice. So Fred felt that it would do no harm to approach the officials. It was a very divided issue. Therefore, no application was made other than to request that Dorothy be allowed to stay until Fred's deadline. On May 23 they received an affirmative reply to that petition, so both Fred and Dorothy were able to stay in Silchar until June 9.

It was a hectic time trying to pack all of their stuff for shipping and then disposing of those things that they could not send or take with them. At the same time, Fred was continuing his class in the college and there were many committee meetings. The eight farewell services were overwhelming. At least twenty families invited them to eat a meal in their homes. But the Lord gave grace and strength through those traumatic days.

They left Assam the afternoon of June 9, 1978 with much heartache. Besides a whole busload of people from Silchar, some came from Alipur and from three of the nearby local churches to the airport to see the Waldocks off. There were about 60 there to wish them well and say goodbye. As the plane taxied down the runway, the door to Assam closed firmly. But they <u>trusted</u> that the Lord that they served would faithfully open a window somewhere.

CHAPTER FOURTEEN
Closed Doors and Open Windows

"The future is still not certain, but we walk as He leads." – Fred Waldock, May 1977

After leaving Assam, the Waldocks flew to Calcutta. Their plan had been to clear Ken's baggage while in Calcutta as the ship was due about that time. But then they learned that the ship would not arrive until the end of the month so they took their chances on reservations and booked a trip to Tumkur before going to Landour.

Getting reservations was a problem but the Lord undertook. Fred sent a telegram to Mrs. Anchan informing her that he and Dorothy would like to visit Tumkur before going to Landour.

She had sent a letter to Landour, thinking they would go there first, saying she wanted some definite answers before Fred and Dorothy came to visit. Unfortunately they didn't get that letter first. When they arrived in Tumkur, Mrs. Anchan had a houseful of guests – her brother and family had come from Zambia so she was more than busy. Still she was gracious and booked a hotel room for the Waldocks and prepared delicious meals for them. The secretary of R.I.M.M., Mr. Paramasivan, flew in from a business trip he was on, to meet with the Waldocks. Mrs. Anchan and Mr. Paramasivan took Fred and Dorothy on a tour of the clinic, dispensaries and storerooms the afternoon they arrived but it wasn't until about 8:30 p.m. that night that they were free to come to the hotel room and talk.

Mrs. Anchan was very firm that a national should be in charge of the medical work – not a missionary. Mr. Paramasivan was just as firm that Mrs. Anchan should have a key position because of the time and effort she had put into the ministry. And yet it seemed a necessity for her both physically and financially to turn over the work to another. They broke off discussion at midnight. Mrs. Anchan and Mr. Paramasivan said that they would bring their final points for discussion the next day.

Mrs. Anchan's brother and family were leaving on the train the next afternoon, so Fred and Dorothy were on their own that day until they were called for lunch. After that they returned to the hotel until Mrs. Anchan was free to resume talks at the hotel at 5:30 p.m. The second time they met the meeting was more relaxed and it seemed that the transfer of the ministry could work out if approved by the Field Council and Baptist Mid-Missions. Fred and Dorothy were willing to start the work in Tumkur, but they did not want to get tied down with administering a medical program at the expense of neglecting a church-planting ministry. Therefore, there needed to be someone to take over the medical side of the work. Their other concern was finances. Yes, they had left Assam but their hearts were very much there and they could not wean themselves from that work that easily. They knew the financial strain there and the need to complete unfinished projects so they were unwilling to take their designated work funds out of Assam to put into a new work. Fred felt that they must trust the Lord to finance any new work through whatever means He chose but not to sacrifice their responsibilities to the Assam field.

They knew they needed to establish a base somewhere in South India so that the BMM missionaries getting kicked out of Assam would have a place to go.

Fred and Dorothy's residential permit expired June 15. They went to the Regional Foreign Registration Officer in Calcutta. Fred told them their story and the official was very considerate and helpful. He accepted their application for a renewal for six months under his jurisdiction. That gave Fred and Dorothy time to make definite plans as to where to settle.

Dorothy and Fred arrived in Landour on June 21. They sent out a prayer letter asking their supporters to pray for direction and particularly about Tumkur. Although they enjoyed the coolness of the hills and being with family, Fred and Dorothy were desirous of knowing where the Lord would have them next. The waiting was hard but they were trying to exercise patience.

They wrote their friends at Temple Baptist Church July 1, 1978, *"It is still very hard to realize that we won't be going back to Assam, in fact it is just now beginning to hit us. We continually thank the Lord for you dear ones there and for your faithfulness in supporting us and now we are especially counting on your prayers as we seek the Lord's definite guidance for our future place of service. We are confident that the Lord is going to open just the right door for us as we trust Him. Our warm greetings to all there. In Christ's love and grace, Fred and Dorothy Waldock."*

Fred sent a report of their trip to Tumkur to the Executive Committee members and asked for a vote concerning whether he and Dorothy should continue with negotiations concerning taking over the Rural India Medical Mission. One couple that had previously been for taking over R.I.M.M voted "no" without giving a reason and then remained silent for over a month. Fred and Dorothy were taken aback by the negative vote. They were not just interested in R.I.M.M for themselves but that it would be sort of a beachhead for BMM in South India.

Fred and Dorothy made definite plans to go to Bangalore on August 31 and even made train reservations in faith that they would receive five specific letters before then. Some of these letters were essential to their going but when not a single letter arrived they took it from the Lord that this was not His timing.

The wait continued into September and they were restless, anxious to get into their next phase of work. Fred wrote, *"These have been trying days for us but the Lord has been bringing many blessed passages of Scripture to our attention in various ways. He indeed is faithful. After having been so occupied with many things in Assam it is hard to just seem to be waiting."*

They did receive good news from home, however. Lois was now engaged to Tim Sebens – a Northwest Baptist Seminary student. Tim and Lois each wanted the Lord's perfect will for their lives. Fred and Dorothy praised God for that and were confident that their engagement was of the Lord.

In September the Baptist Mid-Missions Trust India voted not to take over the Tumkur property. The minutes were forwarded to Fred and Dorothy without comment. Fred and Dorothy were in the dark to know what step to take next.

However, they felt that they could investigate the possibilities better from Bangalore than from Landour. So when they were able to arrange for the rental of a cottage in Bangalore, they moved. They arrived in the city the first week of October. They really had to be careful of their next step. They had been notified before leaving Landour that their application for an extension to their registration in Calcutta had not gone through after all. But to register in a new place one had to be attached to an existing work. This point had been reiterated by many missionaries that Fred had consulted with. Many advised Fred not to even try to apply without that connection. The only existing work that BMM had in South India was the ministry that the Johns were doing in Trivandrum in the extreme south of India.

So with their registration running out, Fred and Dorothy continued to seek the Lord as to what the next step should be. They knew the Lord had something for them but what that was continued to be the big question. They looked for houses to rent in an extension to Bangalore, which was the largest and fastest growing extension in all of Southeast Asia. There was almost no Christian witness at all in this area, so it would be, in the Waldocks' minds, an excellent place to locate.

On October 10 they received a telegram from Ken saying that 14-year-old Caryl had been operated on again for another cyst. This was the second operation in nine months. It was the big puja season and the trains were heavily booked, so Fred called the airport duty officer and asked him if there was a seat on the Delhi flight which was due to leave in 40 minutes. A seat was available. Dorothy packed quickly and in ten minutes they were off in a motor scooter headed for the airport. A motor scooter had just come into the compound; otherwise they would not have been able to get one at that time of night. When Fred and Dorothy got to the airport, they had just closed up the counter but they kindly made out a ticket and Fred and Dorothy rushed to the security check with only five minutes to go. The Lord was good and Dorothy made it on the plane.

Fred wrote, *"We have really been thrust on the Lord. Is He trying to tell us something? The message last Sunday was just for us. When the Lord tells you to wait and you don't know what to do, don't move. That was just what we needed but it is oh so very hard."*

Shortly after Dorothy returned from Landour on November 23, she and Fred moved into the house of a missionary with another agency who was soon to be going on furlough. It was an answer to prayer for everyone involved. The cottage that they moved into was surrounded by fruit trees – guavas, pomegranates, grapes, custard apples, lemons – and all kinds of flowers. Dorothy thought it was especially lovely. Just outside the door was a frangipani bush that gave off an almost overpowering fragrance each evening. The weather in South India in November was pleasant – about 80 degrees in the daytime and around 62 degrees at night. The mosquitoes were bad but not as bad as in Silchar.

The cottage was small but adequate for Fred and Dorothy and Caryl when she came to Bangalore Dec. 6. The housesitting arrangement was nice because it would give them time to find a house, get furniture and fix it up before moving in.

Fred received a telegram from Ken saying that the ship with their freight had arrived in Calcutta so Fred took the train to Calcutta. At Madras he found out that the express train to Calcutta had been cancelled due to terrible floods that had hit Calcutta in October. The only other train was being diverted by a different route but it was jammed full and so Fred ended up flying to Calcutta.

All this traveling back and forth and living out of suitcases was quickly eating away at their funds. They needed to get settled soon. They had just about run out of time with their registration. Officials in Calcutta said that they should apply for a transfer immediately. Dorothy and Fred went to the office on November 10. One of the first questions the officer asked was whether Baptist Mid-Missions had any established work in Bangalore. Then he asked if the mission was recognized by New Delhi. Fred told him that they were registered under the Societies Act but the official said that wasn't enough and again asked if they were approved by the Government of India. Fred was told to submit a letter stating fully why they were asking for registration in Bangalore. The procedure could be a long, drawn out affair.

Special prayer was needed as it would only be of God if the residential permits were granted.

Fred and Dorothy continued to seek a place to live. They went to see the rent control officer with a single missionary worker from the Evangelical Nurses Fellowship. The officer was very friendly and suggested that they go see a house recently built by a relative of his. He telephoned and made an appointment for the next morning. The house was in Koramangala – an extension to the east of where they had previously looked. The house was nice and was in an area that would soon be building up.

The one who showed it to them suggested that they pay a friendly visit to the co-owner, a Mr. Albert Manoraj, the Inspector-General of Police – the highest police officer in the district. Mr. Manoraj was very friendly and wanted to know all about the Waldocks. He looked at their papers, which they had with them as they were on their way to submit them to the Foreign Registration Officer. Immediately Mr. Manoraj called the District Commissioner of Police and told him that the Waldocks were coming to see him and to send their papers through for registration!

Many of the Waldock's prayer warriors had written saying that they had been praying since Fred and Dorothy's Christmas letter and they felt the Lord was indeed answering those prayers. What was even more amazing was that Mr. Manoraj was retiring January 31 so the Lord arranged for him to use his influence on behalf of the Waldocks while he still maintained that position.

Fred and Dorothy desired to return to the United States for medical checkups and to raise additional support for work funds. They did not want to cut back on their contributions to the work in Assam but would need more funds to begin again in South India. But this mini-furlough was contingent on getting their residential permits for Bangalore. They planned to get a return visa, good for three months, rather than a 'No Objection to Return' permit. An added bonus was that they would be able to participate in Lois' June wedding.

Dorothy took Caryl back to Landour on January 29. They hoped they would get there before the birth of Ken and Mary's second child. They missed the January 31 arrival of Kenneth Mark by a few days.

The day Dorothy and Caryl left for Landour, Fred developed some peculiar symptoms – dizziness and near fainting. He was walking down a street and all of a sudden his vision became black and then objects started dancing around and he ended up in a cold sweat. Fred didn't tell Dorothy about the spell until later. After a couple of these spells happened in a period of about six weeks, Fred noticed that his left arm also felt numb. As the numbness increased he'd get a peculiar feeling of inner shakiness.

Fred went to the Southern Baptist hospital in Bangalore and they put him through a number of tests in view of his past history. They did a number of lab tests, an x-ray of the chest and head, an electrocardiogram, an EEC and a complete work over by a neurologist. Fred mentioned to the doctor that they had been planning to go back to the United States in June and he said that they should go before that. He also advised Fred to get a 'No Objection to Return' permit so that he could stay longer than three months in case his doctors advised prolonged treatment or surgery. When Fred told him that they needed to have their residential permits before they could get a NOR, the doctor wrote a letter for Fred to take to the officers concerned. It read, "Since 21 February, 1979, Mr. F. Waldock has been under my care for symptoms which indicate very poor circulation to the brain. This could be due to arteriosclerosis or to a cancerous tumor he had in 1973. He needs to return to his doctor in the States as soon as possible, as he could suffer a stroke at any time. Signed D.M. Ward, M.D. Head of Department of Medicine."

The doctor worded the note stronger than necessary so as to get action on their residential permits. Fred took this letter to some top officials in Bangalore who were quite sympathetic and the highest officials concerned pushed it right through. It was then sent to Delhi on March 17. The officials recommended that Fred go to Delhi to follow it up before it got buried on someone's desk.

Fred, Dorothy, Olive and Helen had a day of prayer on March 22 and Fred left on the train that night for Madras. The Lord undertook and he was able to get train reservations and so arrived in Delhi Sunday noon. The women met for prayer again on Monday morning.

Fred went to the office involved on Monday at 11 a.m. and within three minutes had the answer that the permits had been granted and sent back to Bangalore. Praise the Lord! Fred sent Dorothy a telegram with the news, which she received five hours later and he also sent a letter, which she received on Tuesday.

On Wednesday, Friday and Saturday afternoon Dorothy went to the Foreign Registration Office in Bangalore but no permits had arrived. She then went to the highest officer involved and he suggested that Fred try again in Delhi.

The residential permits were finally granted on April 5, 1979! Not only was this fantastic news for the Waldocks but it was also great news for the other BMM missionaries in India. Helen Sension and Olive Brittain would now be able to shift out of their ministry with Berean Baptist Bible College, where they had been on loan for the past six years. Doris Bruce, currently on furlough, would also have a place of ministry when she returned. This was indeed a miracle of God. Although Fred and Dorothy were concerned for Fred's health, they definitely believed that his medical problems were according to Romans 8:28: "And we know that all things work together for good to those who love God, to those who are the called according to His purpose."

There was encouragement in regards to ministry as well. Although the Waldocks had been told not to start a church planting work before receiving their residential permits, they could witness and teach on an informal basis. A brother of one of the Tamil students at the Northeast India Baptist Bible College in Silchar had been meeting with the Waldocks each Sunday afternoon after church. At the end of March Joshua put his faith in Christ as His personal Savior. Dorothy also started a class for ladies who worked for missionaries in the area. Most of the women were Roman Catholic and had had no previous Bible teaching. They were praying for true salvation to come to some of these ladies.

Brother Gilbert from the Home Office met with Fred and Jim Garlow in Calcutta after his trip to Bangladesh. They had time to meet together in a relaxed atmosphere, as there wasn't any urgency to hurry and get business finished. They were able to freely discuss things as they came to mind. There were many problems and difficulties in Assam – several key national leaders had quit. Fred's heart was heavy for his national brethren.

On Monday morning while Jim and Fred were taking care of some business, Fred had another one of his dizzy spells. He did manage to get some things done and get back to the hotel in time to catch his flight home. On the way in from the airport in Madras he had another one of the swirling black out spells. It lasted for about 20 minutes. He was able to get reservations to Bangalore and finally ended up on the night bus and got home about 7:30 the next morning. On good days he felt sort of dumb about the whole thing but when one of those spells hit, he knew that something wasn't right and that he needed to see his doctor at the University of Washington.

Fred and Dorothy left Bangalore on April 27 and went to Landour to pick up Caryl. She took a quarter's worth of work with her to do on her own so that she would be able to maintain her scholastic standing and enter the 10th grade in July. They arrived in Tacoma on May 5.

Both Fred and Caryl had medical checkups. The report for Caryl was good. She was fine despite the two surgeries in India. Fred's reports were inconclusive. Until the doctors could find the reason for the dizziness and near black out attacks, he was not allowed to drive.

Excitement was building for the wedding of Lois and Tim. It was wonderful to be there for the event. All of the family had the joy of helping her in the preparations. Fred had the special privilege of performing the wedding ceremony on June 30, 1979.

Verses in Daily Light for July 28 were a real encouragement to Fred and Dorothy – "We know not what we should pray for as we ought. He shall choose our inheritance for us." The Lord would open up just His right doors for them as they started an entirely new ministry in a new place.

Nothing significant was found in any of Fred's medical tests. The doctors started him on medication for migraines because of a familial history of the disease. The symptoms, which had been such a concern, subsided and by the end of July it was thought that no further treatment would be needed.

They shared with their Temple Baptist Church friends their tentative plans for the work upon returning to India. They wanted to open a Christian bookstore and start home Bible studies leading towards planting a church. Fred's administrative responsibilities would also consume a large part of their time. While on this mini-furlough they desired to raise more support for work funds and for the purchase of a vehicle. Using public transportation in Bangalore took a lot of time.

Fred had not been able to do as much deputation work as he had hoped because of the indefiniteness of the hospital appointments. Although he had hoped to raise additional funds for the new work in South India, they had actually lost some support. It had nothing to do with leaving Assam. Since their furlough in 1977, three churches and two elderly individual supporters had dropped their support. All told, they were down about $190 a month from where they had been just two years previously.

Fred and Dorothy left Tacoma for India on the morning of August 28, 1979. This would be the start of an entirely new chapter in their lives. The door to Assam was closed behind them but a new door into Bangalore, South India awaited them.

CHAPTER FIFTEEN
Starting Over

"Victory is not just at certain times but <u>always</u> in all circumstances in Christ. 'But thanks be to God, who always leads us in triumph in Christ, and manifests through us the sweet aroma of the knowledge of Him in every place.' (2 Corinthians 2:14)" – Fred Waldock, March 1982

They arrived in Delhi August 30, 1979. They had train reservations for Bangalore for the 6th of September so they spent a few days with Ken and Mary and Caryl in Landour.

Then they started their journey down to Bangalore, bringing Doris Bruce with them. They received their registration papers without any problem. Praise the Lord.

Monday afternoon the Waldocks and their three coworkers spent the afternoon in prayer and in discussing together their goals and plan of approach. More than anything, they desired God's plan for them as they started anew in Bangalore.

They spent three days house-hunting. They concentrated on a new area about six miles to the south and east of Bangalore. It was one of Bangalore's rapidly growing areas. They asked for prayer that God would direct them to the right area and to adequate living quarters. The price for houses was high and going higher all the time. Therefore, they planned to have Doris Bruce live with them and share the cost rent.

At the end of September they finalized a contract to rent a three-bedroom house in the extension called Koramangala, which was building up quickly. Fred and Dorothy wanted to be where the people would be. After seeing about 15 houses, it finally boiled down to just one. They felt it was adequate for their needs at present. In addition to the three bedrooms there was another small room that could be used for an office and guest room. There was a large front room and dining room combined. Fred and Dorothy felt that they would be able to seat about 50 in that room, which would be good for meetings.

The rent was $200 a month. This was more than they wanted to pay but Bangalore was more expensive than Silchar. The practice in Bangalore was that the equivalent of ten months rent must be paid as a deposit, refundable when the renter left.

It was a brand new house. In fact, it would not be completed until November 1. Fred and Dorothy had the privilege of choosing paint colors and the design of shelves. The landlord was a young government officer, a deputy secretary for the state of Karnataka. He and his wife were pleasant people and Fred and Dorothy thought that they would be easy to deal with.

The Lord was so good to provide for their needs until the house would be ready. The guesthouse that they were staying at was only available for one month. However the Lord provided a place for them in the interim. A missionary nurse that they had met earlier invited them to use her house for free for the month of October, as she would be away in the extreme south of India for the entire month.

Even before they moved into their new house, Fred and Dorothy began to lay the foundation for ministry. They started Bible studies and a literature ministry. One great need was for a vehicle – they felt they were spending too many hours waiting for public transportation.

The second week of October Fred and Dorothy went out to see the house. Looking at it they had to pray in faith that it would actually be done by November 1. The walls had yet to be painted and the electrical fittings, door moldings and cabinet shelves still needed to be installed. It was discouraging. The missionary nurse who had loaned them a house would be back on November 2 so they would not be able to extend their time there. In faith, they went to furniture dealers, hunting for used furniture suitable for their house and budget.

The house was not ready on November 1; so Fred and Dorothy made a trip to Madras to see about making arrangements to order books for their proposed bookroom. It would be much closer than ordering books through Assam.

They finally moved into their new home on November 16, even though it still wasn't completely ready. It was a big job moving in and unpacking and getting things in order. They were able to find much of the furniture they needed through auctions. They did have to buy a new refrigerator. It had cost more than they had hoped. They had tried for two months to find a used one for sale but there just weren't any. By this time they had exhausted almost all of the funds they had received from the sale of their things in Silchar.

They enjoyed it immensely whenever they received word from Assam. About that time Gobin and Urirei left the work in Silchar to claim an inheritance, since Gobin's father and uncle had both died. Gobin's eldest sister, who was still a Hindu, was the only one who cared for Gobin. She advised him to move back home immediately or else the other relatives would take all the property that rightfully belonged to him as the only son. The village of Lahkipur was a completely Manipuri Hindu village. Gobin and Urirei wanted to represent Christ there.

The India Field Council meetings were held in Bangalore January 4-7, 1980. Brother Gilbert and Brother Joel Kettenring came out to India from the Home Office for the meetings. Brother Gilbert was retiring and Brother Kettenring was to be his successor. There was some good-natured ribbing going on during the conference. At the conference they discussed the possibility of developing an extension seminary of Northwest Baptist Seminary of Tacoma, WA there in Bangalore to provide upper level theological training for Indian nationals from Assam and elsewhere in India. Ken wrote to Dr. Herman Austel at the seminary to inquire as to whether they would be willing to get such a program underway. It was also agreed that they would move the registered office of Baptist Mid-Missions to Bangalore. Fred remained the Field Council president and Dorothy again took over the position of treasurer.

Although Ken and Mary realized that they had an important responsibility running the MK hostel, they were anxious to be involved in a ministry of Bible teaching. If the extension seminary got underway, perhaps Ken and Mary would be allowed to transfer to Bangalore.

A great delight to Fred and Dorothy was a change of heart in Caryl. For a year and a half she had been going through a time of rebellion. But early in February, Dorothy and Fred had a wonderful opportunity to talk with her. She completely broke and wept and asked her parents and her Lord for forgiveness. The last three weeks of her school break she was a different girl.

In March, with the help of six Bible college students the missionary team visited around 400 houses with personal invitations and Bible study courses. The 16th of March they held their first Sunday morning service in their house with 23 in attendance. Soon they were averaging around 34 people and seeing new faces every week. Ten to twelve came to Wednesday evening Bible study and prayer meeting. They had two families coming as well as several couples. A few were born-again but most were nominal Christians. Fred and Dorothy were blessed and challenged by the apparent hunger to hear the truth of the Word.

By March they had received Dr. Austel's reply. Northwest Baptist Seminary would like to start the program by 1981 or 1982 at the latest. They would give a Masters of Arts in Biblical Studies degree. It was suggested that it be a three-year program with at least two professors coming out to India for three months each summer. That would give the students 36 hours with 12 hours of directed studies. Fred felt that the extension seminary would be much better than sending nationals abroad for training. He felt it had much potential and it gave Fred more hope for staffing the Northeast India Baptist Bible College in Assam in the future.

In the providence of God, He had a special encouragement for Ken and Mary in Landour. Caryl took her stand for Christ as soon as she returned to school and the Lord gave her great victory. Shortly after that two other MKs came back to the Lord. The kids started a prayer meeting during the school lunch hour. The MKs were excited that they were having opportunity to witness to other young people. They had a very fruitful Bible Club retreat. Some kids were saved and a number got right with the Lord.

The change in the devotional time at the hostel was incredible. The girls didn't want to stop asking questions and sharing. Ken would have to stop them so that they could get to their studies. Praise the Lord. It was a real answer to prayer for Fred and Dorothy.

The last two weeks of April Fred and Dorothy helped with a Vacation Bible School in Wilson Gardens where they had been having a Bible hour for about 50 children every Sunday afternoon. They had around 45 Beginners and Primaries for the first week of Vacation Bible School and around 65 Juniors and Teens the second week. During the week one lovely little 8-year-old girl from a Hindu home came and asked to accept Christ as her Savior. They took five young people from their Koramangala group the second week and four of them eagerly made a personal decision for the Lord. They asked prayer for the fifth one – a 13-year-old girl who admitted that she was still unsaved.

Since Good Friday of 1980 the services were running more than 30 people. Fred and Dorothy praised the Lord for the continued interest. Fred estimated that about 70 people had come at one time or another in the seven weeks since they had started services.

In June they added Sunday school classes for four different age levels. Most of those who were coming were nominal Christians from liberal churches. They were happy to have church services locally rather than have to go so far into town. But most important, people were opening up their hearts to the truth of the Word, which many had not been taught before.

Caryl came down to Bangalore for her month break between school years. In years past the Waldocks had always gone up to Landour for this month, but with the services just getting going so nicely it seemed better to bring Caryl down to Bangalore. Bangalore was much cooler than Assam because it was located at 3,000 feet above sea level. April and May were the two hottest months when the temperature went up to about 95 degrees. In June the rainy season began and the temperature usually dropped to the low 80s. On the coldest winter night the temperature would not be below 60 degrees. Because of the temperate climate, flowers bloomed all the time. Also fresh fruits were readily available. The Waldocks were quite proud of their papaya tree –

within ten months of planting the seed it bore more than 100 papayas! The greatest difficulties in living in Bangalore were mosquitoes and transportation.

Buses went by their house but they were crowded beyond description and seldom on a predictable schedule. Sometimes Fred or Dorothy would have to wait for an hour to get a bus for town and then hardly be able to get on the bus for the crowd that had been waiting.

For months the Waldocks had been saving for the purchase of a van. Fred had purchased a motorcycle over the summer. Then in the early fall, a missionary that was going on furlough for a year gave the Waldocks the use of his car. What a tremendous provision! In India, a buyer had to have the full price of the vehicle (about $10,000 for a diesel van) before being able to place the order.

Ken and Mary celebrated the birth of a baby girl, Jeannette, on December 9. Ten days later the family came to Bangalore for their Christmas vacation. On New Year's Eve they had a testimony time with several giving testimony of the Lord's blessings in the past year. Fred and Dorothy had seen wonderful changes in the lives and relationships of many and it was so uplifting to hear these personal testimonies.

The Waldocks' prayer and goal for the coming year was to bring each one in their congregation into a fully surrendered relationship to the Lord. They believed, "If He is not LORD of ALL, He cannot be LORD at ALL."

The first Sunday in 1981 they added an evening service. They now had six Sunday school classes, using three bedrooms, the garage, living room and kitchen. One class was in the Tamil language and the rest were in English. They were running 45-50 in Sunday school. Each week the living and dining room area was converted to a meeting room. The dining room table went out the front entrance and was used as a registration and book table.

The annual conference that spring had the theme of "Triumph Amidst Turmoil." Five of the national leaders were invited including Sambhu Dey, Sana Singh and Promode Malakar. Fred rejoiced in the reunion and the blessing it was to sit together in conference with these leaders after three years. There was very good, frank, and open participation in all the sessions. It took the better part of three days to hear and discuss the reports from the various ministries in Assam. With only three BMM missionaries still in Assam, the work and ministries were reviewed in a more frank and realistic manner from the standpoint of the national workers. Fred counseled and prayed with the national workers till after midnight every night.

They held two Vacation Bible Schools in April and May – one in Wilson Gardens and for the first time, one in Koramangala. Many of their regular Sunday school children were away on vacation that week so more than half of the 40 registered children were new. A number of them came back for Sunday school. As far as they knew, four accepted the Lord. One of those saved was a young man, Peter, who dropped in on the third day of VBS with a neighbor boy who had been coming. He continued to come the rest of the week and accepted the Lord. Peter came from a liberal Christian background and his wife of four months was a Roman Catholic. The VBS at Koramangala was well attended. By the start of the closing program there were over 100 children sitting on the floor and about 50 adults standing and sitting behind. Fred and Dorothy realized that they would not be able to hold another program in the house. There just wasn't enough room for the children to perform.

The following Sunday Peter brought his wife, Deborah, to the services and after a few weeks she also accepted the Lord! They both eagerly began to learn the Word and desired to be baptized. They were very concerned for the salvation of their parents, brothers and sisters.

After the two Vacation Bible Schools, Fred, Dorothy and Ken conducted a family camp at a Boy Scout camp about 25 miles from Bangalore. Even though the group was small they felt it was very profitable both for the few married couples and especially for the 'young hopefuls'. Biblical teaching on family relationships cut hard across much of the tradition and customs of even Christian families in India.

The Bangalore missionaries pooled their resources and were finally able to afford a nine-passenger 1976 Matador Diesel van for the ministry. The Waldocks insisted that it could carry 20 people or more quite comfortably. It was good timing as the owner of the vehicle that they had been borrowing would soon be returning and there were some repairs on his vehicle that needed to be done.

During the middle of June Fred and Dorothy traveled up to Landour to spend Caryl's vacation time with her and to help Ken and Mary pack up to move to Bangalore. When they went through Delhi the temperature was 116 degrees! There were only two BMM missionary children remaining at Woodstock so Doris Bruce volunteered to fill in at the hostel for a few months so that Ken and Mary could move to Bangalore. It seemed best for them to transfer to Bangalore a year or so before going on furlough to enable them to get their No Objection to Return permits from there. Fred and Dorothy would need them to take over the work in Bangalore when they went on furlough next year after Caryl's graduation from Woodstock. They were praying much that the government would transfer Ken and Mary's residence.

In September 1981 the elder Waldocks were notified that they needed to vacate their house by December 1 as their landlord wanted to live there. So less than two years since moving in, they were back to house hunting. In November, they finally found a place that would be suitable. The new place had a large living-dining room area that would seat more than 70 people with an overflow space on the veranda for another 20. It was a little way off the main road but they thought that might prove to be a blessing. The traffic in front of their old house had increased so much that it had become increasingly difficult to hear during services. They moved into the house on Thanksgiving Day; then made pumpkin pies and had a Thanksgiving fellowship service Friday night with 42 people joining them.

Caryl and Doris Bruce arrived December 10 and pitched in to help with the Christmas program preparations. Christmas week was more than full with caroling. The custom seemed to be that the carolers should visit the home of each adult and child that came to any of the Bible clubs or services. Two different groups of carolers went out for six nights and visited more than 100 homes in Koramangala and Wilson Gardens.

Tuesday, December 22 they had their own traditional American Christmas dinner with six missionaries, four MKs and Mary's Mom and Dad. Three fat hens were a delicious substitute for turkey. Thanks to parcels that had arrived during the year, they even had cranberries and mincemeat pie. Bangalore, unlike Assam, had no lack of fresh vegetables so the 'poor, deprived missionaries' feasted and rejoiced in the goodness of the Lord to them in this past year.

In the spring of 1982 Fred began a series of sermons entitled, "Life on a Higher Plane." In a sermon preached on March 21, 1982 Fred spoke on the necessity of a yielded life. *"As the hymn writer put it, 'Lord take my all, the gift is small. For Thee, for Thee Thy sacrifice has paid the price for me, for me.' That is yielding. That is full surrender. What causes that decision? A new understanding and dimension of love has possessed you which results in full surrender to Christ's rightful claim upon your life. Fully yielded. Completely Christ's by right of creation and purchase. Because I am His, I yield to Him. He has the title deed to my life. I am His property. I'm not my own. I am a redeemed one. Realizing this and yielding to His claim and call, I move out and He moves in.*

"Listen, Christ could just take over but He won't do that. He wants us to voluntarily relinquish that which is not my own but is rightfully His. In Romans 12:1 we read, 'I beseech you, therefore, brethren, by the mercies of God that ye present your bodies a living sacrifice, holy, acceptable unto God, which is your reasonable service."

Fred and Dorothy left Bangalore May 24 to join Caryl in Landour for her last concerts and programs and the graduation ceremony. For 24 years, Fred and Dorothy had children at Woodstock; now that was finally coming to an end.

Just before they left India, they received word from Ken and Mary that their residential permits for Bangalore had been granted! Praise to the Almighty God who makes a way for His servants.

Fred was able to get a good deal in tickets so that the three of them could see a bit of Europe on their way back to the United States. From Delhi they flew to Amsterdam. From Amsterdam they were able to visit Fred's aunt in London and Baptist Mid-Mission stations in Munich and Paris. They also spent some time in Switzerland with friends before flying from Amsterdam to New York.

While the Waldocks traveled throughout Europe, the first session of the Northwest Baptist Seminary extension in India got underway with 24 students. The majority of the students were from the Waldocks' previous work in Assam. The first two professors to come out to India were Dr. Phil Williams and Dr. Elvin K. Mattison. Ken, as the director of the extension seminary, would supervise the directed studies that the students would do in between summer sessions.

Dave met his parents and sister at the airport in New York and took them to his home in New Jersey for about 10 days. There they were also able to visit with Hedley, and their stepmother, Ruby.

They made the trip west in a VW camper and arrived in Tacoma the first week of August. Fred made a deputation trip to California. Several people made gifts toward the press that was soon to be delivered to the work in Assam. The cost for the press had been $50,000 and about $10,000 of that was still needed.

In September the Waldocks were able to have dinner with Dr. Williams who had gone out to India to teach. The folks at Northwest Baptist Seminary were thrilled with the results of the first seminary extension in India. Dr. Williams showed some slides and a good portion of the dinner conversation centered around the extension seminary.

By November all the funds had come in for the press! The Christian Literature House Society took delivery of the machine in December. Around 40 manuscripts in the languages of Northeast India were waiting in Silchar to be printed.

Fred and Dorothy left Tacoma on January 20, 1983 for a very lengthy deputation trip. They left Tacoma, not in fear, but with some apprehension, realizing that they would be traveling through winter, spring and summer conditions. Packing to be prepared for all kinds of weather was some job. They committed the entire itinerary to the Lord and many of their friends also faithfully prayed. Fred believed that the timing and dates of this itinerary were programmed in Heaven. They claimed the promise of Psalm 121:8 "The Lord shall preserve thy going out and thy coming in from this time forth, and even for evermore."

As part of their itinerary they participated in the Baptist Mid-Missions Triannual conference in Des Moines, IA in March where they were awarded service pins in recognition of 35 years of ministry. At the conference Fred gave a report on India to the General Council as well as served as a missionary representative to that body. Their travels took them to churches in Idaho, Texas, Tennessee, North Carolina, Florida, New Jersey, Connecticut, Ohio, Iowa, Ontario, Montana and back to Tacoma. The entire trip put 12,310 miles on their little Escort. It was simply wonderful the way that the Lord looked out for them. Several times they just missed severe weather. They never had to cancel a meeting and were never delayed due to weather or any other reason. Many meetings were added to their already full schedule. They praised the Lord for the precious fellowship that they had in churches and especially in so many homes. Often, without getting up from the supper table, they talked missions until midnight. They trusted that the Lord touched many lives and that many more people would be praying for the needs of India.

Dorothy took opportunities for ladies meetings. She was transparent about the difficulties and struggles that missionaries face and the constant need for prayer. She spoke about the need to pray that missionaries would be able to work together despite dissimilar personalities and ways of doing things and that missionaries would be able to carry on despite the uncertainties of permits and government regulations. She talked about committing schedules to the Lord. Taking John 10:7-14 for her text she said, "*I am the door – by me if any man enter in He shall be saved. He shall go in and out and find green pastures. Go in for refreshing and renewal – out for service – to face the battles of life, the storms, the frustrations. You can't stay in the sheepfold all day. You have to go outside to find the pastures. And there is where the dangers lurk, where the enemy can strike at any time, where a sudden storm can blow up. He shall find pasture – the place of refreshing, nourishment, renewal of energy. Outside the sheepfold. Even safety because He never sends the sheep out to find the good pasture. He goes before His sheep; He leads them out with His staff in His hand, to protect, to guide, and to grab them when they start to fall.*

He takes them to the good pasture, the still waters where they can enjoy drinking and stands guard over them while they eat and grow and mature to the place where they will be profitable for their owner. If we battle the storms of life continually without resorting to the nourishment and rest all along the way – the kind that only comes from the Lord – we are temperamental, crotchety, hard to get along with and not much value to our Master."

On Saturday, May 7, 1983 at the Los Angeles Baptist College commencement exercises, the honorary degree of Doctor of Divinity was conferred on Fred. The degree was conferred in recognition of thirty-five years of faithful and sacrificial missionary service in the land of India. Joel Kettenring wrote his congratulations from Cleveland, *"Let me congratulate you on receiving your honorary Doctor of Divinity degree from Los Angeles Baptist Bible College. I am convinced it is an honor you well deserve and rejoice in the Lord with you for the bestowal of this honor. We do recognize that whatever has been accomplished through our lives and ministry has been of the Lord, but I believe this recognition for you is well deserved and is likewise glorifying to the Lord. May the Lord through this even make you a greater instrument in His service."*

The Waldocks received their return visas. On May 29th Fred spoke at Temple Baptist and shared their hopes and dreams for their next term of service in India. The congregation gave a love offering of $1,300 to help them with the expenses of returning. The Waldocks were so appreciative of the financial and prayer support of their beloved home church for more than three decades.

The Lord gave them a verse as they were preparing to return to India. Isaiah 42:9-10: "Behold, the former things are come to pass, and new things do I declare. Before they spring forth I tell you of them. Sing unto the Lord a new song and His praise to the end of the earth."

Fred shared this verse with the people of Temple Baptist, *"It is our prayer that each and every one of us will be able to testify to its reality in our lives not only down the road somewhere but daily as we claim it by faith."*

God was good to let them be with Lois for the birth of Kristi Lynn on June 10 – a week early. On Saturday night, June 18, 1983, around 40 relatives and friends gathered at the airport to see Fred and Dorothy off for another term of service. For the first time, they were leaving all of their children behind in the States.

Fred spoke in two different churches in Honolulu on the 19th after arriving on the island at 3 a.m. From there they flew to Singapore arriving in the wee hours of the morning. From Singapore they flew to Madras where Ken and Nathan met them. They had a five-hour layover in Madras so there was ample time for Ken to update his dad on all that had transpired. They reached Bangalore on the 23rd.   The church was ready to be organized and the future looked bright. It was with great joy and anticipation that they looked forward to what God would have for them in the term to come.

CHAPTER SIXTEEN
The Fruit of Faithfulness

"Many years ago the Lord gave this verse to Dorothy, 'Faithful is He that calleth you who also will do it.' (1 Thessalonians 5:24) Many, many times the Lord has blessed, challenged and comforted our hearts down through the years with this verse. How faithful He is! And He is the same yesterday, today and forever the Faithful One. What wonderful things He has done! And what great and wonderful things He is still going to do and wants to do with us and through us! It also demands our faithfulness to Him." – Fred Waldock, August 1984.

Fred and Dorothy had a delightful welcome back to Bangalore. The night after they returned a formal recognition service for the organization of Bethel Baptist Church of Koramangala took place. The new church had 14 charter members.

Ken and Mary and family and Doris Bruce left for furlough on Monday – just four days after Fred and Dorothy's arrival. The week following Fred and Dorothy tried to adjust and get going again.

On July 7, 1983 the Norm Benson family arrived in Bangalore in preparation for the second session of the Northwest Baptist Seminary Extension in India. Professor Benson was thrilled to be in India and wanted to learn and see and be a part of all that he could during his six weeks in the country. Dr. Miller and his family also arrived in Bangalore, eager to be used of God in training men and women for ministry.

The plane out of Silchar, which was to bring students for the extension seminary, was canceled. It was uncertain when the students would be able to come. But, in time, the seminary got underway. Twenty-one students from the previous year returned enthused and excited to again dig into the Word of God. Four new students very quickly integrated themselves into the student body. Fred and Dorothy were praising the Lord for this opportunity for these national brethren to have this advanced theological training to enhance their ministry as pastors and Christian workers. Many of the students who came were already in full-time service for the Lord – seven as pastors or assistant pastors, some as youth directors in their churches, three as teachers from their Bible college in Assam. One woman was in charge of all the women's work in the association of churches in her area. She walked through the jungle for three days before she could get a bus to travel another three days. Then she went by plane to Calcutta and another two days on two different trains to arrive in Bangalore. Her people were so hungry to get the true teaching of the Word.

Fred was pleased with how the students from such varied backgrounds got along. Despite their varied customs and diets, they all sat down at the same table and ate the same food without complaint.

Although the style of teaching was different than what the students were accustomed to, the inductive method was showing some very positive results. The traditional Indian way was to diligently study what other people thought and then summarize those findings. At the extension seminary they were challenged to wrestle with the Scriptures and come to their own convictions based on what the Scriptures said. Controversial opinions were raised and the resulting deep discussions did much to sharpen the students' convictions. As Fred mingled with the students during their out-of-classroom time, their feedback made him envious to join them. Fred rejoiced in their growth and maturity. There was much evidence that assured the missionaries that God was in this program.

Since returning to Bangalore, Fred and Dorothy were getting "claustrophobia". The living room of their house, which they had thought was so roomy and adequate, was getting cramped during Sunday services. They commented, *"It is a GOOD – but desperate feeling, especially on special occasions when you try to crowd everyone in comfortably. Our goal for the near future will have to be, as we mentioned while home, a multi-purpose building, with sufficient room for services and the Christian Literature House on the ground floor and two apartments for living quarters on the second floor. Please pray with us regarding this."*

For two months the work in Bangalore was buffeted by illness and injury. A viral flu hit many of the congregation. Three of the lady missionaries spent time in the hospital, one for major surgery. One family man had a serious accident and was off from work for a month and a half. His son broke his arm. Another young man had surgery. With so many down, Fred and Dorothy felt as though they were just marking time. It wasn't until the end of November that things began to get back to normal.

As always, much effort was invested in the Christmas programs of Bethel Baptist Church. Christmas was a time to reach those who might not come to regular services and Fred and Dorothy continually redeemed the opportunity.

A wedding rounded out the festivities. Sambhu Dey married Molly Kuruvilla, one of their faithful workers in Bangalore. She had worked with Helen and Olive for about eight years. Sambhu and Molly were recommended for higher-level training at Northwest Baptist Seminary in Tacoma in preparation for teaching at Northeast India Baptist Bible College. Sambhu would eventually assume the position of principal at NEIBBC.

The first week of April 1984 Fred was experiencing pain in the leg where he'd had melanoma surgery ten and a half years before. Upon investigation, he discovered a lump. He consulted two doctors in Bangalore who agreed that it should be taken care of right away. Sunday, April 15, after the morning service he took the train to the Christian Medical Hospital in Vellore for an appointment Monday morning. The diagnosis was that the melanoma had reoccurred.

Fred made immediate plans to return to Seattle and his doctors at the University of Washington. Friends encouraged him with Genesis 28:15: "I am with thee, and I will keep thee in all places...and will bring thee again into this land..." Within an unprecedented time – three days – he had his necessary permits and airline booking and by Friday was home in the United States. Bethel Baptist Church, by this time, had an assistant pastor who could carry on with the ministry.

The following Monday Fred was at the hospital and was scheduled for surgery in a week and a half. Dorothy came from India to be with Fred. When they did surgery, they confirmed that the melanoma had returned. One of the two tumors was attached to the main nerve in the thigh. This had caused the pain that had alerted Fred to the existence of the tumor. He praised the Lord for that. The surgeon was afraid that there would be weakness in the leg because it had been necessary to cut the nerve sheath to remove the tumor. However, the Lord intervened and Fred had full strength in that leg. Praise the Lord!

Although the surgeon thought that he had been able to remove all the cancer, they decided to do radiation therapy just in case. The radiation treatment was five days a week for six weeks. In addition they gave hyperthermia (microwave) treatment for 35 minutes once a week. This was a new treatment that they were finding to be very effective against melanoma. Yet, the doctors could not say whether the cancer would reoccur or not.

On May 25th an infection developed in Fred's leg at the site of the surgery and radiation treatment. On Tuesday, May 29, his surgeon admitted him to the hospital and operated to open the wound and to establish drainage. The tissues checked out normal so it was just a matter of time to heal again before the radiation could be continued. He was in the hospital until May 31. They requested prayer, as Fred had hoped to be back in India in time for the extension seminary the first week in July. Unfortunately, the infection delayed the completion of the radiation therapy and Dorothy returned to India on June 14 without Fred. Ken, Mary and family flew back to India on June 18, just a few days before the third summer session of the extension seminary. Dr. Austel, dean of Northwest Baptist Seminary, and Dr. Mattison of NBS spent six weeks teaching. On August 17, Dr. Austel conferred the Master of Arts in Biblical Studies degree on sixteen graduates. The Waldocks were thrilled and praised God for the success of the program. They anticipated rich and lasting fruit as it continued.

It was September 8 before Fred could return to Bangalore. His leg was quite raw and weepy looking up until the day he was to leave. He wondered how he would be able to sit so long on the plane. But just the day he left, it completely dried up, and except for the first day in Bangalore, he didn't have to have a bandage on it. By the end of September it was finally completely healed over.

The church continued to grow. By the end of September there were 82 in Sunday school and 62 in the morning service. They started two new Sunday school classes, one for Tamil-speaking children that met in the garage and one for Senior High school students that met at a neighbor's house. They were praying that a number of those who were attending the services regularly would withdraw their membership from liberal churches and join with them, knowing that only the Lord could give them the conviction and courage to do that.

In October they began to gather *daily* for prayer at 8 a.m. Usually six to eight came and they sensed the Lord really working in lives. They began a children's church ministry to make more room in the living room for adults.

Six of their active members went on to other ministries – two were teaching in the Bible College in Silchar and two were studying there. Molly Dey was with her husband, Sambhu, at Northwest Baptist Seminary in Tacoma. The sixth one was a laboratory technician working in Saudi Arabia. There were new members' classes being held, however, and they expected another six or eight to join soon.

In November Fred and Dorothy made a trip to Delhi to request permits to enter Assam for the occasion of the Silver Jubilee of the Fellowship of Baptist Churches. The Assam representatives in government were very friendly and helpful. They said that they would put in their recommendations for the Waldocks. However, the Minister of Home Affairs would make the final decision. This was a very difficult time in India with continued tension following the assassination of Mrs. Gandhi and preparations for elections to be held at Christmas time.

The Jubilee celebration was to be January 10-13, 1985. Fred and Dorothy knew that the Lord could move the hearts of kings if it was His will for them to go. They prayed earnestly to this end.

Fred wrote his personal goals for 1985, *"My major prayers and concern for 1985 is that I will be all that God wants me to be in these last years on the field to do my utmost to build up Bethel Baptist Church into a strong indigenous Baptist Church that will reach out in evangelism in this and other areas.*

Secondly, I feel keenly the responsibility to continue to pray and work for the 'continuing on' of the work of BMM in Northeast India under national leadership."

Fred and Dorothy prayed much about the granting of their permits to visit Assam but still they heard no word. Brother Promode spent three days in the capitol of Assam trying to get the permits approved. On Saturday night, January 5, he called the Waldocks and told them to proceed to Calcutta as the government had given approval to grant the permits.

Accordingly, Fred and Dorothy went to Calcutta. But when they went to pick up the permits the officer in charge said that he could not grant them without a confirmation from Delhi. A wireless message was sent to Delhi. Fred phoned a government official friend to have him check into it but by January 11 Fred still had no reply.

Fred and Dorothy had been to Delhi several times and had been assured that Delhi would grant the permits immediately if the Assam government had approved. Yet, the permits were not granted before the completion of the Silver Jubilee Celebration and Fred and Dorothy returned to Bangalore very disappointed.

The permits came through three weeks later but an even greater blow was before them. It appeared that the cancer had come back. This happened just as they were preparing for a special Spiritual Life Conference with their national representatives from the ministries in Assam and with their Field Administrators from the Home Office. They had been planning this conference for two years and were looking forward to fellowshipping with some that they had not seen since leaving Assam in June 1978.

But they knew that it was the Lord's will for Fred to fly back to Seattle for further assessment and treatment as advised by the Cancer Research Center in India. The Lord gave wonderful grace and peace as Fred flew home February 8, 1985.

Fred arrived in Seattle just before noon and was met by his family and friends. Preliminary studies were done at the University of Washington hospital that same afternoon. A full CAT scan was done on the 11th that showed no sign of metastasis whatsoever. Praise the Lord. The areas of doubt and suspicion were most probably due to the aftereffects of the radiation. 1

Peter 1:3-7 was a special comfort to Fred during these days. "Blessed be the God and Father of our Lord Jesus Christ, which according to his abundant mercy hath begotten us again unto a lively hope by the resurrection of Jesus Christ from the dead, to an inheritance incorruptible, and undefiled, and that fadeth not away, reserved in heaven for you, who are kept by the power of God through faith unto salvation ready to be revealed in the last time. Wherein ye greatly rejoice, though now for a season, if need be, ye are in heaviness through manifold temptations: that the trial of your faith, being much more precious than of gold that perisheth, though it be tried with fire, might be found unto praise and honour and glory at the appearing of Jesus Christ."

All the arrangements had been made for the special conference in India so Ken took over and filled in capably for Fred. Ken was very happy to meet some he remembered from his growing up days in Assam. They, in turn, were now able to meet his wife and family. Fifteen delegates from the work in Assam came and shared their heartaches and hopes for the work there. Dorothy wrote, *"The problems seem insurmountable in the natural but we know that nothing can be solved in the natural when you are doing the Lord's work and we are driven to His throne for wisdom and help in time of need."*

The annual Field Missionary Conference followed the Spiritual Life Conference. Soon after, Dorothy's sister Florence arrived from Canada with a nurse friend and they all had a good time visiting some tourist attractions first in Bangalore and then around Delhi.

On Sunday, Feb. 17, Fred and the congregation of Temple Baptist Church had a blessed day of praise and thanksgiving. Many tears of love and praise were shed. An offering was taken to help with the expenses of getting Fred back to India.

After her guests left, Dorothy met Fred in Calcutta. Together, they were able to take advantage of the permits to Assam and did a whirlwind visit for six days. Fred spoke nine times in churches, the Bible College, board meetings, et cetera and Dorothy spoke three times. The financial burdens were heavy upon the national workers now that all the missionaries had been forced to leave. The financial concerns had also affected the spiritual ministries in some measure.

It was a great joy to visit with loved ones and their families after nearly seven years. The permit did not include the Makunda Leprosy Colony as that area was now under a new district. As they returned to Bangalore, their burdens for the work in Assam were renewed and increased.

The week after Easter they held a Vacation Bible School. There were about 45 children attending, some of whom were Hindu neighbors of Ken and Mary. One girl accepted Christ as her Savior. The Waldocks had a few days to recoup and then they plunged into a very busy week at youth camp the first week of May. There were some decisions made to follow the Lord more closely and to put the Lord first, even before family. This is a very difficult decision in the Indian culture. However, they were concerned about a growing spiritual apathy on the part of some in Bethel Baptist Church.

Fred and Dorothy wrote, *"Even though our living conditions are much easier here, the work seems more difficult. Education, materialism and financial success are more important than faithful attendance to the things of the Lord. And now along with more educational advantages the extracurricular activities have multiplied, taking the thoughts and time of those who previously attended the services. We are not seeing solid church growth. A life of real dedication and surrender to the Lord for His will is seldom seen. We cry to the Lord for the working of His Spirit in using the Word to bring conviction."*

The extension seminary program was not as large as years past. Only 11 students were instructed by Professors Norm Benson and David Gower. Many students had graduated from the program the year before; also some of those that they thought might be attending dropped out.

The church in Koramangala was involved with mothering a small church plant about two hours from Bangalore in an area called the Kolar Gold Fields. This church, Immanuel Baptist Church, had been started by one of their members a couple of years before and was officially organized as a church in 1985. That man felt the Lord leading him to another area and the church was without a pastor for a time. People from Bethel Baptist filled the pulpit and prayed for a new pastor. The Lord answered their specific request and supplied a Tamilian couple as pastor and wife.

The people who worked in the mines were poor and could not fully support a pastor, so Bethel Baptist Church was helping with the salary of the pastor and also in getting the new man and his family moved out to the Kolar Gold Mines. One need of the pastor and his wife was transportation so that they could go visiting in that spread out area. By faith Bethel Baptist Church undertook the challenge to provide a bicycle for the couple. There was great excitement in the Sunday school about the project, with each class pledging to pay for a certain part of the bicycle. It was a real step of growth for the church, which was still not very big, to help out a daughter church in this way. In addition to the bike, enough was given to help purchase hymnbooks, benches and other necessary supplies.

Fred had been praying for revival in their work for a long time. He was asking the Lord to show him areas in his own life and service that might be blocking the Holy Spirit and hindering a revival. Fred felt that he had only a few more years on the field as he anticipated turning 64 on January 23, 1986. He yearned for the Lord to make these last few years mightily blessed of Him.

Dorothy's goals for the new year were similar. She wanted to pray even more *"for more power in our ministry for the Lord to bring real conviction as the Word is preached and taught to the believers as well as the non-Christians who sit in our services."* Many who came regularly were professing Christians but had been born into a Christian family and had no real experience of salvation. Very few of their young people were wholly dedicated to the Lord. *"We long to see the power of God and His Word unto definite decisions for salvation and dedication of lives. We pray for young people we can disciple and train in the church work."*

Fred arranged a meeting with seven representatives from the ministries in Assam at the Lee Memorial Mission in Calcutta in January 1986 because he was so burdened for the situation there. Some of the leaders had personal grievances and they seemed to be at a low spiritual ebb. The financial problems in the Assam ministries were a huge concern.

Fred wrote, *"I felt that it [the meeting] was essential and that time should be given to prayer and waiting upon the Lord. I purposely did not go with a fixed agenda nor with a series of set messages and neither did I request others to do so. I felt we had to seek the face of the Lord and give time to let Him work. I did not want to rush into such a meeting to listen to a long list of grievances and complaints and then come to some, perhaps, hasty conclusions. The Lord certainly seemed to be leading along this line."*

Quite naturally the sessions began on a somewhat subdued and guarded note. Fred began the first meeting with an extended time of simply sharing blessings of God in their lives and ministries over the recent months. This was followed by a time of earnest prayer. Fred felt the working of the Spirit from the very first session. They met again in the evening and began with somewhat the same pattern. Fred asked Ken to be ready to bring a message from Nehemiah that he had recently preached at Bethel Baptist Church if the Lord seemed to lead in that direction. That message fit so beautifully into their situation and need. The next morning they again had a time of meditation particularly thinking on the greatness and goodness of their God. After a season of prayer, Fred spoke on "Renewal". The Lord prepared them for the discussions that followed.

After that they again engaged in a precious time of prayer. God's presence was felt. Hearts were examined and at one particular moment there was not a dry eye in their midst. It was not prompted by a message or any particular remarks. It was purely a work of the Spirit of God.

After the meeting, Fred met Dorothy in Madras so that they could give Isabelle Swanson a proper send off. Miss Swanson was retiring after serving 36 years in India. The Annual Field Conference was held with only eight remaining missionaries. What a change from earlier days when BMM had over 35 personnel on the field. The winds of a new policy further restricting foreign missionaries were wafting in the air. When Ken traveled to Bangkok, Thailand in October and tried to get a permit to leave India and a return visa, he had been interrogated by a high officer concerning his status as a missionary and of Baptist Mid-Missions in India. The official had said that all missionaries would be gone within a year. (As it turned out, that official left first. He had been badmouthing his superiors which resulted in his transfer to another area.) Now it had been reported that only missions approved by the National Christian Council of Churches would receive renewal of their yearly permits. Fred's permit was due that month and the others would be applied for in May and June, so they would soon see how far this policy would be carried out. Dorothy's renewal had been applied for in June 1985. They were still waiting for a response ten months later.

Fred wrote, *"You can realize that this stirs up a multitude of thoughts in our minds. There is much to take care of. When a request for extension is refused they sometimes only give you 7 or 15 days to leave. Some have been even shorter and a few have been longer."*

The Waldocks held a VBS in the spring. They started out with 47. Every room in their house was arranged to hold classes besides two classes in Ken's office, which was above a bank. There was very good attention and participation. The interest accelerated as the week progressed. They held the closing program on Sunday night. They particularly asked the Lord to send in many of the parents and friends of the children. The Lord answered. Their front room was filled with 75 parents and friends. Nearly all the children came, probably over 80. With 12 teachers and helpers they had over 167 present for the closing meeting! To say that the house was packed was an understatement! The Waldocks were rightly proud of the children. Seven accepted the Lord.

All of the missionaries' residential permits were still pending by this time. Dorothy had not had a valid residential permit for over a year. They were aware that the government authorities were investigating them.

A far more serious and disturbing situation arose in July. In May Fred had received a letter from Sambhu and Molly stating that they expected to return to India from Tacoma, WA sometime around June 12. They heard nothing more until he received the minutes of some of the meetings in Silchar and saw that Sambhu's name was listed as being present. But no word came directly from Sambhu – which was totally out of character for him.

Shortly after that, Fred was summoned to the police office. He had no idea why the police might want to speak to him. Their first question was whether Fred knew Sambhu Dey. Fred was required to give full details of everything he knew about both Sambhu and Molly ever since he had known them. He was asked why they had been in the States and when they were coming back to India. Fred was even asked to supply a picture of them. Fred had been listed as the contact person for Sambhu's and Molly's visit. After the officer had written up two full pages of information, Fred was permitted to leave.

Within a few days Fred received a letter from Sambhu telling of his arrival plans. Then one evening a Central Intelligence Department officer came. He was dressed in civilian clothes. This man could neither speak nor understand English very well. He carefully folded down the top sentence of the letter he had to let Fred read it. It read: "Mr. Sambhu Dey, an American citizen, wants to go to Punjab, Haryana, Tripura, Assam and Manipur..."

Fred was surprised. He immediately told the officer that the Sambhu Dey that he knew was an *Indian* citizen. The officer was indignant that Fred would suggest that the CID had their information wrong. When Fred saw his attitude, he suggested that because of the language barrier it would be better for them both to go over to the police station so that they would have an interpreter. Fred didn't want the man to be putting down information that wasn't true.

He agreed to go to the police station. Once they got there, they went through the whole story again. Fred knew that this whole business would be on file. With all the terrorism going on, especially in Punjab, at that time, it was no wonder that Fred was being questioned.

After the visit to the police station, Fred received another letter from Sambhu. Fred had written stating that he had not heard from Sambhu since May. It was then that they realized that their mail had been intercepted because Sambhu *had* written with full information about his arrival.

The summer extension program was small that year – only 10 students when they had expected 20. But the professors were glad for the closer relationships that they had with each student due to the smaller class. Two students, Alung and Leela, graduated that year. There were about 80 people at the graduation ceremony.

When Sambhu and Molly arrived in Bangalore on August 11, Fred met their train and then took them to the police station as had been requested. The next day a CID officer came to question Sambhu. They went to the police station but when it was determined that Sambhu did not have his passport with him, he was asked to come back the next day. After taking all the necessary information and conducting an interview, they told Sambhu that he must have some enemies who were trying to get him in trouble. The CID told Promode when they investigated in Silchar that someone within was writing detailed reports of the mission and all its activities. The name of the informant was not disclosed. After that, the whole thing blew over and Sambhu and Molly returned in August to the United States to continue their training at Northwest Baptist Seminary.

On August 21, 1986 Ken and Mary received their extension permits good through May 7, 1987. Praise the Lord! Fred and Dorothy hoped that their extensions would be forthcoming soon. But August and September went by and still Fred and Dorothy heard nothing about their permits. There was serious labor trouble at Makunda in Assam, and with Sambhu's past connection with Makunda, well anyone could be writing reports. Since July, Fred and Dorothy knew of at least one important telegram and other letters that had never arrived. They guessed that they were probably still under surveillance and perhaps that was why their permits were delayed.

In September Fred and Ken met with Gerry Weber (their administrator from Cleveland), Jim Garlow and 14 leaders from Assam in Calcutta. While there they learned more about the trouble at Makunda. Several years before Communists from the district had organized the agricultural workers into a union, recognized by the Assam government. From the beginning the union made unreasonable demands. The matter went before a labor tribunal and the workers won a higher pay scale and greater retirement benefits among other things. This, plus other factors, had thrown Makunda into $12,000 worth of debt. During the past two years some of the Christians on the medical staff had also joined the union. On August 26 union members violently beat the agricultural supervisor, Basanta Singh. His wife and sons were also injured when they tried to protect him. This resulted from Basanta's refusal to withdraw misconduct charges against the union president and members. A short time after this beating, three policemen from the nearby police outpost came to Basanta's house with an accusation against his son, Pradip, suggesting that he had stabbed a worker and a union sympathizer. These charges had been filed by Basanta's attackers in order to shift the attention from themselves and accuse the innocent party. However, since the police had no warrant, no arrest could be made.

From there the situation went from bad to tragic. A son of one of the Christian families at Makunda had witnessed the beating of Basanta and his family. The son disappeared one day and a concentrated search was made for him. After a week and a half his murdered body was found in the large fishpond. About this same time, seven out of the eight buildings of the Rehabilitation Center were set on fire and completely destroyed. The union members hoped to drive the Christians off the land so that they could occupy it.

In Bangalore, they continued to see people coming to Christ, including an earnest young man from a strict Hindu background. Ken was meeting with him two hours per week for individual Bible instruction.

On October 15, the mission birthday, the five remaining missionaries in India had a full day of prayer together remembering Baptist Mid-Missions' ministry around the world. In the evening at their regular church prayer meeting, they reviewed the work of BMM giving a brief account of the early beginnings and then brought their people up to date on the outreach of the mission today. It was a joy to recall and review the ministry of each of the fields. Fred and Dorothy identified strongly with their larger mission family and indeed designated $1,000 to "Operation Move-Out" a fundraising effort to enable the Home Office of BMM to move from downtown Cleveland to a new site in Middleburg Heights, OH.

In November Fred and Dorothy had the delight of seeing Ken baptize his son Nathan and also a recent convert from Hinduism. The church was holding its annual meeting at this time and Fred told the church that he would be submitting his resignation as pastor. They would be leaving on furlough in the spring, and it was time, in Fred's mind, to turn the reins over to Ken. He also felt that the church should call an assistant pastor. The church had other ideas, however. They refused to accept his resignation and asked Fred to continue on as their pastor until furlough. The Indian brethren felt strongly that Fred, as the senior and eldest man, should be their leader.

The plans for the Christmas season seemed unusually full that year. Both Fred and Dorothy didn't feel that they had the reserve energy that they used to have. The years in India had taken a lot out of them and they were tired. Dorothy's blood pressure was acting up again and Fred's cancer checks were inconclusive. The doctor wanted to do a tissue biopsy early in December.

Both Fred and Dorothy were eager to get home on furlough and be among their family. They often thought of retiring. Fred would be 65 in less than a month.

By the end of January they still had no word about their permits! They had been officially investigated though - the first time in their history in India. Of greater concern, however, was Fred's medical condition. By early February it was apparent that there had been some significant changes in the area of the previous cancer. It was possible that another tumor was developing.

Fred took his concerns to his regular doctor and he agreed that some changes were apparent and advised Fred to return to the United States as soon as possible. Fred also consulted a doctor who attended the services at Bethel Baptist Church. She agreed that further testing was needed and went with Fred to Vellore to see the same doctor (a cousin of her husband) who had seen Fred in 1984. They were so kind and concerned. At first the doctor suggested that another scan be taken but after examining Fred he was convinced that Fred should return to the University of Washington Hospital as there seemed to be a growth under the scar tissue which was causing changes and exposure of deeper vessels. The doctor also said that if his suspicions proved to be correct, there were no drugs available there to properly treat it. When Fred asked if he could wait until April to return to the States, the doctor emphatically stated, "Certainly not."

They made plans to leave Bangalore February 25, 1987. Upon arriving in Tacoma, Fred went through a full month of numerous tests at the University of Washington Hospital, including five days as a volunteer in a special research program specifically designed to pinpoint melanoma wherever it might be located in the body.

It came as a complete surprise to Fred and Dorothy when the doctors said that they found no evidence of melanoma in the areas where the previous surgeries were done and where the doctors in India had suspected further growths. Instead, his former surgeon was concerned about three lesions that appeared on the x-rays of his lungs. Fred had frequent x-rays of his lungs in India and the doctors hadn't detected these lesions so perhaps they were fairly recent. Because it is the nature of melanoma to spread to the lungs and brain, other scans and tests were done which ruled out the brain.

He had surgery on March 30 to remove the lesions on his lungs. David flew in from New Jersey for the week. It was a real blessing for Fred and Dorothy to have the whole family together at the hospital, except for Ken who faithfully held the ropes in Bangalore.

Fred came through surgery very well despite the fact that there were four lumps on the lungs instead of three. Fred remained in the hospital for ten days.

How thankful they were for the Lord's continual faithfulness and leading in their lives. God had used a wrong diagnosis in India to take them back to the United States where the true problem could be found. Because they were on furlough, there would be no rush to return to the field. Fred would be able to recover fully. He began walking two to three miles a day to increase his lung capacity.

The Waldocks 12th grandchild, Kimberly Louise, joined the Seben brood on May 21. Caryl also had happy news. Joseph Parkinson, a student at Northwest Baptist Seminary, had proposed marriage and she had accepted! Fred and Dorothy were pleased. They were confident that the Lord had given their youngest child the right man. Joe loved the Lord and had a heart to serve Him. The wedding was planned for December 19, 1987.

For Fred and Dorothy's 40th wedding anniversary the family surprised them with a wonderful evening in a beautiful restaurant on the bay. David and his family took their vacation in Tacoma that year, so everyone was there except Ken and Mary and family. Twenty-two members of their family, plus two other couples were there to surprise Fred and Dorothy when they arrived. Edna

Hemminger was the only representative of the original wedding party.

In July they traveled to Canada for Prairie Bible Institute's "Homecoming '87". It was the 40-year reunion of Fred's graduation from college and the 45th year reunion for the high school where Fred had been among the first students. It was a huge reunion with approximately 3,000 registered guests.

Caryl's long-anticipated graduation from Pacific Lutheran University with her B.S. in nursing occurred in August. Fred and Dorothy were delighted to be at the pinning and graduation ceremony. Fred and Dorothy's ministry had often kept the family apart. It was so good of the Lord to fill this furlough time with so many milestones and happy times with precious family and friends!

A scan of Fred's lungs in August confirmed that they were clear. Tests in the original area of cancer also showed no metastasis whatsoever! They praised the Lord for His mercies.

In preparation for retirement, the Waldocks did a lot of house hunting. The Lord led them to a fine older Christian man who had a condominium for sale outside of Gig Harbor, WA. After negotiations they discovered that by buying it on time their payments would be cheaper than renting. The condo was in a little development on Henderson Bay. It was suitable for Fred and Dorothy's needs and was large enough for Ken and family to use on furlough.

After receiving medical clearance, Fred and Dorothy started deputation ministry in the fall. They spoke earnestly of the needs in India, especially of the desperate need for a church building in Bangalore. The home where they were meeting was bursting at the seams. Three believers were baptized September 6th. Ken reported that the Northwest Baptist Seminary Extension session with 14 dedicated young men was one of the best sessions yet. One graduated that summer with a 4.0 grade point average.

Joe Parkinson and Caryl Waldock were married on December 19, 1987. Fred performed the ceremony.

CHAPTER SEVENTEEN
His Perfect Will

"We believe that the LORD, Who has brought us through many hard places in the past, is able to meet every need in this situation. Our trust and joy and victory are all in Him. Let us believe God. He is able and He will fulfill His perfect will and plan for our lives." – Fred Waldock, May 1988

Just before the wedding, Fred had learned that he had to undergo chemotherapy for new evidence of malignancy in his lungs. Once a month, Fred had chemotherapy by I.V.

Despite the chemotherapy, they persevered with deputation plans. They visited churches in Washington, Idaho, Florida, North Carolina, Connecticut and Ohio. They were at the Baptist Mid-Missions Triannual Conference in Owatonna, Minnesota and received their 40-year pins for missionary service.

The Bangalore missionaries stepped out in faith and requested a loan of $30,000 from BMM to purchase land and start construction of a multi-purpose building that would house Bethel Baptist Church, the extension seminary and the Bible school night classes. Mid-Missions granted the loan on the basis that the missionaries promised, by faith, to repay a certain amount of the loan each month.

A cancer checkup in March was not encouraging. Fred's cancer was not responding to conventional chemotherapy. Fred was considered for participation in a study at the University of Washington using expensive Interleukin-2 treatments. Those were long, hard days of decision-making. Fred and Dorothy thanked the Lord for His sustaining grace and peaceful assurance of His presence and leading.

Because Interleukin-2 was considered experimental treatment, the group insurance plan for the Mission would not cover the long period of hospitalization and special care. After much prayer and consultation with the family and some supporting churches, they felt that Fred should proceed with the treatment anyway. They believed that the Lord, Who had brought them through many hard places in the past, was able to meet every need in this situation. They affirmed, *"There is nothing too hard for Thee, Lord. Our trust and joy and victory are all in Him."*

Their hearts were greatly touched in May when they received a letter from a church in Texas that included a check of $1,000 to help defray the costs of Fred's medical care. The letter came at just the time when they felt the need of some sort of confirmation from the Lord about taking this serious step in Fred's treatment.

The Interleukin–2 treatments were delayed because a lesion was discovered on Fred's larynx which had to be irradiated first. The lesion could swell considerably during the IL-2 treatment and be life-threatening.

Fred and Dorothy still hoped to be able to return to India by August 23 when their visas expired but that would depend on how the treatments went. Since Ken and Mary were due for a furlough, Joe and Caryl made plans to go out to India on tourist visas in August to relieve them.

Fred entered the critical care unit to begin the Interleukin-2 therapy on July 4th. At first the doctors were very pleased with his ability to handle the rather difficult treatment, but eventually a cumulative effect took hold and Fred's kidneys and liver shut down. David sat with his Dad through those long, harrowing nights. Lois, Caryl and Gordon added their support to their Dad and Mom. Fred was finally well enough to leave the hospital 20 days later. Since he would need six weeks of checkups, it was now clear that they would not be able to return to India before their visas expired. They requested a medical extension to their visas, which was granted.

Joe and Caryl left for India just five days after Fred left the hospital. Early in August, Fred had a thorough check-up. To their great disappointment, it seemed as though the Interleukin-2 treatment had not been effective against the cancer in Fred's lungs and chest. Fred was scheduled for more scans and another assessment in a month.

Dorothy wrote, *"We know He is able and will do that which is best for us. We continue to count on you to bear us up before His throne of grace to find His help in time of need. We are so mindful of His love and mercy to us each day of our lives."*

By the end of September, Fred was experiencing chest pains on a regular basis. The doctors could not find the cause of it. Ken and family arrived from India on October 4th. It was good to have them at the house in Gig Harbor.

On the morning of October 25, Mary, Jeanette and Dorothy went to a missionary ladies brunch at University Place Baptist Church where Mary was the speaker. Ken, Fred, Nathan and Mark dropped them off and then went for nine holes of putt-putt golf. It was so sunny and warm and beautiful that Fred just couldn't resist the urge to try nine holes of real golf on the Gig Harbor course. He had been trying to regain his strength after the strenuous cancer treatments and just wanted to prove to himself that he could do it.

Ken and Fred returned from the course around 5:30 p.m. Soon after that Fred suffered a massive stroke in the living room. Paramedics arrived quickly and took him to the hospital. Doctors gave little hope for him to last the night, but Fred held on in a coma for five days surrounded by his family who loved him.

Fred was promoted to Glory on Sunday, October 30, 1988 just a few hours before Joe and Caryl arrived back from India. The funeral was at Temple Baptist Church on November 2. Five missionaries representing Baptist Mid-Missions took part, as well as four professors who had been to India to teach in the Northwest Baptist Seminary Extension program. A slide presentation of the work in India, prepared by one of the professors, depicted the work that was so dear to Fred's heart and which had consumed so much of his life. The music and program glorified the Lord and was a challenge for missions.

The pastors in India sent the following tribute: *"We fondly recall that Rev. Dr. Waldock has left a glorious history of working as a model missionary in the virgin fields of southern Assam for about 25 years and thereafter serving at Bangalore of South India for another ten* years. He was a man of very tender heart with understanding of nationals, a missionary of very sociable character and a source of inspiration to many in the Lord's work. He was instrumental in developing Makunda Leprosy Colony, organizing Makunda Baptist Church and thereafter initiating the literature ministry with printing press at Silchar town and the Silchar Baptist Church and founding together with the other missionaries the Northeast India Baptist Bible College and forming Baptist Mid-Missions Trustees India Society. He also helped a lot in the ministry of Burrows Memorial Christian Hospital and other ministries particularly the Fellowship of Baptist Churches in Northeast India."

Rev. Darrell Beddoe wrote, "One of this generation's great men of God has passed from this life – missionary Fred Waldock. Born on the prairies of Alberta and raised in the shadow of Prairie Bible Institute, Fred took a strong belief in sacrifice for the cause of Christ to the muddy rice fields of Assam and the open sores, poverty and isolation of its lepers. Together with the inspiration and hard work of his wife Dorothy, they raised a family and helped rear indigenous churches, a hospital, book room and Bible school.

Courageously loving the Lord, His Word and His Church, Fred seemed ageless and energetic, always looking for a better way to reach Indians for Christ. His preaching was always immersed in solid Biblical thinking and passion; his relationships were filled with the same. How he survived the frustrations of bureaucracy and the caste system, only the Lord and Dorothy know.

While he was battling cancer, it never seemed as through the cancer could win. Only God's call to come home could have removed him from the front line. Fred always had plans and they always focused on his call to India and Indians; he could always laugh – at himself and the frustrating situations he faced. He was inflexible on the truth of God, but able to accept changes, both at home and abroad, that staggered others."

In lieu of flowers, the family suggested that memorial gifts be given to build the church and extension seminary facility in Bangalore. Around $4,000 was given. The family had a private burial. Fred's headstone carried this inscription, "Chosen to Go Up Higher, John 15:16."

On the day of Fred's memorial service, as the Waldock family was returning to the car, Ken mentioned that Darrell Beddoe had told him that the Board of Directors of The Master's College (formerly Los Angeles Baptist College) had unanimously chosen to dedicate their newest dormitory in the name of Frederick W. Waldock. Dorothy said, "You know your Dad wouldn't want that."

Ken said that he had told Darrell that but that Darrell had said that they wanted to name it after someone the students could emulate their lives after. Two weeks later, Ken was in Southern California for deputation travels and stayed at The Master's College. He was told about the dedication and again Ken stated that his Dad wouldn't want anything like that because he wouldn't feel that he was worthy of such recognition. But the people at The Master's College were adamant that they wanted the students to pattern their lives after Fred's dedication and faithfulness. They told Ken that it was already decided.

A friend of Dorothy's, Harriet Ishii, phoned from the college and told Dorothy to make reservations for Ken, Mary and herself to fly down Dec. 3rd and stay until Dec. 6th for the dedication. When Gordon heard about it, he said that he wanted to go as well, since he hadn't been able to go when Fred was awarded his honorary Doctor of Divinity degree in 1983.

Their flight was delayed about an hour and a half because of heavy fog so they arrived late for the special dinner the college was putting on for their donors. But they had places waiting for them. They were there for the special program and Christmas concert. After the program, Ken, Mary and Gordon caught up with friends while Dorothy went to bed.

On Sunday they were able to catch up with old friends at Placerita Baptist Church. Monday morning they had the dormitory dedication during the chapel hour at The Master's College. Dr. John Stead gave a resume of Fred's life while a large picture of Fred was displayed on a big screen. On either side were pictures of Indian nationals from their area. Then as all of the Waldocks were brought on to the platform, they unveiled a large redwood sign with Fred's name on it that was to be installed in the dormitory. Ken gave an acceptance speech.

Although Dorothy would turn 65 on February 23, 1989 she wasn't quite ready for retirement yet. Her heart was still in India, as it would be for the rest of her life. She returned to the land of her call. She flew direct to Delhi and soon realized that after nearly two years she was back in IST – India Standard ("stretching") Time. A variety of familiar sounds and smells assaulted her senses as she spent ten hours in the bleak, cold Delhi airport waiting for her delayed flight to Bangalore.

She had to admit that it had not been easy for her to go ahead on her own and make decisions, but the Lord truly was her refuge and strength. She had to constantly analyze what her role and work were to be. She was no longer the mission treasurer nor the wife and helpmate to the Pastor and Field Council president.

She moved into the house that the congregation used for church meetings. Ken and his family had lived there previously but had moved when it was needed for church facilities.

Her first day back in Bangalore, the verses in *Daily Light* were God's special message for her. "Be strong and work; for I am with you, saith the Lord of Hosts." "Strong in the Lord and in the power of His might." "The joy of the Lord is your strength." (Haggai 2:4, Philippians 4:13 and Ephesians 6:10)

She determined that her main ministry would be to visit families of members and Sunday school children to encourage regular attendance and full commitment to the Lord. She challenged Christians to live in such a way that they would be ready to meet the Lord at any time. As Fred had been taken suddenly, so could they.

She also taught piano lessons and helped out in whatever ways she could. One day she called on a family whose two daughters, Joanna and Jyothi, had been coming to Bethel Baptist Church Sunday School for about eight years before their mother had decided that she wanted Jyothi to go to her church, which was very liberal. Joanna continued to come to Bethel Baptist as often as she could. When Dorothy called on them, the mother said that she wanted Jyothi to return to Bethel Baptist because she could see what a difference it had made in Joanna. Soon the mother and the two girls were at church. The father had been threatening for two years to leave the family and had just recently followed through with that threat.

Dorothy was seeing victory in the lives of some. One lady whom Fred and Dorothy had been trying to encourage over the last five years or more suddenly had a complete reversal in her outlook on life. She praised the Lord in everything and rejoiced in the way that the Lord met her needs. Dorothy went with her to a doctor's appointment. The lady told her Hindu doctor how the Lord had removed her tension and had given her new strength. He checked her over and took her off most of her heart medications and then said she could come back in three months for a checkup instead of the usual monthly checkup. Her difficult problems were still there, but the Lord's presence and the Word of God were sustaining her. She was a brilliant woman and voraciously read whatever Christian literature Dorothy could put in her hands.

A number of the young college graduates, who were earnest Christians, were facing great difficulty as their parents sought to arrange marriages for them. The young people were trying to hold out for born-again partners but they were hard to find if the parents were adamant about sticking to clan, educational requirements and high-paying jobs.

In April, the hottest month, they held two Vacation Bible Schools. Dorothy was only involved at the one held at Bethel Baptist. One junior girl, who had accepted the Lord the previous year, came again. She hadn't been allowed to attend Sunday school. She told how she was trying to live for the Lord but her Hindu family and friends made fun of her and tore up the Bible she had been given. Ken was able to visit the home. Her father was very friendly and decided to allow the girl and her sister to attend Sunday school. Praise the Lord!

A visitation program in June resulted in several more families attending the church. In July, twenty students arrived for the extension seminary. There were more students from South India this year for which they were very glad.

Also in July, David's wife Mary and their daughter Jennifer came out to India to spend a month with Dorothy. Dorothy went to Delhi to meet them and took them by deluxe bus 150 miles north to Mussoorie, so that they could see where David had gone to school. July is the beginning of the monsoons and usually it starts with heavy rains, but for the two and a half days that they were there it rained very little and they were able to see the school and some of the staff and even hiked up to the top, which is more than 7,400 foot altitude, to drink in the beauty of the valleys and the snow-capped Himalayan mountains that separate Tibet from

India. David had made a list of different places and people he wanted Mary and Jen to see and they were able to accomplish most of that.

They returned to Delhi and took a tour taxi to see Jaipur and Agra, two historically famous cities, which also included the Taj Mahal. The temperatures soared to around 115 degrees in the middle of the day so they didn't spend any extra time there other than to see the main monuments. A heavy rainstorm on the trip back to Delhi from Agra brought some relief.

The next three weeks they spent in Bangalore involved in the church and extension seminary. After the seminary graduation, Ken took his kids out of school and the whole family went to a government reserve and stayed in a jungle hut in the Niligiri Hills. They had a tour through the reserve and saw wild elephants, bison, boar, deer and lots of monkeys. Everyone but Dorothy hiked to the top of a high hill in front of their hut so that they could see the countryside for miles around. On the way back to Bangalore they visited a bird sanctuary and a huge dam with gardens and fountains. It was a special time for the whole family.

Dorothy began to consider when she should go home and retire. Dorothy applied for a permit to visit Assam one last time before leaving India. The permit was granted in November, although only for one week rather than the two she had requested. It was decided that the trip to Assam would be January 20-27, 1990.

The trip to Assam was the crowning joy of Dorothy's return to India. She traveled by plane to Calcutta and spent the night there at a guest house. By 5 a.m. she was at the airport for the 55-minute flight to Silchar. Promode, Dak Ful, Sambhu, Tapon, Selungba and Ajit were waiting to greet her.

Many friends from the Bible College gathered at Sambhu's house for his daughter's first birthday party. Sambhu was now the principal of the Northeast India Baptist Bible College. Molly also taught full-time at the college. They had two little girls. Sambhu and Molly's house would be a home base for Dorothy.

After the party Sambhu gave Dorothy a quick tour of the Bible College facilities and they had a late lunch. After that they had the dedication of the first floor (second floor for Americans) of the Christian Literature House. How long Fred and Dorothy had prayed for that project to be done! The addition had space for offices for the Christian Literature House and Bibles International, storage space for literature, and guest facilities for visiting translators. Dorothy spoke during the dedication. Afterwards, there was tea and sweets and lots of picture taking.

Later in the day there was a welcome meeting at the Bible College. Many friends came to talk. It was a long but very happy day.

The next day was Sunday so Dorothy went to Silchar Baptist Church. Dorothy was asked to share about the history of the church. She spoke of the beginning of Silchar Baptist Church; the leasing of the present building; the salvation of Gobin, Tapon, Dr. Das of Alipur, Pastor Nobin of Alipur Baptist Church and many others. She rehearsed how the Lord had opened the door for the purchase of the property for the Christian Literature House and Northeast India Baptist Bible College. She explained that it had been her and Fred's desire to see Silchar Baptist Church be a model and training ground for the Bible College students as they prepared to teach and preach the Word of God back in their own villages.

Dorothy's voice had been giving her increasing problems in Bangalore making it very difficult for her to speak at times. But the Lord marvelously undertook while she was in Assam. Even though she spoke two or three times almost every day, her voice held up fine to the last!

Dorothy had lunch with Alung and Themlieu, pastor and wife of Ebenezer Baptist Church. Their church was located near the railroad station among the Rongmei Naga people. The Naga sweepers were looked down on by the rest of society. While Fred and Dorothy had been in Silchar many of the Rongmei Nagas had joined Silchar Baptist Church. But in recent years, the Rongmei members of the church and Sunday school had gone back to the rail station and built a new church. When Dorothy had first heard about that she had been sad because the railroad station was such a filthy, chaotic place.

However, when she attended the afternoon service there she was greatly encouraged. The building was nice and airy with woven-bamboo walls and a thatch roof. It was a bit apart from the railroad colony so it was quiet and neat and very nice. They could reach out to many Rongmeis working there who would not feel comfortable attending the church in Silchar. After the service they gave Dorothy garlands for her neck and a beautiful woolen panek and a white cotton Rongmei shawl. They shared tea and sweets and everyone gave glory to God for letting them be together again.

On Monday Selungba came in the morning with a jeep and took Dorothy and several others to the Annual Conference of the Fellowship of Baptist Churches held at Khumba Baptist Church, a small congregation near the airport. Most of the members of that church were tea garden laborers. They had, with the help of others in the Fellowship of Baptist Churches, put up a large woven-bamboo meeting hall with sheets of plastic for the roof. It was nice and bright and airy. The members of the Khumba Baptist Church had forgone their annual Christmas feast so that they could provide all the food free to delegates and guests. Dorothy was very impressed at all they had provided.

Some of the members shared rooms in their houses to give some of the leaders places for their families. For the women, they had built a nice, large bamboo house and put straw on the floor. It was here that Dorothy spoke to the women as they sat on their bedding. Many of the women Dorothy had known from before so she was glad for the opportunity to visit with them again. She spoke in Bengali with Themlieu sitting next to her to help out with the few words that eluded her. Pastor Nobin's wife translated her words into Manipuri. Dorothy spoke to the main group later on.

On Tuesday Dorothy visited Emmanuel English School – the fulfillment of a dream that Deb Singh had for reaching Hindus and Muslims through an English school. They had started in March, 1987 with nine students. Less than three years later, the school had about 150 students. When Dorothy visited it was opening day of the school year. Dorothy cut the ribbon for the opening of the new library building. The kids were all lined up in front of the building by classes for the occasion. They had all brought loads of flowers and had made them into leis for Dorothy. Each class put two leis around her neck. She finally had to unload some of them and put them around her arms.

From the school Dorothy went to Gobin and Urirei's house about a mile from the school. Gobin was the coordinator for Bibles

International and Urirei worked at the Emmanuel English School. At the house were Deb Singh and his wife, Pasat, and their three daughters.

Later that day Selungba took Dorothy out to Alipur for tea and fellowship and a welcome meeting at Alipur Baptist Church. It was a very festive time with special numbers, speeches and gifts followed by tea and sweets out in the church yard. She spent the night at Alipur in the Kenoyer's former bungalow.

After breakfast the next morning they left for Makunda via Silchar. Dorothy had to report where she was going to the police. They insisted that she check in going to and coming from Makunda. To Dorothy, it made her think of what life must be like in the Soviet Union.

The Makunda Leprosy Colony had been given over to another Christian organization a few years before. The Society could no longer make a go of it after many labor troubles. The Makunda Baptist Church was hanging on but had been without a real pastor for too long. The acting pastor-leader had not had much training; but, with the help of others, was holding on. While at Makunda, Dorothy slept in the same room that she had slept in 29 years before. Even some of the furniture was the same! Dorothy was able to fellowship with some that she had known years ago and to catch up on what had become of their children.

The road was dusty and Dorothy felt that she was wearing a good portion of it, but there was no time to clean up before a scheduled lunch with Ajit. She had a good visit with him. He had suffered heart problems but somehow managed to keep going and was active in the annual Fellowship of Baptist Churches conference and working half time at the Bengali Correspondence School.

The rest of Dorothy's time in Assam was a dizzying schedule of meals at people's homes, visiting until it was time to go on to the next stop. Dorothy relished the opportunity to see and hear the testimonies of those in whom they had planted the Word of God, now mature and passing the faith on to their children and others. What was left of the time, Dorothy spent with Molly and Sambhu. Both Molly and Sambhu taught full-time at the Baptist Bible College. This was a particular strain on Molly since she also had her home and two little girls to take care of. Dorothy admonished Sambhu to have Molly teach only part-time.

Another need of the Northeast India Baptist Bible College was auxiliary lighting for the library. In Silchar, the lights went out for half an hour to an hour three or four times a day. Sambhu mentioned the need for auxiliary lighting for the library so that the students could get their studying done. There were some new lights coming out in India that were continually plugged into the electric outlets for recharging. When the electricity went off, these tube lights would immediately come on. Dorothy was delighted to contribute $1,000 from her work funds for the purchase of lighting.

The week passed all too quickly and it was time for Dorothy to depart. In Silchar, Dorothy had to report the time of her departure. Even though Assam was opening up to foreigners, they were still being very cautious and vigilant with missionaries.

The plane was delayed due to fog so they put Dorothy and her party – 10 or 12 of them – in a special side room and assigned a lady security officer to sit with them until departure time. The security guard did not let Dorothy out of her sight even to go to the bathroom. When it came time to leave, she carried Dorothy's handbag through security and escorted her right out to the plane. This would have been rather uncomfortable for Dorothy except that the lady assigned by the airport security was also a member of Khumba Baptist Church. Dorothy had met her at the Fellowship of Baptist Churches conference at the beginning of the week! So they had a great time of fellowship while they waited for the plane.

Dorothy praised the Lord for the way that He had taken care of her in that one very hectic but wonderful week in Assam. She was able to visit every mission station except Binnakandi. She was able to see most of the people she had wanted to see because of the one day at the Fellowship of Baptist Churches conference. Even the trip back to Bangalore was arranged by the Lord. When she had come through Calcutta the week before, she had tried to call her unsaved friends, Aroti and P.L. Das. Their phone line had been out – not unusual – so she had sat down and wrote them an air form telling them that she would be coming through again in a week. So they were at the airport to meet her on the return trip and took her to their house for the night and brought her back to the airport the next morning.

Again, because of heavy fog all planes were delayed. The airport was hot and stuffy even though it was January. With the plane being delayed, her flight arrived in Bangalore just as Ken was through with the morning service. He sent Nathan and Jayram by motorcycle to the airport to let Dorothy know that he would be by to pick her up just as soon as he delivered some of the people home from the service. Dorothy had just cleared her suitcase when he drove up. So the Lord was with her every step of the way.

The spring in Bangalore flew by and all too soon it was time for Dorothy to pack up and leave India. Dorothy truly praised the Lord for what He had done for her in the year and a half since Fred went home to be with the Lord. It had been good to be back in India, surrounded by church people, and busy in the work. She had witnessed several of the young people break from the tradition of their parents' Orthodox churches. With their parents' permission, they received baptism and joined Bethel Baptist Church. She'd been able to help with the weddings of three of their young people who had married true Christians rather than allow their parents to arrange marriages through brokers.

A recently retired friend from Tacoma, Loretta Prettyman, came out to visit India for three weeks. Then in the middle of May they set out together for home via the Holy Land. This was a trip that Fred and Dorothy had planned to do for several furloughs but it was never possible due to his need for medical checkups.

In spite of much tension in the Holy Land, Loretta and Dorothy covered much territory by tour bus and on foot to visit most of the places about which Dorothy had taught in her Bible Geography and other Bible classes. It was very moving for Dorothy to walk where Jesus had walked and taught and performed miracles. They stood on the Mount of Olives where Jesus had ascended to Heaven after completing His work of redemption. It was awesome for Dorothy to think to the future when Jesus would stand there again when He returns to this troubled world to put down the forces of evil and set up His reign of righteousness.

Dorothy left Loretta in London to spend another month with relatives. She arrived in New York on June 5th to stay with David for several weeks. She was able to attend the graduation of her eldest granddaughter, Jennifer. From there she flew to Clearwater, Florida to spend ten days with Fred's stepmother Ruby before going to the BMM Triannual Conference near Cleveland in July.

Dorothy decided not to put in for retirement at that Triannual Conference. Since no new missionaries could get visas for India and because Ken and Mary needed to take a short furlough in the first part of 1991 to raise additional support, Dorothy thought of perhaps returning to India to help out the nationals while Ken was in the United States. So she delayed her retirement plans. She had received a "No Objection to Return" permit before leaving India, so it was possible she would go back in.

She stayed in the home of Quentin and Marleah Kenoyer. Three of the Kenoyer children came home while she was there. Dr. Gene and Bette Burrows and John and Cora Wilkens, all previous missionaries with Fred and Dorothy in Assam, also stayed with the Kenoyers. They had delightful fellowship together as they caught up after so many years apart. During the conference, Jim Garlow, John and Cindy Burrows and Tom and Mary Ruth Walker joined the India contingent. It was indeed special for Dorothy to fellowship with all these people and many memories came flooding back.

For the first time, Dorothy sat on the General Council to represent the India Field. She had a part in interviewing the new candidates for BMM. It was a blessing to her as she saw the dedication and caliber of the ones the Lord had chosen to send into His harvest field.

Dorothy wrote, "*As I heard the challenge of our Mission leaders and returning missionaries, telling of fields that are wide open to the Gospel and, in many cases, like Russia and Romania, the people grasping for Bibles and study books and true Bible teaching, it almost makes me wish I could start my missionary life over. So many fields are crying for new workers and too few are preparing to go. My heart aches for India where new missionaries cannot go and the government is outwardly and militantly anti-Christian.*"

After all the traveling, it was time to unpack and settle in at the condominium in Gig Harbor. At times the unwanted tears came. It was hard to be in the house alone without Fred. But the Lord was good. Ken's son, Nathan, arrived from India to start high school in August. His family was scheduled to begin a five-month furlough in January. Because the school years were different in India and the United States, this was the only way Nathan could be in the same school for the entire year.

Dorothy was glad to have Nathan around. He filled the house. She kept him busy picking wild blackberries, skateboarding to get the mail, and helping with chores.

On August 26, 1990 Dorothy became the happy grandmother of her 14th grandchild when Joe and Caryl had their first daughter – Aimee Elizabeth, a beautiful redhead. Dorothy was thankful that she could be there for the delivery.

That fall after Nathan started school, Dorothy began the monumental task of sorting 40 years of slides and prayer letters to put them in some kind of order. Her children had requested that she write a history of their family life in India. She did a little speaking in women's meetings but her voice was getting progressively worse to the extent that she didn't feel she could speak in meetings anymore.

She had a real burden to see younger missionaries trained and supported so that they could go out to their fields. She felt that if she retired soon, then some of her churches could use those funds to send young missionaries out. At Ken's request, she decided not to go out to India while they were on furlough but to stay in Gig Harbor to care for their children who would be enrolled in school, thus freeing Ken and Mary to travel more extensively on deputation. Ken needed to build up his support considerably to meet the ever-growing needs on the field.

She and Nathan went over to Moscow, Idaho with Gordon and his family to spend Thanksgiving with Lois' family. It was a delightful time for Dorothy to be surrounded by her children and grandchildren. She savored these family times all the more because of the many times their family had not been able to be together on the field.

Ken and family arrived in January 1991. Now the condo was full and Dorothy was happy with the arrangement. She officially retired from active ministry with Baptist Mid-Missions effective March 31, 1991 after 43 years of missionary service.

The spring flew by in taking care of Nathan, Mark and Jeannette. All too soon, Ken and Mary and family left for India on the 17th of June. Soon after, Dorothy rushed over to Moscow, Idaho to be with Lois for the birth of their sixth child. Dorothy missed the arrival of her fifth grandson, Josiah Timothy, by just a few hours.

Dorothy felt led of the Lord to return to India in October 1991 for four and a half months. During that time she did visitation in the homes of those who came to services but who had never stepped out of their old church traditions to join Bethel Baptist. She wanted to make sure that they were truly born again.

Dorothy was able to have an influence for Christ in many ways. She traveled to the wedding of a church member in Delhi. Jayram and his sister, Anu, were members of Bethel Baptist Church, having been saved out of an orthodox Hindu background. Anu had recently married a young man who had no regard for any god. He adamantly refused to let her come to church. Jayram was a captain in the army, posted in Kashmir and about to marry a girl from the Seventh Day Adventist church in that area. The mother of Jayram and Anu, a widow, had been very friendly and open to the gospel but because she lived with her Hindu parents was not free to fellowship with people from Bethel Baptist Church. She had wanted someone from the church to go to the wedding so Dorothy was the delegate. The church had prayed much and the Lord answered by giving Dorothy much opportunity to talk with Anu and her mother, to Jayram before and after the wedding and even to the Hindu grandfather, who asked many pertinent questions. Dorothy shared with Jayram the differences in teaching between Baptists and Seventh Day Adventists. Jayram's bride was not sure of her salvation so he took her through the Bible verses and she accepted the Lord before they were married.

Dorothy remained in India until the end of February 1992. She had planned the timing of her return so that she could be home for the birth of Caryl's baby. Little Emylee arrived just four days later.

Dorothy became active at Temple Baptist Church, helping in AWANA and with a new program for Senior Citizens called "Keen-Agers." She, with the help of others, planned a number of outings for the group, visited shut-ins and edited a monthly newsletter so that shut-ins and others would know of their activities.

Life was full with family, Temple Baptist Church and keeping the churches informed about the ministry in India. But, unknown to Dorothy, the Lord had yet one more missionary project for her to do.

CHAPTER EIGHTEEN
The Last Big Missionary Project

"In His perfect plan for you is true joy and blessing and contentment" –
Dorothy Waldock, August 1993

At the BMM Triannual in 1990, Dorothy had heard how new
fields such as Russia and Romania were opening up to the gospel.
She had written, "It almost makes me wish I could start my
missionary life over. So many fields are crying for new workers
and too few are preparing to go."

That burden was, in a way, fulfilled in Dorothy's last
missionary project. The Lord sent her Mary Amesbury, a greener-
than-grass missionary appointee with Baptist Mid-Missions, who
was headed to the very field that had sparked something in
Dorothy's heart - Russia. Mary, a friend of Caryl's, needed a place
to live while on deputation. It worked out for her to come and
share the condo with Dorothy.

Although it wasn't realized at the time, Mary had met the
General Council of Baptist Mid-Missions at the same church in
Cleveland as Fred and Dorothy had 44 years earlier, although the
church was now in a different location and had a different name –
Cedar Hill Baptist Church.

Dorothy's assignment from the Lord was to take this
immature Christian – saved only four and a half years – and
prepare her for effective missionary service. Dorothy soon
realized that Mary was a diamond in the rough. Yes, she loved
the Lord and had seen God work in miraculous ways in her life,
but oh how she lacked gentleness and grace and tact. She knew so

little about being a Christian woman who could be under submission to others. Yes, this new assignment from the Lord was going to be a big job for Dorothy.

Dorothy put Mary in Nathan's old room. A bookshelf filled with challenging Christian literature – missionary biographies, especially - filled one wall. The very books that had so encouraged and challenged Fred and Dorothy would now challenge Mary and begin to shape the missionary she would become. Dorothy began to pour her life into Mary's. Dinnertime became a classroom. Because of her throat problems, Dorothy had to eat slowly. In between bites she would share of her and Fred's experiences in India. She told her protégé of the joys...and of the struggles. She sensed that Mary needed to understand the tough times that would come as a missionary. She wanted her to be prepared for it. Mary lacked the necessary stoicism that had enabled Dorothy to persevere through all the trials that she and Fred had experienced.

Dorothy began to train Mary in running a household, assigning her duties around the house and teaching her to cook. She modeled sacrifice, frugality and improvising with what they had on hand. When the element in the dryer burnt out, Dorothy used it as a lesson in making do without. They hung the laundry on the banister upstairs to dry. It ended up being an excellent lesson, for there were no dryers in Far East Russia.

It was a wonderful blessing from the Lord for Mary to have Dorothy in her life. By mid-December the relationship had definitely become that of mentor and disciple. Dorothy was at times frustrated by the scope of Mary's training, but she never let on. She just persevered in her teaching and praying. They came to love each other, even though they didn't have words for it. Mary respected Dorothy very much and drank in her wisdom like a sponge.

Dorothy and Mary rejoiced together when God gave Mary her first supporting church. Dorothy and Fred had invested tremendous amounts of time and effort into securing churches to partner with them in God's work in India. Dorothy understood the challenges of deputation. She encouraged Mary as much as she could to develop strong relationships in the churches.

When the possibility of doing a survey trip to Russia came up, Mary asked Dorothy for her opinion. Dorothy thought the $1,300 that would be needed for the ticket might be better saved for outfit and passage. Survey trips were a new concept to Dorothy. In years past, missionaries never got to see the field before they went for their first term. They went forth in faith.

Dorothy challenged Mary to pray it through and assured her that if it was God's will, He was certainly able to provide the money. God did provide all of the funds that were necessary. Right before Mary went to Russia for the survey trip Dorothy noticed that Mary seemed to be struggling with some kind of illness. They thought it was a cold or bronchitis. It would clear up only to reoccur a week or so later. The symptoms reoccurred with a vengeance in Russia. But even with the time of ill health, Mary truly fell in love with Russia. The survey trip was a valuable addition to the training.

When Mary came back to the United States, she began to study the Russian language. Dorothy challenged her to really invest time and energy in getting the language well. She knew that being able to speak the language of the people would greatly expand her usefulness to the Lord.

Dorothy modeled perseverance in prayer to Mary. Dorothy wrote once, *"We become a candidate for God's power when we have a problem. God's power is delivered by interceding prayers."* Many a morning Mary would come downstairs to find her praying on the couch for her family, the work in India, for Baptist Mid-Missions and for Mary, herself.

Mary's health continued to be a concern. She attempted to do a summer intensive Russian course but her health broke down and she had to withdraw from the course. One day when Dorothy, Lois and Mary were in the kitchen, Mary slid to the floor with her back to the refrigerator. She whined, "I don't think I'll ever be well." Dorothy wasn't joining in her pity party. With a sparkle in her eye, but love in her voice, she said, "You're not dead yet." The pity party was over. Dorothy knew Mary well enough by then to know when she needed a pat on the back and when she needed one applied a little lower on her anatomy. If she was going to survive on the mission field, then she needed to be a fighter. Dorothy couldn't afford to baby Mary. Her usefulness for the Lord would depend on her ability to be steadfast. Fred and Dorothy had persevered through numerous bouts of cancer, heart disease and other illnesses. Despite it all, God had given them fruitful ministries. He would do the same for Mary if she refused to give up. Dorothy's "tough love" was just what Mary needed. It would be seven years before the correct diagnosis of fibromyalgia was made. Dorothy's words "You're not dead yet!" came back to Mary again and again and gave her the resolve to stop whining and just do what she could.

From May to August in response to specific prayer, the Lord took Mary's support from 30% to 90%. Dorothy was excited and pleased to see the Lord undertake in this way. Even though Mary had nearly all her support, her missionary colleagues did not. Baptist Mid-Missions felt it would be wise for Mary to wait for her coworkers. So just a few days before the fall semester began at Washington State University, Mary moved to Pullman, WA to enroll in Russian language classes. The university was just eight miles from Tim and Lois Seben's church in Moscow, ID.

It wasn't easy for Mary to leave Dorothy but they both knew that much had been accomplished in 11 months. Dorothy's life had been characterized by a sense of duty to the Lord and that quality had now been instilled in Mary. Dorothy knew what it was to surrender to the Lord and to trust the sovereignty of God. And now, so did Mary.

Dorothy gave Mary a card for her birthday. In part she wrote, *"You have reached another milestone – 30 years, and it is very evident the Lord is leading you step by step. In His perfect plan for you is true joy and blessing and contentment. May you continue to seek and know that plan throughout this coming year. I am praying for you as you prepare for serving Him in Russia. My love and prayers and the Lord's richest blessings throughout the years ahead, Dorothy Waldock (Proverbs 3:5-6)"*

It wasn't long after Mary moved out that Dorothy's health began to go downhill. Her last assignment from the Lord was nearly complete. It would soon be time to go Home.

Dorothy went to Moscow, ID for the birth of Lois' last child – Kaylee Ruth on September 22. Caryl gave birth to Joseph Ryan just a few days later and Dorothy was able to be there for that birth as well. Joe had just been installed as the new pastor at East

Wenatchee Baptist Church. So, with the exception of Gordon's family, all of Dorothy's children were no longer living close by.

Dorothy went to Moscow again at Thanksgiving. She came down with a severe case of laryngitis that made breathing difficult so Lois and Tim took her to the E.R. and she was kept in the hospital overnight. The ENT doctor recommended that Dorothy go to her doctors at the University of Washington. Lois and Tim brought her home on the 29th. It was discovered that Dorothy's larynx had atrophied again and was not opening wide enough to let sufficient air through.

Dorothy moved in with Gordon and Joan because her children didn't want her to live by herself with no one to know if she had trouble again. The family came to Gig Harbor for Christmas and everyone stayed at Dorothy's house. Dorothy was still not truly well. It was decided that Kati – the Sebens' eldest – would stay with her grandmother for a couple of weeks so that Dorothy could be in her own home. Mary could take Kati back with her when she returned to classes.

Just a few days after New Years, Kati called Mary and asked her to come over and drive her grandmother to the hospital. Her doctor wanted to run some tests that would require a hospital stay. Mary rushed over to the house and waited while Dorothy finished writing her annual report for Temple Baptist Church. She wanted it done before she went into the hospital. Duty first – even to the last.

During one of the tests several days later, Dorothy lapsed into a coma. All of the family came with the exception of Ken and Mary who would not be able to get N.O.R. permits quick enough. After several days in the coma, it became obvious that she would not recover. Her family and Mary gathered around her bed.

A few days after that, Jesus called Dorothy home to her eternal reward. She was buried next to Fred on January 14 and a memorial service was held at Temple Baptist Church on the 15th.

Jim Garlow wrote the following testimony: *"She had a high energy level and a tremendous ability to work and plod. Realizing the need to communicate with the nationals, Dorothy studied and mastered the Bengali language so well, that it was said she spoke Bengali beautifully for a foreigner. Dorothy was a tremendous all-around missionary, and she was especially used of God in a strong ministry among the women. Her influence and ministry were very effective and her dedicated life was greatly used by God."*

Gary Anderson, president of Baptist Mid-Missions, wrote in tribute: *"Dorothy Waldock modeled for all of us spiritual qualities necessary for effective Christian service. Among those qualities were three that especially facilitated her missionary endeavor.*

Dorothy was captivated by the work of God waiting to be finished. India and its teeming population was as much a concern to her as it was to William Carey whose work in India two centuries earlier gave rise to the modern era of missions. While great victories have been won there for Christ, Dorothy was not so impressed with what had been accomplished as she was moved by what remained to be done.

Her place in India was for Dorothy a God-assigned share of His work. God's role was to draw the target; her role was to shoot at it. Before ever arriving on her field of service she had surrendered to God the right to do with her life whatever He pleased. What may have initially been accepted as duty became the passion of her heart. God's will was unconditionally her will.

Dorothy was constrained to stick with the work of God until her share was finished. The challenges of ill health never took her determination from her. The fact that Fred preceded her to Glory did not dissuade her. Retirement only meant transition into a new phase of ministry. Her plans for this year included a stint in India. Her final days amongst us gave evidence that she did not consider her work finished. God must have judged it so.

We praise God for the influence Dorothy's life has had and will continue to have. The end of her life in no way marks the end of her influence. Her children and grandchildren will forever reflect her life having been poured into theirs. The churches and ministries in India who received their present leaders through her evangelistic and discipling efforts will forever bear her fingerprints. Those of us who were her coworkers and loved ones will always have her example to emulate. Her impact for Christ will far exceed her own lifetime."

I cannot write the words "THE END" in regards to the lives of Fred and Dorothy Waldock, because the story is still being written in India, America and wherever those whose lives they have touched happen to be. The story of Fred and Dorothy Waldock continues on in me, in David, Ken, Gordon, Lois and Caryl, in their children, in Promode, Gobin and Urirei, in Hranga, in Sana, in Tapon, in Ajit, in Sambhu and Molly and hundreds of others. To God be the glory. Great things He has done.

Not The End